Using the INTERNET *in Your* JOB SEARCH

Fred E. Jandt
Author of *Win-Win
Negotiating* and *The
Customer Is Usually Wrong!*

Mary B. Nemnich
Employment Specialist
and Popular Lecturer

E-mail address: jobnet@aol.com

JIST Works, Inc.

Using the Internet in Your Job Search

Copyright © 1995 by Fred E. Jandt and Mary B. Nemnich

Published by JIST Works, Inc.
720 North Park Avenue
Indianapolis, IN 46202-3431
Phone 317-264-3720   Fax 317-264-3709

Library of Congress Cataloging-in-Publication Data

Jandt, Fred Edmund.
    Using the Internet in your job search / Fred E. Jandt, Mary B.
Nemnich.
        p.   cm.
    Includes index.
    ISBN 1-56370-173-1
    1. Job hunting–Computer network resources.   2. Internet (Computer
network)   I. Nemnich, Mary B.   II. Title.
    HF5382.7.J36   1995
    650.14'0285'467–dc20   95-18721
                                                                 CIP

Printed in the United States of America
99 98 97 96 95   2 3 4 5 6 7 8 9

Errors and Omissions: We have been careful to provide accurate information in this book but it is possible that errors and omissions have been introduced. Please consider this in making any career plans or other important decisions. Trust your own judgment above all else and in all things.

ISBN 1-56370-173-1

CONTENTS

PREFACE

Mary Nemnich got her first professional job through a referral from the state Employment Development Department. Fred Jandt got his first professional job by applying for a position listed in a professional newsletter. Both ways of finding a job still exist. But today there is an exciting new option: finding your job by using the *Internet*—the interconnections among approximately 41,500 computer networks worldwide.

Literally thousands of positions are listed on the Internet. Thousands of resumes of job seekers are available on the Internet. Thousands of employers personally read their e-mail daily. And thousands of job seekers using the Internet are finding exciting new jobs all over the world.

You might expect the Internet to be as simply organized as your local library. But navigating the Internet takes some skill since the Internet is many times larger than your local library, giving you access to the world's libraries, governments, businesses, and individuals. Because of the Internet's size and the way it developed, it is not as easy to use as walking into a library. You need some new skills to access the world of information now available to you. The purposes of this book are to help you become proficient at using the Internet and to give you one more tool for finding that next job. *Using the Internet in Your Job Search* is a step-by-step guide from gaining access to the Internet to finding job listings on the Internet to even applying for these jobs by e-mail.

Current economic conditions have made finding work in today's labor market particularly tough. You need to be more competitive than ever to find a job. Using the Internet in your job search will furnish you with access to more employment opportunities than ever before— giving you the edge.

We've found all kinds of jobs on the Internet from internships and part-time employment to executive positions in government and the private sector. This book combines easy-to-understand, hands-on information on using the Internet with pragmatic advice on adapting job-seeking skills to the new world of the Internet. We've tested all the information ourselves and included real-life examples from successful and unsuccessful Internet job seekers.

We've written this book for both job seekers and employers. Other individuals who will find this book useful include government and private employment agencies and teachers and career counselors.

Personal computers and the Internet are innovations of the past 25 years and continue to change at a fast rate. We've done our best to ensure that the information in this book is up-to-date, but changes will have occurred by the time you read this. Look at the positive side: Using the Internet to search for a job is proof positive to employers that you can learn new skills and adapt to a rapidly changing environment!

Mary Nemnich wants to acknowledge the good-natured cooperation of her children, Alex and Alissa, and the unfailing support of her husband, Lee Albert Nemnich, who also provided technical advice for the book. Both Mary Nemnich and Fred Jandt want to thank the e-community—the supportive community of Internet users who shared their experiences and helped make this book possible.

CHAPTER

1

Getting Connected

There's no doubt that technology affects our lives in ways we haven't even begun to consider. Have you thought about—and are you using—new technologies in your job search?

One of us, Mary Nemnich, has been an employment specialist with the State of California Employment Development Department for some 20 years, working with both job seekers and employers. Today she uses television to introduce job seekers to potential employers!

It was way back in the 1930s that the first experimental television broadcasts of sports and political events began. But it wasn't until after World War II that U.S. citizens discovered television. Cable systems originated in the 1940s to extend the reach of television signals into remote areas. By 1952, one-third of all families had a television set in their homes. Today, of course, cable can bring hundreds of channels to every home. So today, Mary produces "Job Connections," a televised job bank on community-access cable television. In each program she showcases local employers and has individual job seekers market themselves directly to employers. Her show recently won a Helen Putnam award for excellence—an award sponsored by the League of California Cities.

Fred Jandt has been a communication professor in New York and California for some 25 years. He used to refer job-seeking graduating seniors to campus placement centers to look through binders of vacancy announcements sent to the campus by employers. Today he teaches students how to locate vacancies on the Internet!

Big mainframe computers date back to the 1950s. By 1977 the first personal computers were introduced. Today about one-third of U.S. households have a personal computer. Some 18 percent of men and 9 percent of women use a personal computer at home almost daily.

Recently one of Fred's graduating students wanted to relocate from Southern California to the Boston area. She had tried for months to find an entry-level job. Fred showed her how to find job listings on the Internet. She applied for a job she saw listed and was employed in Boston within a month.

There's no doubt that technology is dramatically changing the job search process. What you can learn from this book is how to use the Internet in your job search.

Understanding the Internet

What is called the Internet today was started about 25 years ago in the Cold War Era by the Defense Department Advanced Research Projects Agency (ARPA) to link researchers with computer centers to share hardware and software resources over telephone lines. Before that time magnetic tapes or punch cards had to be exchanged by mail. Access was limited to the military, defense contractors, and universities doing defense research. In the early 1980s Milnet, an unclassified military network, was spun off ARPAnet, but connections between the two networks continued. That interconnection was known as the DARPA Internet. And what we know as the Internet today is an expansion of the concept of interconnections between these two computer networks.

In the late 1970s and early 1980s more computer networks were developed for the academic and research communities, and these too became a part of the Internet. Established in 1986, the National Science Foundation Network (NSFnet) replaced the original ARPAnet by 1990, and by 1991 NSFnet itself ceased to exist. But what remained was the Internet—the interconnections among computer networks that by then consisted of about 8,000 networks around the world. So in a very real sense, the Internet is not a "thing"; it's the interconnections among computer networks worldwide.

When you're on the Internet from your spare bedroom in your home in Texas, you're not aware of the interconnections that allow you to apply for a job in Germany. To the user, the Internet seems to be a direct connection.

The growth of the Internet has been astronomical. By 1994 there were 3 million computers and 41,500 networks on the Internet. The number of users—more than 20 million—has been increasing some 20 percent a month!

You might be wondering who bears the cost. The National Science Foundation has been supporting the backbone of the Internet for upwards of $10 million dollars a year. As the NSF withdraws support and commercial free-market forces take over, the nature of the Internet will certainly change.

Adapting to the Internet

Before we begin, we must discuss the most common mistake job seekers with a little knowledge about personal computers and a little knowledge about the Internet can make. We can see this mistake if we look back to the histories of the introduction of different new technologies. The quality of silent movies in the late 1920s was superb, whereas the talkies were crude and simplistic. But by the 1930s virtually all movies were talkies. Some producers and stars made the transition, but a whole new set of faces with theatrical experience became the new stars because they had the skills that the new technology demanded. Those who didn't adapt to the unique characteristics of the new technology–those who acted the same way and just added speech–weren't successful.

In the 1930s everyone agreed that television would never replace radio. Radio was the "theater of the imagination." But the transition was dramatically fast as major radio stars switched over to the new medium. Some survived, but many didn't adapt to the new visual requirement that the new technology demanded.

What's the lesson from these shifts from silent movies to talkies and from radio to television? It's that each new technology has unique requirements.

How does that lesson apply to job seekers using the Internet? You know how to prepare a resume. If you know how to use a personal computer, you probably have that resume on disk. When you learn the basics of using the Internet, you'll learn that you can send a resume electronically to an employer.

You work so carefully on your printed resume to give employers just the right "picture" of you as they review it with your letter of application. You're proud of that resume and it's probably pretty good–so good in fact that you feel you should use it with your electronic job application. You've just made the same mistake as the silent movie stars who didn't realize that each new technology has unique requirements. An employer looking at a printed resume takes in at a glance the whole page or two. An employer looking at an electronic resume sees the first screen and will make a judgment based on the first 20 lines of your resume!

In this book we want to help you make that transition from silent movie star to the talkies, from radio star to television, from printed resume to electronic resume, from a job seeker relying on out-of-date local print vacancy notices to a job seeker electronically scanning current job vacancies anywhere in the world.

In this first chapter we'll describe the ways anyone can gain access to the Internet. Even if you have access now, such as at your current job, you should review this chapter to learn about other ways. Not only does the cost differ, but the extent of your access can vary. And for those of you planning to rely on your access at work, remember that your employer may not appreciate you using company time and resources for your new job search. We'll end the chapter describing what you're getting access to and how you'll be identified there.

Using a Computer

Do you have a computer? Have you considered buying a PC? Too expensive? Too complicated? What cost $3,500 in 1991 is now available for $1,500 or less. Even the large discount stores now sell computers. Factory-equipped personal computers can be running in less than half an hour. If you need help, the major manufacturers have toll-free help lines.

If you're ready to purchase, consider getting the same kind of computer your kids use at school or you use at work. Here are some other things to consider:

- *Invest in a good monitor*. Skimping on a good monitor can affect your eyes and cause headaches. Most complete systems come with color monitors. Look for what is easy for you to read.

- *Invest in speed*. Speed means how quickly your computer processes information. Speed can be indicated by a number ending in "86" and by "megahertz" (MHz). For IBM-compatible computers today, the 486 is the standard. You can also compare the megahertz ratings. The higher the MHz, the faster the computer processes information.

- *Invest in storage*. The amount of information a computer can hold is measured by "megabytes" (M, Mb, or megs) of hard-drive memory. The higher the megs, the more information the computer can store.

Remember, too, that as more and more people buy computers for their homes, more and more people replace their old computers with newer, larger ones. That means that there are many used systems available. Check the newspaper classifieds and computer swap meets. The advantage of buying a used computer is that the price will be much less, and you should be able to negotiate as part of the price that the seller install the computer in your home and help you get started on it. The disadvantage is that there is no guarantee, so be sure that the seller agrees to install it and to get you going on it.

You don't need to invest in a computer right away to have access to the Internet. Almost all colleges and universities offer computer labs to students. You usually don't have to be a computer science student to use these labs, so check with your local college or university. Learn the conditions for using its computer labs and under what conditions you may have access to the Internet.

If you're not in college now, you can enroll for one class. That will be considerably cheaper than investing in a new computer right away. Some colleges may open their computer labs to alumni. If you're a graduate of a college in your community, check with the alumni office. Alumni office staff members may be able to help.

And as public libraries become increasingly computerized, some provide computer access to patrons. Some government buildings provide access to citizens. Do some checking.

Using a Modem

A *modem* is a device that connects your home computer to a computer network through a telephone line. Technically, a modem converts digital signals produced by computers into analog sound waves that can be transmitted over telephone lines. Modems are rated by speed and such features as error correction and data compression.

Error correction and speed are most important. Error correction features help filter out telephone line noise to ensure error-free transmission. Speed refers to the time it takes to transmit the information. Many people have modems rated at 2400 bps (bits per second), which is considered slow by today's standards. Recommended speed today is 14,400 bps. Transferring a file from one computer to another that takes eleven minutes at 2400 bps takes less than two minutes at 14,400 bps. IBM-compatible 14,400 bps modems sell for as little as $60.

Today's modems also allow you to send and receive faxes. If you buy a modem, it will probably come with a trial subscription to one of the commercial online services such as Prodigy. Keep in mind, though, that your modem's speed is limited to the speed of the modem at the other end of the line. Today, Prodigy and America Online use 9600 bps. CompuServe does have 14,400 in some communities, but in others is limited to 9600 and 2400.

Installing a Telephone Line

If you're planning to access the Internet from your home, you'll need a telephone line. After you install your modem in or beside your computer, you will plug the modem into a phone jack. Deciding whether you need a separate telephone line should be based on such factors as how many people use the telephone in your home and how many incoming telephone calls you receive. If you have call-waiting on the same line as your modem, for example, an incoming second call will break your modem's connection unless you remember to turn off call-waiting.

Installing Communications Software

Some modems come equipped with the communications software necessary to connect your home computer to another computer. If yours doesn't, you'll need to buy a communications package that works with your modem. The easiest way is to check that the software specifically mentions your modem's brand and model number in its list of compatible modems. If it doesn't, get advice from a knowledgeable dealer so that everything will work for you.

Your communications software must provide terminal emulation, which basically permits your home computer to act as a terminal on the computer system you're connected to. The most commonly used terminal emulation over the years is known as VT-100, the standard for computer-to-computer communications.

Now that you've thought about access, the next step is how you actually get connected to the Internet. There are several ways to get connected: commercial online services, freenets, and bulletin board systems.

Using Commercial Online Services

Commercial information services charge a monthly fee. They themselves provide you with a wealth of information, including news and financial data, bulletin boards to post messages, and mail to other subscribers. Some services have job vacancy announcements. Others provide gateways to send mail to people on other networks. And some of these services also give you access to the Internet.

Prodigy (more than 2 million subscribers), a joint project of IBM and Sears, is targeted to home users. Prodigy provides a link to the Internet to send and receive messages from people on other networks. Prodigy charges $14.95 a month for unlimited access to most basic services and an additional fee for a few other services. Call 800-776-3449 for more information.

CompuServe (about 2.25 million subscribers) is the oldest, largest, and most comprehensive of the online services. Like Prodigy, CompuServe is linked to the Internet to send and receive messages from people on other networks. You can access your CompuServe account through the Internet from another computer system. CompuServe costs $8.95 a month for unlimited access to basic services. The more valuable services cost more. Call 800-848-8990 for more information.

NovaLink Interactive Networks provides online entertainment and information along with multimedia access to the Internet (Santa Claus has a NovaLink address: santa@novalink.com and also www.novalink.com). The cost of NovaLink is $9.95 monthly for five hours of usage. For more information, call 800-274-2814.

America Online (fastest growing with some 2 million subscribers) provides full Internet access. America Online provides newsgroups, WAIS and gopher databases, telnet, file transfer, and World Wide Web. America Online charges $9.95 a month for five hours of access by local phone call from more than 600 U.S. cities. Additional hours cost $2.95 each. Call 800-827-6364 for more information.

In 1994 Microsoft, the world's largest personal computer software company, introduced Microsoft Network as part of Microsoft's new personal computer operating system Windows 95. Buyers of Windows 95 will be able to subscribe to the Microsoft Network or any other online service with the click of a mouse. Information will be available with Windows 95.

Also in 1994, MCI Communications introduced InternetMCI to give customers access to the Internet. The estimated price was $49.95 for the Internet software and access charges of $19.95 monthly for seven hours of use. More information will be available from MCI.

Delphi is an economical access provider that gives access to all Internet services and has a large support staff. Delphi and any of dozens of smaller commercial operations provide some access to the Internet. For Delphi, call 800-695-4005 for more information.

Netcom offers an Internet suite of NetCruiser—an easy-to-use Windows program—combined with Netcom's Internet service to provide access to most Internet resources: e-mail, ftp, telnet remote access, gopher server searches, USENET news, World Wide Web, and others. NetCruiser charges a $25 startup fee, and then $19.95 a month for basic services. For more information, call 800-353-6600.

PSInet Pipeline is a New York-based Internet provider. Pipeline offers an easy-to-use Windows access program with pull-down menus and icons to connect with most Internet services. Pipeline offers a number of price plans starting from $15 a month plus $2 an hour for access from the New York area. For an additional hourly fee, the service can be used anywhere in the United States. Call 212-267-3636 for more information.

Institute for Global Communications, probably the best-known and most efficiently coordinated computer effort for peace and the protection of the environment, provides complete access to the Internet. Cost is $12.50 monthly plus telephone charges for six hours of use. Special rates are available for groups, students, and low-income people and organizations. For more information, call 415-442-0220, fax 415-546-1794, or write to 18 DeBoom Street, San Francisco, CA 94107.

The entire French Minitel system is easily accessible in the United States from local dial-up numbers. There's a onetime fee of $20 to establish an account. Charges are based on the specific services used at rates ranging from 19 cents to more than $1 per minute. From Minitel, you can access the Internet. For more information, contact Minitel Services Company, 888 Seventh Avenue, 28th Floor, New York, NY 10106, or call 212-399-0080.

Using Freenets

The first and best-known freenet, Cleveland Freenet, was developed at Case Western Reserve University in 1986 to permit thousands of local Cleveland citizens to chat with each other and to visit the courthouse, library, and arts and community centers. The Cleveland Freenet also provides access to the Internet. Some freenets offer Internet access; others are local only and feature discussion groups about local issues. Some of the freenets aren't even free.

Another example of a freenet is the Sailor project of the Maryland public library system that calls for terminals to be available in public libraries. Maryland citizens will also be able to call in from home using local telephone numbers. Complete access to the Internet will cost a Maryland citizen about $35 a year. Another example is Alaska's State Library and the University of Alaska in Fairbanks' joint project State-wide Library Electronic Doorway (SLED). In time, every public library in Alaska will have computers tied into the Internet for public use.

The International Internet Association (IIA) is the largest nonprofit provider of free Internet access and services in the world giving easy access to a full suite of Internet services, including e-mail, USENET news, ftp, gopher, WAIS, World Wide Web, and others. IIA provides 800 access 24 hours a day, seven days a week from any point in the Domestic United States, including Alaska, Hawaii, and U.S. Territories. The electronic address of the IIA is iia.org (Note: not iia.com).

Most freenets are funded and operated by individuals and volunteers. And most are members of the National Public Telecomputing Network (NPTN), an organization working to make computer network services as freely available as libraries. For more information, call 216-498-4050, fax 216-498-4051, or write to Box 1987, Cleveland, OH 44106.

Using Bulletin Board Systems

There are an estimated 50,000 to 100,000 public dial-up bulletin board systems (BBSs) in North America today. There is a BBS for every conceivable lifestyle and interest. Some of the bulletin board systems offer Internet access. Some bulletin board systems are free, some suggest donations, and others charge a fee. Prices range from $30 to $75 a year.

Most bulletin board systems are small operations that provide a low-cost alternative to the national online services. They don't provide anywhere near the services of the online services, but they provide an alternative. Bulletin board systems are linked together through networks such as FidoNet, which was developed by Tom Jennings and basically given away out of his personal philosophy of "radical communications."

One of the most helpful BBSs on the Internet is the WELL (Whole Earth 'Lectronic Link) started by *Whole Earth Review* and located in

Sausalito, California. It's an excellent place to learn about the Internet. To join, call 415-332-8410 by modem, login as new user, and then follow the prompts.

Boardwatch Magazine conducts an annual survey of its readers to determine the more popular BBSs. Here are some samples:

EXEC-PC (414-789-4210) in Elm Grove, Wisconsin, is one of the oldest and largest bulletin boards. It offers Espan Job Search and costs $25 per quarter or $75 a year.

PC-OHIO (216-381-3320) in Cleveland, Ohio, is connected with 22 e-mail networks including the Internet as `pcohio.com`.

For *Boardwatch Magazine*'s list of "The Top 100 BBSs," see figure 1.1.

Some federal government agencies offer their own BBS. Two notable examples are the Food and Drug Administration and the Small Business Administration. The Small Business Administration BBS is designed for entrepreneurs and is available at 800-697-4636.

Looking to join a local BBS? There are ways to find their telephone number. In later chapters, you'll find out how to use these tools, but highlight this now so you can find it later:

> On CompuServe go to the IBM BBS Forum; on America Online use the keyword BBS; and on the Internet go to any of the BBS newsgroups.

Now that you've decided how to get connected, you need to know more about what you're getting connected to.

Determining Your Internet Address

Just as you have a mailing address, you will have an address on the Internet. Actually, the addresses are easy to understand. Let's look at one of Fred's addresses:

        `fjandt@wiley.csusb.edu`

First of all, know how to "read" the address aloud. Fred's address is read aloud as "f-j-a-n-d-t at wiley dot c-s-u-s-b dot e-d-u." A period is read aloud as "dot." Commonly known words—such as wiley—are said as a word; others—such as Fred's name, fjandt—are spelled out letter by letter.

Just as your mailing address tells us what state and city you live in and where in that city you actually get your mail, your Internet address gives us location information. Refer back to Fred's address. We'll look at the elements *from right to left*, which is from most general to most specific:

- The last part of Fred's address is `edu`. That tells you he's at an educational institution. Others are com for commercial, gov for governmental, mil for military, org for organizations, and net for networks.

- Next is `csusb`. That refers to California State University at San Bernardino, the educational institution where Fred works.

- Next is `wiley`. There are several computer systems at Fred's university. Wiley is simply the name of one system used on that campus—the system Fred is using.

- Finally, there is the userid, or user name, `fjandt`. That's simply an abbreviation of Fred's full name. Many people choose to use the first letter of their first name and then as much of their last name as their system permits. For example, Mary uses mnemnich.

Some addresses will have an additional two letters at the end, such as `jp`. That's because most countries require a two-letter country code in addresses. All Internet addresses in Japan end in jp—the two-letter code for Japan.

Let's look at another example:

> `123456@microsoft.com`

Reading from the right, it's a commercial organization known as Microsoft, and the person's name is 123456.

In addition to words you can read, every computer on the Internet has a unique number called its *IP* (Internet Protocol) address. The IP address identifies a specific computer on a specific network. IP numbers look like this:

> `128.174.33.160`

If you know the IP number, you can enter that as the address. What happens if you enter the address incorrectly? Well, just like the U.S. Postal Service, your misaddressed mail will be returned to you by a "postmaster." By the way, to continue the comparison with the Postal Service, electronic mail is known as e-mail, but print material delivered by the Postal Service is known as *snail-mail*. That comparison shows one definite advantage of the Internet!

Some computer systems are case-sensitive. This means that letters shown in capitals must be entered as capitals and those shown in lowercase must be entered in lowercase. Be careful to copy down addresses exactly as you find them. Computers are very powerful, but very literal—in some systems FJANDT would not be recognized as fjandt, and MNEMNICH would not be recognized as mnemnich.

Choosing a Password

One final word: You must have a password. Without the security a password provides, anyone who knew your address could send messages in your name. Also, anyone could order merchandise from JC Penny's in your name. Security is provided by carefully choosing a secret password.

Passwords should be random and not linked to you in any way. For example, if your friends know you love cats and if you use your cat's name Yahtzee as your password, a friend could enter only your pets' names and quickly find your password. A password also should never be shared with another person. You might be able to trust your friend not to use it, but what if your friend accidentally allows a third person to see your password? You don't know whether that third person might use your account for all sorts of things you wouldn't know about or approve!

Providing a Message Header

All e-mail messages are sent with what is known as the header. The header includes a TO: line, a FROM: line, and other information. The following is a sample header:

```
Message 646
From carranza@ucssun1.sdsu.edu Sat Nov 12 16:24:42 1994
Date: Sat, 12 Nov 1994 16:24:22 -0800
From: Reyes Carranza <carranza@ucssun1.sdsu.edu>
To: fjandt@igc.apc.org
Subject: Re: permission

Sure, why not. Is there anything special you want me to do?

Reyes
```

Finding Others' Addresses

Sending messages to other people means that you need to know their addresses. How can you find out other people's e-mail addresses? Unfortunately there isn't a single, simple directory. The reasons are many: people's e-mail addresses change, some desire security, some organizations prefer to use e-mail for internal use only, some organizations don't have the staff available to compile and update lists, etc. But here are some things you can do:

- Look at business cards and letters. It is becoming very common today to list e-mail addresses on business cards and letters.

- Call and ask. Simply call the receptionist and ask if an e-mail address is available for the person you're trying to reach.

- Search on your computer. Try the following methods:

1. One method is WHOIS. Enter at a telnet prompt (*see* Chapter 3) the following:

    ```
    whois.internic.net
    ```

    At a **whois** prompt, enter the last name of the person or the company you are trying to reach. Note that some of the results of the search you'll see are in the form of e-mail addresses you'll easily recognize or a string of numbers you'll recognize as the IP address.

2. A second method is finger. If you know the name of the computer the person you're searching for is on (for example from WHOIS), you can try a finger command to search for a person. But, not all computers have finger, and not all those who do have it list all the people on that computer. To try it, enter the following:

    ```
    finger <some part of the person's name or
    userid>@<computer address>
    ```

    You'll find limited success.

3. A third method is PSI's White Pages Services. You can telnet (see Chapter 3) to:

    ```
    wp.psi.com
    ```

    and login as **fred**.

4. A fourth method is to search USENET (see Chapter 3) if the person has ever posted an article in a newsgroup. To try this method, send a message to the following:

    ```
    mail-server@pit-manager.mit.edu
    ```

    In the body of the message enter:

    ```
    send usenet-addresses/<name of person>
    ```

However, don't expect success with these methods. The most reliable way to get another person's e-mail address is to ask the individual for it!

Now that you have a user name, a place to go, and a way to get there, Chapter 2 walks you through the use of two commercial online services: CompuServe and America Online.

Boardwatch Magazine's list of "The Top 100 BBSs"

PLACE	TITLE	PHONE	DESCRIPTION	LOCATION
1	Software Creations	508-368-7139	Home BBS for Apogee, and many other shareware producers	Clinton, MA
2	EXEC-PC	414-789-4210	World's largest BBS, 35Gig, most anything you need	Elm Grove, WI
3	deltaComm BBS	919-481-9399	Support board for Telix Communications software	Cary, NC
4	PC-OHIO	216-381-3320	Internet, 3000 message areas, 400 file areas, 250 doors	Cleveland, OH
5	GLIB	703-578-4542	Information serving the gay, lesbian, and bisexual community	Arlington, VA
6	Westside	213-933-4050	SprintNet access, very large file base, many great features	Los Angeles, CA
7	Albuquerque ROS	505-299-5974	Home of ROS BBS, 60000+ files, active social issues	Albuquerque, NM
8	Odyssey	818-358-6968	Where adults come to play and meet, active chats	Monrovia, CA
9	Wizard's Gate BBS	614-224-1635	FREE, no fee, ASP BBS, full access on first call 12Gig	Columbus, OH
10	Pleasure Dome	804-490-5878	Sexually explicit, adults only, ladies free	Norfolk, VA
11	Blue Ridge Express	804-790-1675	Message areas, 84+ file areas, 21000+ files	Richmond, VA
12	Deep Cove BBS	604-536-5885	Internet, 7Gig file area, CD-ROMs, ZyXEL modem sales	White Rock, BC
13	Totem Pole BBS	313-238-1178	4Gig, 97 file areas, 419 message areas, 24 doors	Flint, MI
14	Planet BMUG	510-849-2684	100 forums, gateways to OneNet & BMUG Boston	Berkeley, CA
15	Prostar BBS	206-941-0317	Home of MajorNet, 200000+ files, Interlink chats, 100+ games	Auburn, WA
16	Chrysalis	214-690-9295	Internet, Connex, 30Gig, chat, encyclopedia	Plano, TX
17	OS/2 Shareware	703-385-4325	5000+ OS/2 files, 25 areas, 50 message area	Fairfax, VA
18	Microfone Infoservice	908-494-8666	FidoNet, 14 CD-ROMs, online games, since 1982	Metuchen, NJ
19	Nashville Exchange	615-383-0727	Internet, USENET, FidoNet, 10Gig files, online games	Nashville, TN
20	Eagle's Nest BBS	303-933-0701	FREE access to all, 1.3Gig, very nice single-line system	Littleton, CO
21	Plains Bulletin service	701-281-3390	Great Plains Software support for GPS Partners	Fargo, ND
22	City Lights	612-633-1366	Adult lifestyles & echoes, 600 message areas, 5.7Gig, 35000+ files	Arden Hills, MN
23	Lifestyle	516-689-5390	Adult lifestyles, personal ads, e-mail, personal contacts	Lake Grove, NY
24	Monterey Gaming System	408-655-5555	Chat, messages, e-mail, online games, fun entertainment	Monterey, CA
25	Windy City Freedom Fort	708-564-1069	Adults only, over 4000 original scanned graphics	Northbrook, IL
26	Micro Message Service	919-779-6674	Internet, excellent Ham Radio area, 7Gig, family BBS	Raleigh, NC
27	Liberty BBS	714-996-7777	Nationwide chat, e-mail, news, games, Internet	Anaheim Hills, CA
28	File Bank	303-534-4646	Astronomy, Ham radio, programming, adult files	Denver, CO
29	Cracker Barrel	703-899-0020	Medical/Diabetes info, real-time games, 88 message areas	Falmouth, VA
30	Source BBS	310-371-3737	General interest, FidoNet e-mail, new files daily	Torrance, CA
31	America's Suggestion Box	516-471-8625	Focused on collecting & distributing consumer feedback	Ronkonkoma, NY
32	Garbage Dump BBS	505-294-5675	Adult chat, dating registry, games, national access	Albuquerque, NM
33	Windows On Line	510-736-8343	Premier Windows file service, 10000+ 3.x files	Danville, CA
34	Springfield Public Access	413-536-4365	Internet e-mail, focus on Genealogy, Ham Radio, Windows	Springfield, MA
35	O.U. BBS	405-325-6128	Internet, telnet, 3Gig files, online games, PIMP, chat	Norman, OK
36	AlphaOne	708-827-3619	Online shopping, 30+ games, 200+ echoes, 30000+ files	Park Ridge, IL
37	Advanced System BBS	702-334-3308	Internet, FidoNet, 16Gig, TBBS enhancements	Reno, NV
38	Godfather	813-289-3314	FidoNet, USENET, adult areas, graphics, GIFs, new files	Tampa, FL
39	Fantasy Party Line	713-596-7101	Social gatherings, live chats, great users	Houston, TX
40	Hello Central	206-661-7218	Adult recreational computing, fun without the kids	Bellevue, WA
41	Datamax/Satelite	215-443-9434	Live ftp & telnet, 10Gigs, large adult area	Ivyland, PA
42	Tampa Connection	813-961-8665	Matchmaker Pen-Pal Network, 11000+ user database	Tampa, FL
43	H H Infonet	203-738-0342	Professional, technical, & business oriented, Windows files	New Hartford, CT
44	Radio Wave BBS	609-764-0812	ASP BBS, Rime, 4Gig files, 4000+ newsgroups	Delran, NJ
45	Executive Network	914-667-4567	10Meg new files daily, 4000 message areas, Internet	Mt. Vernon, NY
46	Invention Factory	212-274-8110	250000+ files, newsgroups, large adult section, USR V.32bis modems	New York City, NY
47	Father and Son BBS	215-439-1509	FidoNet echoes, 10Gig, large adult area, chat, OS/2 files	Whitehall, PA
48	Legend of Roseville BBS	313-776-1975	4.5Gig, message areas, files	Roseville, MI
49	Radio Daze BBS	219-256-2255	Worldwide echoes, 6.3 Gig, 65000+ files, USR HS modems	Mishawaka, IN
50	COSNUG BBS	719-578-6088	Mainly for Seniors, open to the public	Colorado Springs, CO
51	Rusty and Edies BBS	216-726-2620	All shareware, 9Gig, huge adult section, USR 16.8 modems	Youngstown, OH

PLACE	TITLE	PHONE	DESCRIPTION	LOCATION
52	Space BBS	415-323-4193	Internet e-mail, 3000 newsgroups, Rime, Ilink, a most active BBS	Menlo Park, CA
53	Techtalk	407-635-8833	Six CD-ROMs, USR 16.8 modems, PIMP, Internet, techtalk.com	Cocoa, FL
54	Hotlanta BBS	404-992-5345	Social chat system for open minded & adventurous adults	Roswell, GA
55	24th Street Exchange	916-448-2483	General IBM MS-DOS files and support, ASP BBS, FidoNet, chat	Sacramento, CA
56	Mog-UR's EMS	818-366-1238	Internet, 2.8Gig, 6 CD-ROMs, 15 nets, 300 file areas	Granada Hills, CA
57	After Hours	512-320-1650	Best little BBS in Texas	Austin, TX
58	Starship 11 BBS	201-935-1485	General interest, 10Gig, Chat, 100+ message areas	Lyndhurst, NY
59	Prime Time BBS	818-982-7271	Live multiuser games, chat, InterLink, files	Burbank, CA
60	3rd Eye BBS	615-227-6155	Adult system serving the responsible swinging lifestyle	Nashville, TN
61	Arizona Online	602-294-9947	Massive adult area, 20000+ files, 3Gig online	Tuscan, AZ
62	Digicom BBS	812-479-1310	Product Support BBS list, adult area with games, 2.7Gig	Evansville, IN
63	Cajun Clickers BBS	504-756-9658	Online games, 4.4Gig, no fees, 11000+ files	Baton Rouge, LA
64	Channel 1	617-354-8873	3500 message areas, 120 online games, Internet, 30Gig	Cambridge, MA
65	KBBS Los Angeles	818-886-0872	4.4Gig of shareware, online games, chats, chatlink.	Canoga Park, CA
66	Eagles Nest Communications	401-732-5290	Internet, USENET, RIME, Ilink, Paranet, 50000+ files	Providence, RI
67	Argus	617-674-2345	Active chat, 40000+ files, internet, newsgroups, games	Lexington, MA
68	TCSNet	206-692-2388	Newsgroups, Rime, MetroLink, online services	Silverdale, WA
69	S-Tek	514-597-2409	Montreal's premiere Gay & Lesbian BBS, G&L BBS List	Montreal, QC
70	Infoquest	618-453-8511	RIP, FidoNet, Internet, VNet, 100000 files, many online games	Carbondale, IL
71	One Stop PCBoard BBS	509-943-0211	USR 16.8 modems, 8Gig, 70 doors, 900 message areas	Richland, WA
72	Kandy Shack	714-636-2667	Ilink, U'NI-net, ASP member, 2.4Gig online, USR 16.8 modems	Garden Grove, CA
73	Texas Talk	214-497-9100	Adult chat, matchmaking, games, parties, CD-ROMs	Richardson, TX
74	BCS BBS	213-962-2902	Home of Cal-Link, Ilink, e-mail, general interest	Hollywood, CA
75	Higher Powered BBS	408-737-7040	Ilink, SmartNet, SciFact, FredNet, 1Gig files	Sunnyvale, CA
76	Zoo BBS	312-907-1831	Adult social network, chats, gay, bi, straights welcome	Chicago, IL
77	Toolkit	219-696-3415	Resource for programmers and power users	Lowell, IN
78	Electronic Tribune	505-823-7700	Operated by the *Albuquerque Tribune*, news and information	Albuquerque, NM
79	YA WEBECAD	812-428-3870	PSL library, ASP BBS, 72000+ files, 11.8Gig, adult file area	Evansville, IN
80	Wayne's World	918-665-0061	Large filebase, online games, latest new files	Tulsa, OK
81	TGC Services	812-284-1321	Adult BBS for all users over 18, 2.6Gig, GIFs & animations	Clarksville, IN
82	Computers & Dreams	212-888-6565	Internet, USENET, Rime, 40 doors, 10000+ new files	New York City, NY
83	WinPlus	206-630-8203	Christian values, family fun, everyone welcome	Kent, WA
84	U.S.A. BBS	501-753-8575	Internet, all major filebone areas, online games, 10Gig	N. Little Rock, AR
85	Capital City Online	206-956-1206	Internet, USENET, 1.2Gig 100+ online games, chat	Lacey, WA
86	Nightbreed	512-345-5099	Games, messages, files, users	Austin, TX
87	Cloud 9	619-737-3097	Chat, Internet e-mail, trivia, 50000+ files, online CPA	Escondido, CA
88	Mercury Opus	813-321-0734	Internet, 80000+ files, MS-DOS, Windows, OS/2	St. Petersburg, FL
89	Wolverine	517-695-9952	Official SkyGlobe support, Searchlight sales & support	Midland, MI
90	Heat In The Night	515-386-6227	Free Adult BBS, chats, dates, and fun	Kent, WA
91	BMUG Boston	617-721-5840	East coast BMUG, gateways to OneNet & Planet BMUG	Boston, MA
92	Seaside	805-964-4766	ASP BBS, 100+ online games, 450 message areas	Santa Barbara, CA
93	Psycho Ward BBS	203-371-8769	Free system, 1.3Gig, IBM, Amiga, MAC	Bridgeport, CT
94	File Shop BBS	816-587-3311	RIP, 2200 file areas, 28Gig, 310000+ files, 85 online games	Kansas City, MO
95	Aces Place	209-357-8424	Message areas, new files, helpful staff	Atwater, CA
96	Frog Pond	716-461-1924	Supporting MS-DOS & CP/M with great files and zany users	Rochester, NY
97	CRS	416-213-6002	Canada's largest online system, very large file area	Mississauga, ON
98	Studs	415-495-2929	Adult conversation, AIDS/HIV news and information	San Francisco, CA
99	Collector's Edition	214-351-9859	ASP BBS, CD-ROMs, 28 file areas, online games	Dallas, TX

Fig. 1.1. Boardwatch Magazine's list of "The Top 100 BBSs." For subscription information, call 1-800-933-6038.

Walking Through Commercial Services

In Chapter 1 we talked about getting connected to the Internet. Since many people will gain access through commercial services, we'll take a step-by-step look at CompuServe and America Online in this chapter. We are using these two services as examples, but bear in mind that there are several other commercial providers from which to choose.

Once you get access through whatever means, how you use the Internet is the same. This chapter is just for the new user accessing the Internet through a commercial provider.

Accessing the Internet Through CompuServe

If you select CompuServe as your provider, you will be assigned a numerical userid—in other words, you have no choice. Your userid on CompuServe will look something like this:

        75140,3723

Notice that on CompuServe, your userid includes a comma. Remember that when you give your e-mail address to someone not on CompuServe, you should make the comma a dot. Therefore, your e-mail address should look like this:

        75140.3723@compuserve.com

CompuServe assigns passwords as well. Typically the password will be two words separated by a slash, such as press/money.

CompuServe provides you with a local access telephone number for each baud rate. If you don't know the baud rate, select the lowest baud rate. Dial that number with your modem.

When you're connected, you hold down the Ctrl key while you press C.

You'll see on-screen a prompt for your userid. Type your assigned number and press Enter. Then you'll see a prompt for your password. Notice that as you type your password, the letters do not appear on the screen. (That's to prevent a person looking over your shoulder from learning your password.)

The first screen you'll see is CompuServe's main menu of services. It shows the CompuServe copyright at the top, followed by a menu of available services listed by number. It also might show a What's New This Week screen (see fig. 2.1).

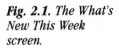

Fig. 2.1. The What's New This Week screen.

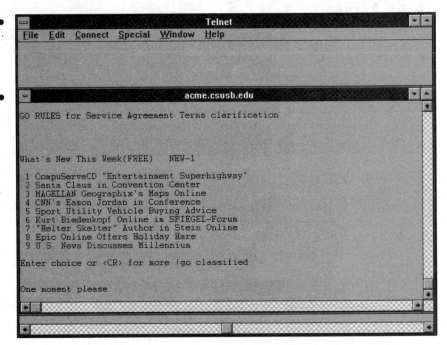

There is a prompt at the bottom of the screen asking you for your choice. You respond by entering the number of your selection.

Note: The item numbers used in this and other examples in the book are subject to change. Remember, the Internet is not like a library, where once a book is published, it can't be changed. Internet information can change at any time—and does!

All CompuServe functions follow this basic format. It is menu-driven, meaning that you will always get a list of choices from which you can make a selection.

You can follow the menus to navigate through CompuServe, or you can use the "go" command with a reference word to jump from one area to another. At the Enter choice prompt, you can type **go** and then type

the name of a destination to get to a specific area. For example, typing
`go classified` would put you directly in the Classified Ads section
of CompuServe (see fig. 2.2).

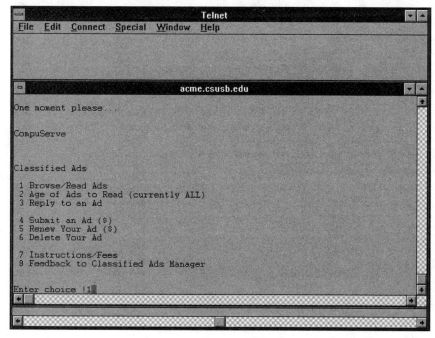

Fig. 2.2. *The Classified Ads section.*

From this screen, you can select Browse/Read Ads by choosing 1. You
soon see the Classified Ads Browse/Read screen (see fig 2.3).

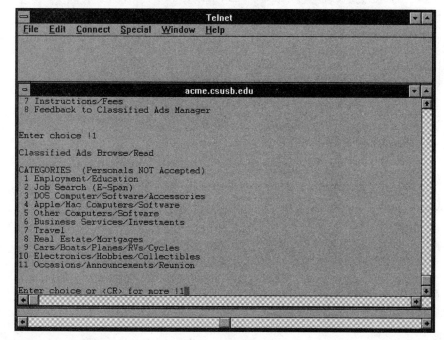

Fig. 2.3. *The Classified Ads Browse/Read screen.*

From that menu, if you choose item 1, Employment/Education, you get the EMPLOYMENT/EDUCATION screen (see fig. 2.4).

Fig. 2.4. The EMPLOY-MENT/EDUCATION screen.

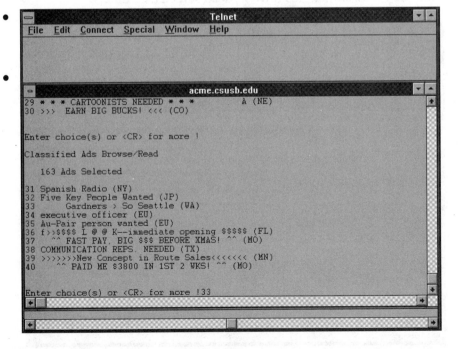

```
─                              Telnet                    ▼ ▲
 File   Edit   Connect   Special   Window   Help



─                          acme.csusb.edu               ▼ ▲
10 Electronics/Hobbies/Collectibles                        ↑
11 Occasions/Announcements/Reunion

Enter choice or <CR> for more !1

Classified Ads Browse/Read

EMPLOYMENT/EDUCATION
 1 Jobs/Positions Wanted
 2 Jobs/Positions Wanted(Cont'd)
 3 Open Technical/Engineer
 4 Open Marketing/Sales
 5 Computer Related Positions
 6 Computer Related Positions(Cont'd)
 7 Other Open Positions
 8 Entrepreneuring Opportunities
 9 Entrepreneuring Opportunities(Con't)
10 Employment Services
11 Educational Opportunities

Enter choice !7                                            ↓
◄                                                          ►

◄                                                          ►
```

Selecting 7, Other Open Positions, gives you an Ads Selected menu (see fig. 2.5).

Fig. 2.5. The Ads Selected menu.

```
─                              Telnet                    ▼ ▲
 File   Edit   Connect   Special   Window   Help



─                          acme.csusb.edu               ▼ ▲
29 * * * CARTOONISTS NEEDED * * *          À (NE)          ↑
30 >>>   EARN BIG BUCKS! <<< (CO)

Enter choice(s) or <CR> for more !

Classified Ads Browse/Read

   163 Ads Selected

31 Spanish Radio (NY)
32 Five Key People Wanted (JP)
33     Gardners > So Seattle (WA)
34 executive officer (EU)
35 Au-Pair person wanted (EU)
36 f>>$$$$ L @ @ K--immediate opening $$$$$ (FL)
37    ^^ FAST PAY, BIG $$$ BEFORE XMAS! ^^ (MO)
38 COMMUNICATION REPS. NEEDED (TX)
39 >>>>>>>New Concept in Route Sales<<<<<<< (MN)
40    ^^ PAID ME $3800 IN 1ST 2 WKS! ^^ (MO)

Enter choice(s) or <CR> for more !33                       ↓
◄                                                          ►

◄                                                          ►
```

This shows a partial list of jobs available. Notice that above the list, it says that 163 ads are available for browsing, but you see on-screen only about 10 at a time. To get through the whole list, you press Enter to page through the list.

If you pick #33, Gardners > So Seattle (WA) by typing 33 at the Enter choice(s) prompt (Note the state abbreviation at the end of each listing), you'll see the next screen, which is the position description (see fig. 2.6).

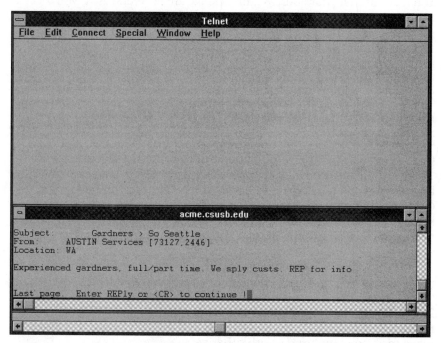

Fig. 2.6. The position description.

Note that at the bottom of this screen, you have the option of entering REP. If you type **REP** and press Enter, your reply will be automatically sent via CompuServe Mail to the person who submitted the ad. You'll see the words Enter Reply, followed on the next line by 1:. Start typing your reply at the 1: prompt.

The screen directs you to type **/EX** and press Enter when you are done entering your message. You will then receive a Reply Action Menu, which gives you the choice of sending, editing, or canceling your reply.

We have walked you through these steps as an exercise in using CompuServe, but we don't want you to reply to any job postings until you have read the material in the remainder of this book. Remember that applying for a job on the Internet is not like applying for a job you see in the newspaper or some other conventional source.

Using CompuServe Mail

The CompuServe e-mail function is easy to use. Simply type `go mail` at the Choice prompt and press Enter. This gives you a menu of choices for composing and sending a message. You will first get the 1: prompt to start typing your message. Type `/Exit` and press Enter when finished. You will see another list of choices, including send, edit, etc. If you choose send, you'll be asked for the userid of the receiver. Next, you'll see a subject line. Type in a suitable, short subject of your message. You'll be asked if your address and message are correct. Lastly, you'll get a confirmation that your message was sent.

To read messages sent to you, enter `go mail`, and you'll see another list of options. Option 1 shows you the number of messages pending. Entering **#1** will bring up your mail.

Accessing CompuServe's Information Resources

CompuServe's strength is the number of information resources it has. There are forums in which people of similar interests can exchange information and participate in discussions. They are run by *Sysops* (system operators) who are in charge of the forum because they have some expertise in the subject matter. This is the Internet equivalent of newsgroups, which you will read about in the next chapter. Here are some sample CompuServe forums:

        `go VET`   Military and Veteran Forum

In this forum, vets may learn about vet services, benefits, and current military information, including careers and military news. It is also a place for discussing topics with other vets.

        `go TRAVSIG`   Travel Forum

This is a forum for people interested in travel. Here, you can find out about destinations and customs, restaurants and hotels.

        `go ROCKNET`   RockNet (Rock Music) Forum

People in this forum exchange inside information about the music industry.

        `go WORK`   Working from Home Forum

A networking forum for people who work at home. Information on management tips, laws, marketing, and contacts.

        `go FLEFO`   Foreign Language Forum

This forum includes information on foreign languages and foreign language learning, including a job bank for translators, educators, and students.

CompuServe gives you access to the world of data. In Chapter 4, you'll read about databases available on the Internet. Here are some examples available to CompuServe members:

    go DEMOGRAPHICS   Demographics

Demographic information for any area of the United States, including population, income, and age of residents.

    go CENDATA   CENDATA The Census Bureau Service

Information on manufacturing, housing starts, population, agriculture, and more. Available reports answer specific questions, such as "What are the occupations with major employment gains for women?"

    go GPO   Government Publications

Catalog of government publications, books, and subscription services. With a credit card, you can order online. It also has free information from government publications on a variety of helpful topics, such as energy conversation and food preparation.

    go GOVERNMENT   Government Information

Information on various government services.

    go TBW   The Business Wire

Press releases and news articles from the world of business, updated throughout the day.

    go TRWREPORT   TRW Business Credit Profiles

Credit and business information on more than 13 million organizations. Includes credit histories, financial information, size, and ownership of businesses. *Note:* There is an extra charge for this service.

Accessing the Internet Through America Online

America Online (AOL) provides a disk for your first sign-on. It comes with a preassigned numerical userid and alpha password like this:

    48-6284-5667
    CUBS-CURIAE

Before you logon, you will be asked for your userid and password, and then led through a series of questions, asking for the baud rate of your modem, and personal information, such as your name, address, phone number, and credit card information. You will also be asked to enter a new password of your choosing, along with the name you want to use online. Your userid will then look like this:

name@aol.com

Generally, AOL provides disks for several hours of free service as a preview. You can often find these disks free in computer magazines. (We found ours in *PC World* magazine.)

For your first logon, the disk packet contains the following instructions:

1. Insert the enclosed disk in your floppy disk drive.

2. From your Windows Program Manager, click **File** and select **Run.** At the prompt, type **A:/SETUP** (or **B:/SETUP**) and press enter.

3. When the installation is complete, click the **America Online** icon, and you're ready to go!

The first screen to come up shows your name and a prompt for your personal password. Type your password and press Enter. (Again, your password does not show on the screen for security reasons.) Next comes a Welcome screen (see fig. 2.7).

Fig. 2.7. The America Online Welcome screen.

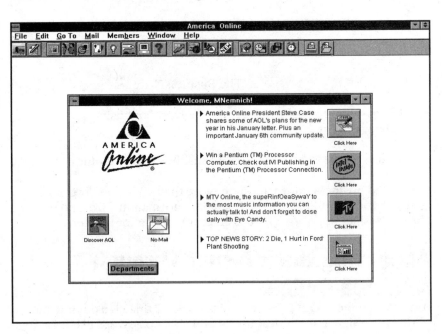

Notice that this screen also has an icon with a message indicating whether you have mail.

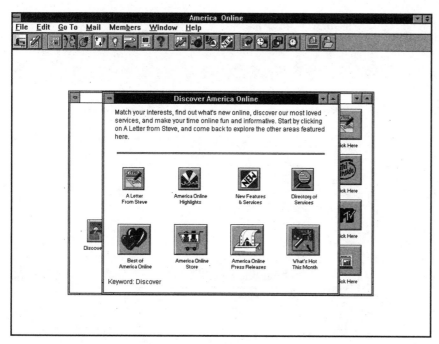

Fig. 2.8. *The Discover America Online screen.*

Click the Discover AOL icon. You will get the Discover America Online screen (fig. 2.8).

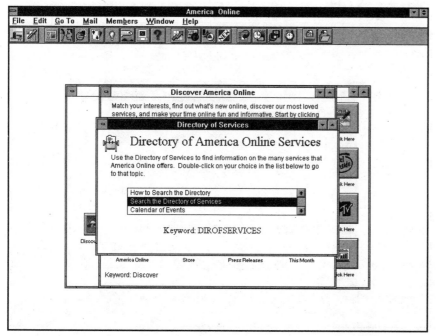

Fig. 2.9. *The Directory of America Online Services screen.*

In the Discover America Online screen, click the Directory of Services icon. Soon you see the Directory of America Online Services screen (see fig. 2.9).

Fig. 2.10. The
Directory of Services
screen.

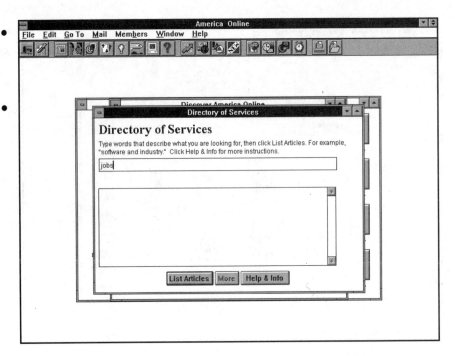

Fig. 2.10. The
Directory of Services
screen.

If you choose Search the Directory of Services, you soon see a Directory of Services screen (see fig. 2.10).

Fig. 2.11. A list of
entries matching the
keyword search.

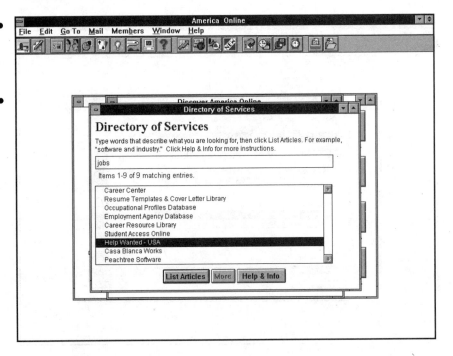

On this screen, you see a prompt for one or more keywords. Enter a word or phrase that describes the area or service you want to search. We entered **jobs** and got the screen on the next page (see fig. 2.11).

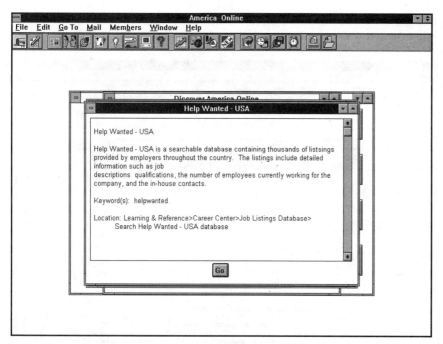

Fig. 2.12. The Help
Wanted - USA screen.

Double-click Help Wanted - USA to get a screen explaining this extensive database of job listings (see fig. 2.12).

Click the GO button at the bottom of the screen to enter the database. You will get a keyword prompt. Enter one or more keywords that describe what you're looking for. Then click List Articles. This gives you a weekly list (see fig. 2.13) of all positions containing the keyword(s) you entered.

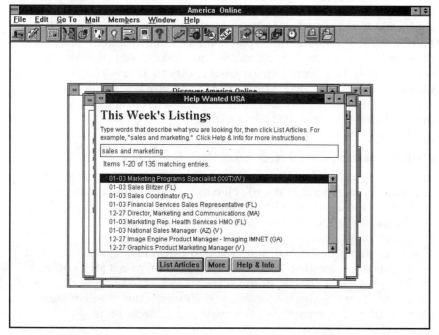

Fig. 2.13. A list of
positions matching
keywords.

Use the arrow key to highlight a position you want to review. Then click the position. You soon see the job announcement (see fig. 2.14).

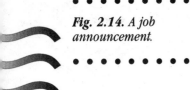

Fig. 2.14. A job announcement.

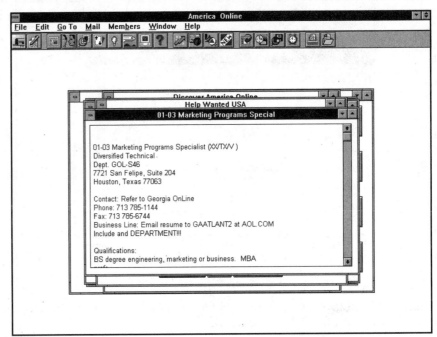

We've shown you how to navigate through several screens to get to a jobs area. There are different ways to do this, using AOL's **G**o To feature. Simply select **G**o To from the menu bar at the top of the screen. Click **G**o To to open the window. Select "keyword" from the list of options. Enter an employment-related keyword to go directly to a job area. If you type `jobs`, you get a listing of options where jobs may be searched, including E-span database, Help Wanted - USA, and the classified ads area. Typing `career` at the keyword prompt puts you right into the Career Center, where you can access jobs plus career guidance and other help. Type `classified` at the keyword prompt, and you enter the Classifieds Online section. Here you can select an option called "business and jobs postings."

Accessing America OnLine's Many Features

In "Career Center," you can get help with resumes and cover letters, information on federal jobs and self-employment, plus an "employer contacts" database. You can also find career guidance services and an employment agency database here.

The e-mail function on AOL allows you to e-mail messages throughout the Internet. On the first screen after sign-on, there is a **M**ail command on the menu bar at the top of the screen. Click **M**ail once, and it opens a window showing all mail functions, including compose, read and check mail, Fax, Internet Mail Gateway, and Address Book.

The Internet Mail Gateway function is the means of e-mailing to other systems on the Internet. There is no additional charge to members for this service. At the Internet Mail Gateway screen, click HOW TO SEND MAIL TO OTHER SERVICES. The screen will tell you exactly how to e-mail to Internet addresses, like this (see fig. 2.15):

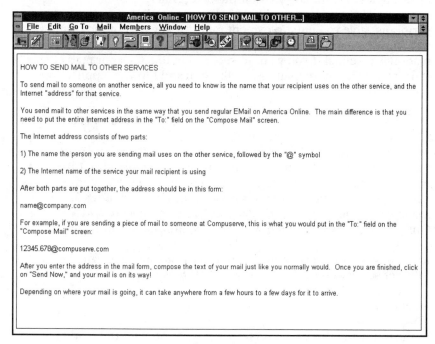

Fig. 2.15. On-screen instructions for HOW TO SEND MAIL TO OTHER SERVICES.

You will use this feature a lot in responding to employers.

AOL has a "talk" feature known as People Connection. Select **G**o To from the menu bar at the very top of the screen. Then select Departments to get to People Connection. When you "arrive" there, you are in a "lobby" of an interactive place where you can engage in conversations or "real time chat" with other AOL users. One icon in People Connection is named List Rooms. Click it, and you see a list of chats you can enter. There are such groups as New Members Lounge, Sports, and Romance Connection. You can even create your own "private room" by typing a title at the prompt. Just pick a room and join any conversation in progress.

Among the many features available on America Online, there is a substantial area called Newsstand, containing many publications, such as *Business Week*, *Time*, *The New York Times*, *The Chicago Tribune*, *National Geographic*, and *Smithsonian*. *Compton's Encyclopedia* is also available, searchable by keyword. All are good research tools for the job seeker.

Using Resources Available Through Online Providers

Every job seeker needs information about employment trends as well as vacancies and employers. CompuServe, America Online, and other commercial providers can tell you what occupations are growing or shrinking, give you unemployment rates for any part of the country, and show housing costs in any part of the country. This kind of information is essential if you want to succeed in today's labor market. For starters, it takes more than just walking in and filing an application to secure a job.

Mary worked with career military officers at a base that was closing. After having been out of the civilian job market for many years, the officers were amazed at the amount of research that is necessary to find the right job. They had to learn about civilian pay structures and benefits packages, as well as company philosophies. For many of these people, a new career also meant relocation. The kind of resources available through online providers such as CompuServe and America Online can put you in touch with all this information and more.

Remember commercial servers differ in the amount and range of Internet services they deliver to you. Before you subscribe to any service, evaluate your needs and what the services can provide—and at what cost.

In the following three chapters, we present you with the world of options available to you on the Internet.

CHAPTER 3

Using the Internet Classifieds

In this chapter, you'll learn how to find job announcements on the Internet. You may be surprised to know that thousands are listed from all over the world. First, we'll look at network news, LISTSERV, e-mail lists, and job listings on BBSs (bulletin board services). Then we'll explore telnet and gopher.

Finding Job Lists Through Network News

Don't let this term mislead you. What is referred to as "news" does not refer to current events but instead to what we will call bulletin boards.

Think of a bulletin board on a college campus or even in a neighborhood grocery store or laundry. Let's say your dog is missing. You can post a message on a bulletin board for anyone who happens to read passing by. If someone has seen your dog, that person might copy down your telephone number and report the sighting to you. Another person having a dog of the same breed might leave you a message to tell you that some puppies are available. And because bulletin boards are open to anyone who passes by, another person might write graffiti on your posting. Think of network news as the electronic equivalent of a bulletin board in your local grocery.

On network news you'll find thousands of discussions, conferences, and interest groups on topics from the Bible to bestiality. Network news is transmitted on the USENET (User's Network). Most people who have access to USENET don't have Internet access. And, even if you have Internet access, that doesn't guarantee you'll have access to USENET.

Network news is divided into newsgroups devoted to a certain topic. Some of the newsgroups are serious discussions; some are frank discussions. Even if you have access to USENET, your Internet access computer may not carry all the newsgroups because thousands are available or because the subject matter of some of the newsgroups is explicit.

If you find you have access, you'll be able to read *postings* (known as articles) and respond to them publicly, or copy down the originator's address and send a private message.

The best place to begin in newsgroups is the group called `news.announce.newusers`, which provides articles on how to best use the service.

At this time, the majority of job listings on the Internet are for computer-related positions. Of course, that is to be expected. But this should not discourage job seekers in other areas. You'll just have to look through a lot of job listings for people with computer skills before you find those most appropriate for you.

Just as the Internet itself is dynamic and ever-changing so are newsgroups. Some of these may no longer exist; many others will be added. We've identified from the thousands available those that have the most job listings:

`ba.jobs.misc`	Small listing of jobs in the San Francisco Bay Area
`ba.jobs.offered`	Large listing of jobs in the San Francisco Bay Area
`bionet.jobs`	Very large listing of jobs in biological sciences
`biz.jobs.offered`	Very large listing of all types of jobs
`comp.jobs.offered`	Small listing of computer-related jobs
`cr.jobs`	Some listings of jobs in the field of conflict resolution and dispute mediation
`dc.jobs`	Large listing of job vacancies largely in the Washington, D.C., area
`edu.popular`	Some job listings for people interested in education for democratic social change.

`gen.jobs.usa`	Listing of jobs in the environmental and social change fields
`gn.jobs`	Green Net's small listing of jobs in Europe
`misc.jobs`	Small listing of computer-related jobs
`misc.jobs.contract`	Large listings of contract jobs
`misc.jobs.misc`	Mostly computer-related job listings
`misc.jobs.offered`	Very large listing of primarily computer-related jobs, but others listed as well
`misc.jobs.offered.entry`	Entry-level positions
`ne.jobs`	Very large listing of job vacancies in the northeastern United States
`uk.jobs.d`	Small listing of jobs in the United Kingdom
`uk.jobs.offered`	Some listings of jobs in the United Kingdom
`web.jobs`	Small listing of jobs in Canada

And here are even more listings that we've heard about from different sources. Unfortunately, we can't guarantee that your site carries these newsgroups or that they are current and active.

`ab.jobs`	Jobs in Alberta, Canada
`atl.jobs`	Jobs in Atlanta, Georgia
`aus.ads.jobs`	Jobs in Australia
`aus.jobs`	Jobs in Australia
`austin.jobs`	Jobs in Austin, Texas
`ba.jobs.contract`	Contract positions in the San Francisco Bay area
`balt.jobs`	Jobs in Baltimore and the Washington, D.C., area

`can.jobs`	Jobs in Canada (also see local groups: `ab.jobs`, `kingston.jobs`, `kw.jobs`, `out.jobs`, `ott.jobs`, `qc.jobs`, and `tor.jobs`)
`chi.jobs`	Jobs in Chicago
`cmb.jobs`	Jobs in Columbus, Ohio
`de.markt.jobs`	Jobs in Germany
`dfw.jobs`	Jobs in Dallas-Fort Worth, Texas
`dk.jobs`	Jobs in Denmark
`dod.jobs`	U.S. Department of Defense jobs
`fl.jobs`	Jobs in Florida
`fr.jobs.offres`	Jobs in France
`houston.jobs.offered`	Jobs in Houston, Texas
`il.jobs.misc`	Jobs in Illinois
`il.jobs.offered`	Jobs in Illinois
`kingston.jobs`	Jobs in Kingston, Canada
`kw.jobs`	Jobs in Kitchener-Waterloo, Ontario, Canada
`la.jobs`	Jobs in Los Angeles
`li.jobs`	Jobs in Long Island, New York
`memphis.employment`	Jobs in Memphis, Tennessee
`mi.jobs`	Jobs in Michigan
`nm.jobs`	Jobs in New Mexico
`nyc.jobs.contract`	Contract positions in New York City
`nyc.jobs.offered`	Jobs in New York City
`ont.jobs`	Jobs in Ontario, Canada

`pdaxs.jobs`	Jobs in Portland, Oregon (*Note*: insert job title such as clerical, management, etc.)
`pgh.jobs.offered`	Jobs in Pittsburgh, Pennsylvania
`phl.jobs.offered`	Jobs in Philadelphia, Pennsylvania
`relcom.commerce.jobs`	Jobs in former Soviet Union
`sdnet.jobs`	Jobs in San Diego, California
`stl.jobs`	Jobs in St. Louis, Missouri
`su.jobs`	Jobs at Stanford University
`swnet.jobs`	Jobs in Sweden
`tor.jobs`	Jobs in Toronto, Ontario, Canada
`triangle.jobs`	Jobs in the Triangle Park area (North Carolina)
`tx.jobs`	Jobs in Texas
`ucb.jobs`	Jobs at the University of California, Berkeley
`ucd.cs.jobs`	Jobs at the University of California, Davis
`uiuc.misc.jobs`	Jobs at the University of Illinois, Urbana-Champaign
`umn.general.jobs`	Jobs at the University of Minnesota
`us.jobs.contract`	Contract positions in the United States
`us.jobs.offered`	Jobs in the United States
`ut.jobs`	Jobs at the University of Texas
`za.ads.jobs`	Jobs in South Africa

You're probably wondering what these job postings look like. Here are some examples:

Topic 441	Casino Clerical Position in Las Vegas	
lance	misc.jobs.offered.entry	12:12PM Aug 30, 1994
(at unlv.edu)		(From News system)

We currently have a clerical position available at a reputable casino here in Las Vegas. The job includes system/database maintenance, Lotus 1-2-3/MS-Excel, filing, and other typical clerical duties. If you are interested, please send me E-mail, and I will provide you with the details.

Thank you very much,

Bryan

Topic 391	Youth Minister Announcement	
allan.klindera	misc.jobs.offered.entry	3:54 AM Jun 30, 1994
(at minserv.com)		(From News system)

Northside Methodist Church in Milton, Texas, is searching for a minister of youth. Interested applicants may submit a resume to Anthony Eldridge, First United Methodist Church, P.O. Box 632, Milton,TX 00000-0000, by fax to (000) 000-0000, or by e-mail to allan.klindera@finders.bbs.utxlub.edu. E-mail responses will be forwarded.

```
*****************************************************************************
R                                                                         R
T     Allan Klindera              allan.klindera@minserv.com      T
3     1234 Main Street            phone:(000) 000-0000            3
V     Milton, TX 00000-0000 USA   fax:  (000) 000-0000            V
S                                                                         S
*****************************************************************************
```

Topic 2012	CAD/Graphics Programmer – West	
Charles	uk.jobs.offered	9:36 AM Oct 11, 1994
(at newcomb.ivory.co.uk)		(From News system)

Position:	Analyst/Programmer for CAD Software package
Skills:	DOS, Windows, C/C++
Experience:	CAD Applications Packaging
Length:	6 months (with 6 months extensions)
Location:	Gloucestershire
Rate:	Good

Charles Osgood || Charles@newcomb.ivory.co.uk || Tel 071-000-0000
Newcomb Designers, Ltd. || Fax 071-000-0000
23 Newington Circle
London, W4 3BH

Topic 124   Agronomist Wanted
krune   biz.jobs.offered   8:21 AM Nov 19, 1994
(at tray.ucw.edu)   (From News system)

USDA, Agricultural Research Service
An equal opportunity employer

1-year temporary full-time position at GS-5 ($19,116) level in Plant Molecular Biology Lab,
Harleytown, WI 00000.

Duties: To assist in a breeding program to develop silage soybeans for sustainable
agriculture. Will harvest and clean seed of breeding lines, weigh and package seed for
distribution, plant field experiments, record and summarize data on performance of
silage soybean lines, hybridize selected breeding lines.

Required Training: Knowledge of reproductive botany of plants and plant genetics, field
plot technique and statistics.

Contact Dr. M. C. Davies
phone: (000) 000-0000

email: krune@tray.ucw.edu

Topic 283   Next Generation Reporter
sue.riley   biz.jobs.offered   10:18 AM Oct 12, 1994
(at newslet.com)   (From News system)

Hi

We are a small publishing company near Princeton, NJ. We currently publish a hardcopy
newsletter (weekly) and a directory; maintain a BBS, four publishing lists, and a network
to other boards; and manage 8 newsgroups. We also have our newsletter online and
maintain a fax service for our subs.

We're looking for a next generation reporter/writer to be located in our office. Should be
familiar with desktop publishing (we use PageMaker), working on the Internet, BBS's,
and LOTS of phone calling to get info for newsletter.

If interested, call, write, or fax to:
sue.riley@newslet.com
Voice   609-000-0000
Fax   609-000-0000
BBS   609-000-0000
P.O. Box 000, Some Town, NJ 00000

Topic 211   Job opening-Librarian/Info Spec
RT   misc.jobs.offered   10:12 AM   Oct 25, 1994
(at newtechinfo.com)   (From News system)

Posting date: October 23, 1994

International consulting firm has IMMEDIATE opening for FT Librarian/Information
Specialist to support and respond to information needs of home-office and overseas project
staff. Responsible for all aspects of library management and technical information services
including collections, databases, and online accounts. Must be expert in online services,
CD-ROM, and Internet. Requires 5 years relevant experience and excellent networking and
communication skills. Foreign languages and USAID experience a plus.

Respond via Internet to RT@newtechinfo.com or by fax to 555-000-0000. Attn RT. Please
indicate availability and salary range.

Firm is based in Arlington, VA, about 210 professionals. Portfolio includes work in 60
countries worldwide. Provides technical assistance and project management services to
projects funded by USAID. World Bank, regional development banks, and foreign
government agencies. Specialty areas include agriculture/agribusiness, environment and
natural resources management, economic development, local government and municipal
development, private sector development, restructuring and privatization.

Topic 229   London Peace Job offered
kc:afd   uk.jobs.offered   6:43 AM   Oct 11, 1994

COUNCIL FOR UNITY & PEACE

The Council for Unity & Peace, a network of over 183 groups working for peace, the
environment, development and human rights, is looking for a

MEMBERSHIP & PUBLICATIONS OFFICER

Candidates must be able to demonstrate commitment to peace, disarmament and
nonviolent conflict resolution. Good writing, word processing and "Windows" skills are
essential; design and database skills preferable. Candidates must have plenty of energy
and enthusiasm.

The post is for three days per week.

Salary is GBP 15,162. Pro rata GBP 9,102.

The closing date for applications is Friday 18 November 1994
An equal opportunity employer

For further details contact:

Council for Unity & Peace, 146 Wellington Close, London K2 6MT

Tel: 071 000 0000 (+44 71 000 0000) Fax: 071 000 0000 (+44 71 000 0000)
e-mail: afd@kc.cup.org

Topic 333   EUGENE, OR: Environmental Engineer
oec   misc.jobs.offered   1:30 PM   Sep 16, 1994
(at newport.com)   (From News system)

Environmental Engineers
REF# 63-312KV

Oregon Environmental Consultants, Inc., has an immediate opening in the Eugene,
Oregon, area for the following:

Environmental Engineer: REF# 63-312KV: EUGENE, OR

This regular full-time position will formulate, implement, and administer
a comprehensive environmental program for the entire facility in order to
ensure the safety of facility personnel and compliance with local, state,
and federal regulations, while fostering an increased awareness of
environmental issues. It is highly desirable that the candidate have a BS in
Chemical Engineering or related field and 3-5 years environmental
experience in an industrial setting. A knowledge of Industrial Hygiene
principles is important.

Oregon's clean, healthy environment makes the University town of Eugene a great home.
You can live in the country and still be only 10 minutes from your office. The ocean,
year-round skiing, and great fishing are all in close proximity.

For this or other opportunities, send your resume to:
Oregon Environmental Consultants, Inc.
3220 Some Street
Portland, OR 90000

email: oec@newport.com

Fax: (503) 000-0000

Phone: (503) 000-0000

Topic 127	Director of Finance	
mmendinas	su.jobs	9:12 AM Aug 15, 1994
(at netcom.com)		(From News system)

The Sea of Cortez Aquarium Foundation, a 501(c)(3) public benefit corporation, is working to begin construction on an exciting and highly innovative project, the Sea of Cortez Aquarium and the Baja Institute of Oceanic Sciences, a combined nonprofit aquarium and research institute to be located in San Jose del Cabo, southern Baja California, Mexico.

The mission of the Sea of Cortez Aquarium is to promote awareness, understanding, and responsible stewardship of the marine environment around the Baja California Peninsula of Mexico, and to inspire appreciation of all the world's ocean environments.

We are seeking a senior-level Director of Finance to join our team. Position to be located in the San Francisco Bay Area. Qualifications for the position include:
* Overseeing corporate fiscal planning and spreadsheet-based budgeting experience.
* Executive-level presentation skills.
* Team player.
* Willing to travel to Mexico on a limited basis.

  At least one of the following:
* Big Six accounting experience with hands-on implementation of IPO or bod issue.
* Experience with investment bank or major brokerage firm.
* Chief financial officer.

In addition, fluency in Spanish, experience in a startup environment, and international exposure are desirable.

We offer a rewarding challenge and the opportunity to make a significant impact in the protection of the marine environment for future generations.

Please respond to Milo Mendinas, Executive Director at mmendinas@netcom.com
Sea of Cortez Aquarium Foundation
Stanford University
Stanford, CA 94304

No phone calls please!

Sea of Cortez Aquarium Foundation

Working to ensure the protection of marine life
through the compassion of a better informed citizenry.

M E X I C O % U S A

Topic 672   Communications Jobs — N. CA
LIC/EB   ucsf.jobs   11.42 AM Sep 22, 1994
(at conscom.net)   (From News system)

Consolidated Communications, Inc., a leader in advanced wireless rural telecommunications, is expanding our Los Gatos, California, engineering development team. We are looking for self-starters for this dynamic startup environment.

Radio Development
Senior Radio Development Engineer

Experience in digital microwave radio circuit and system design. Cost/performance analysis of digital radio transmitter and receiver architectures: TDMA, FDMA, CDMA. Analysis of power, efficiency, intermodulation, spurious. MSEE with 8+ years experience.

High-Speed Modem Development Engineer

Experience in multimegabit-per-second modem circuit design, including TDMA modems, clock and carrier recovery. Cost/performance analysis of modulation techniques: TDMA, FDMA, CDMA, GMSK, OQPSK. DSP implementations of demodulation, carrier & clock recovery techniques. BSEE with 5-8 years experience.

Entry-Level Electrical Design Engineer

Familiar with use of RF spectrum and network analyzers, digital modulation/demodulation, microwave amplifier/oscillator/filter design, phase-locked loop design, and electromagnetic wave propagation. Theoretical and practical balance. BSEE or equiv., microwaves & communications.

System Engineering

Senior System Engineer — OAM&P/Call Processing

Experience in analyzing and specifying, maintaining, and verifying signaling, call processing, routing, billing, and OAM&P requirements for a digital switching system. Review system architecture, hardware, and software designs for compliance. Review system test plans and procedures for coverage. BSEE with 8+ yrs. experience.

Senior Systems Engineer — RF

Experience in analyzing and specifying requirements for radio frequency (RF) links interconnecting nodes of a digital switching system. Specify RF link architecture, including RF propagation effects, multiple access techniques, transmitter power, receiver sensitivity, antenna height and gain. Review RF designs for compliance, and system test plans and procedures for coverage. BSEE with 8+ yrs. Experience.

Please send your resume with references to:
Edward Bronson
Human Resources
Consolidated Communications, Inc.
5678 Some Street
Los Gatos, CA 90000-0000

Some positions require overseas travel. Include position title on cover letter. Principals only. No phone calls please. An Equal Opportunity Employer.

Topic 884   Teacher/Naturalist in Marin County (CA)
Mitchell   misc.jobs.offered entry   10:16 AM May 20, 1994
(at marlow.ucsf.edu)   (From News system)

TEACHER/NATURALIST
Job Announcement

BACKGROUND:
PINE VALLEY is a nonprofit Environmental Education Program that serves Marin County students in the 4th through 8th grades. Students participate in a week-long residential camp experience to explore and learn about the natural environment, to learn how to relate more fully and openly with their peers, and to build their sense of self-esteem and empowerment in their individual lives. The Pine Valley staff members work closely together and consist of the Director, Associate Director, the Counselor Coordinator, the Administrative Coordinator, and approximately nine Teacher/ Naturalists. The site is a 180 acre, full-facility camp with forest, stream, and bay areas. It is located near Sausalito in Marin County, less than an hour north of San Francisco.

SPECIFIC RESPONSIBILITIES
Teaches environmental education during on-site camp program:
— Leads hiking groups of 10 students in the Stream Watershed. Uses multidisciplinary learning games, scientific exploration, and group discussions to teach environmental concepts; uses group challenge activities to build sense of cooperation and self-esteem.
— Leads students in coastal exploration.

Leads a variety of other program activities:
— Facilitates evening group social-interaction activities and discussions.
— Teaches arts and crafts, elective games, and physical activities.
— Leads night walks, "Environmental Skits" activity groups, "Moral Development" discussion groups, and other evening events.
— Aids in organizing and leading campfire songs, stories, and activities.
— Provides instruction in health and safety aspects of living outdoors.
— Supervises students in living activities, meals, cleanup, etc.
— Assists in training of high school counselors.
— Helps in implementing program changes.
— Participates in evaluation of counselors and program.
— Is on call, while in camp, for emergency situations.
— Performs other duties, when asked by Program Director.

QUALIFICATIONS
Bachelor's degree in education, environmental studies, geography, biology, psychology, sociology, or related disciplines.

Experience in working with children 10-14 (experience working with children from a variety of ethnic and socioeconomic backgrounds helpful).

Interest and/or experience in problem-solving with kids' issues.

Certification in Standard First Aid, CPR, Advanced Lifesaving (can arrange for certification).

JOB SPECIFICS

Pay Rate: $275 — $300 per week dependent on experience.

Time Period: Seasonal   —   late September to early December
                                                (Fall, approx. 7 weeks)

                                   —   early February to late May
                                                (Spring, approx. 11 weeks).

Miscellaneous: Free housing available from late September to late
                          May. Board provided during weeks of on-site work.

Send resume and cover letter to: PINE VALLEY
                                                        1234 Some Street
                                                        Sausalito, CA 90000

Contact People: Ian Brannock — Associate Director
                            Kathryn Boyd — Administrative Coordinator

Call: (415) 000-0000 for further information.

EOE: Women and minorities encouraged to apply.

Look at the examples carefully. You'll note that in the upper-left corner, you'll see the e-mail address of the person who posted the announcement. (Not all newsreaders may show this.) That e-mail address may be listed in two lines, such as these:

```
fjandt

(at aol.com)
```

You know that to send a message to that person, the e-mail address would be this:

```
fjandt@aol.com
```

Also read the complete job announcement. Some will specify an e-mail address for applications.

Please note that you could also send a message to the whole group. If you see a prompt for reply on your screen, remember that your reply is probably going to be posted on the whole list for anyone to read. You don't want your application and resume posted as a response to a job announcement if for no other reason than it tells the employer that you don't understand how to use the Internet.

Even if you don't have access to the newsgroups on these pages, you can still post a message to the newsgroups if you have e-mail access. For example, suppose that you want information about stores in your state that sell exotic birds and you know that an address for bird enthusiasts is `rec.pets.birds` but you have access only to Internet e-mail. You can still seek information by directing your request to `rec.pets.birds@decwri.dec.com`. Include in your request your name and e-mail address and ask that any information be sent to you by e-mail. Note that only the first line of your posted request will be visible on-screen, so make certain that the first line indicates the nature of your request.

In some of the newsgroups, you'll notice that people have placed their own job-wanted announcement. You'll also find some newsgroups where people post their resumes. Later in the book, we discuss better ways to do this.

Finding Job Lists Through LISTSERV and E-Mail

LISTSERV takes its name from "list server," an automatic discussion list service that accepts commands requesting different actions, such as subscribing to a list or listing members of a group.

LISTSERV resembles USENET newsgroups except that you must subscribe, and you receive issues through e-mail.

Let's say you're interested in jobs in criminal justice. Your criminal justice instructor tells you to check out the **UNCJIN-L** bulletin board. (The L tells you it is a LISTSERV list.) UNCJIN is the United Nations Criminal Justice Information Network. Your instructor gives you its Internet address.

The automatic list server requires that you subscribe and unsubscribe in a certain way. To subscribe, you send an e-mail message to:

> **LISTSERV@UACSC2.ALBANY.EDU**

In the body of the message, you send only the following:

> **SUBSCRIBE UNCJIN-L**   `<your name as you usually write it>`

Because LISTSERV picks up your e-mail address from the header of your message, you don't include it in the message itself.

Shortly you'll receive in your e-mail mailbox an acknowledgment of your subscription and information about the list. It will also tell you how to unsubscribe from the list; keep this information, or you may be receiving messages from this group for years. Usually you send a message to the same address you used to subscribe, but this time the message should read only **SIGNOFF UNCJIN-L**. It's a good idea to use this command when you're away on vacation, or your mailbox will fill up with messages from the different lists to which you've subscribed.

You're probably wondering how to find the addresses. One way is to send a message to the following:

> **LISTSERV@BITNIC.bitnet**

The message you enter should read only **list global**. You'll receive a huge document of lists.

Another way is to send an e-mail message to:

> **MAIL-SERVER@SRI.COM**

In the message enter only **Send Netinfo/Interest-groups**.

Academic discussion lists can be searched using gopher, which is described later in this chapter.

Here are two gophers to try:

> **gopher nysernet.org**

Path: New York State Education and Research Network (NYSERNet)/ Special Collection: Higher Education/Scholarly Electronic Conferences [Kovacs]

and

    gopher gopher.austin.unimelb.edu.au

Path: Austin Hospital, Melbourne/Research Related Information [Directory of Scholarly E-conferences] (ACADLIST)

Note: A *path* includes each selection you make from each menu in a series of menus. In a path the selections are separated by a slash (/).

A more extensive list can be searched using this gopher:

    gopher gopher.cni.org

Path: Coalition for Networked Information/Coalition FTP Archives (ftp.cni.org)/Publicly Accessible Documents (/pub)/Guides to Network Use/Strangelove, Michael: Directory of Electronic Journals and Newsletters

While LISTSERV uses an automatic list server, e-mail uses an actual person as the list administrator. An e-mail list is simply a group of e-mail addresses of people interested in a particular subject.

To subscribe to an e-mail list, send a message to the list administrator. Because this message is read by a person, you can say whatever you want. Keep in mind, however, that if you address the list itself, your message will be sent to all subscribers. The administrator may have a separate address, or you would add the word *request* to the address, such as:

    <name>-**request@**<address>

Finding Job Lists on Commercial Online Services

America Online calls itself the first electronic career and employment guidance agency in the United States, although it does provide more than job listings. Its job listings include these:

Help Wanted USA—Information on thousands of job openings in all career areas

Career Resource Library & Employment Agency Database

Self-Employment Service

Federal Employment Service

AOL Talent Bank—A way for AOL members to find talent among other AOL members

Finding Job Lists on BBSs

The major BBSs have job search information as well. Here's a list of some we've found:

BBS Name Location Telephone Number(s) and Maximum Baud Rate(s)	Description
Career Connections Los Altos, CA 415-917-2129 (2400) 415-917-2125 (14,400)	Worldwide job listings No fee required
Career Link, Inc. Phoenix, AZ Voice: 800-453-3350	Nationwide and worldwide job listings Updated weekly Fee required; call 800 number for information
Career Systems MA 413-592-9208 (9600)	Nationwide job listings No fee required
Careers Online San Jose, CA 408-248-7029 (14,400)	Job listings and resume fax service No fee required
Careers Online MA 508-879-4700 (9600)	*Computer World* newspaper listings of DP jobs nationwide No fee required
Contractors Exchange San Francisco, CA 415-334-7393 (2400)	Construction and contractor jobs Updated daily No fee required
Dallas Opportunity Network 214-444-0050	Unable to verify— authors

BBS Name Location Telephone Number(s) and Maximum Baud Rate(s)	Description
D.I.C.E. National Network Des Moines, IA 515-280-3423 (14,400)	Nationwide job listings Updated several times daily
Newark, NJ 201-242-4166 (9600) Sunnyvale, CA 408-737-9339	No fee required
DP NETwork (Toner Corp.) San Francisco, CA 415-788-8663 (2400) 415-788-7101 (9600)	DP jobs in the San Francisco and Sacramento areas Updated daily No fee required
ECCO BBS San Francisco, CA 415-331-7227 (14,400)	Nationwide job listings
Employment Board San Diego, CA 619-689-1348 (9600)	Employment information for the San Diego area No fee required
Exec-PC BBS WI 414-789-4210 (9600)	Large variety of job listings in all areas No fee required to access Job Search door
Federal Job Opportunity BBS 912-757-3100	Service of U.S. Office of Personnel Management
Jobs BBS 404-992-8937	Unable to verify– authors
JOBS-BBS Portland, OR 503-281-6808 (9600)	Listings of all sorts of jobs nationwide Updated several times daily No fee required
International Systems Source Denver, CO 507-645-2394 (14,400)	Mostly jobs for information engineers in the Denver area No fee required

BBS Name Location Telephone Number(s) and Maximum Baud Rate(s)	Description
Mouse House Anaheim, CA 714-535-3761	Devoted entirely to Disney, includes job openings
National Technical Search Amherst, MA 413-549-8136 (14,400)	Nationwide job listings with forums and career guides
Online Opportunities Philadelphia, PA 215-873-7170 (14,400)	All kinds of jobs nationwide Updated weekly Registration fee
OPM FEDJOBS - Philly Philadelphia, PA 215-580-2216 (14,400)	Federal job listings (BBS operated by U.S. Office of Personnel Management) Updated daily No fee required
ouT therE BBS San Jose, CA 408-263-2248 (9600)	San Francisco Bay Area job listings Updated every two days No fee required
Résumé Exchange 602-947-4283	Phoenix area resumes and job listings
The Resume File 805-581-6210	Nationwide jobs and resume database and federal job opportunities.

Finding Job Positions Through Telnet

Telnet is what allows you to access another computer through the
Internet. Telnet is similar to using a modem to dial another computer,
but it is easier and faster, and doesn't result in any telephone toll
charges. Telnet was originally developed to allow users to access their
own computer from remote locations. Now, though, telnet is largely
used to access databases on other computers.

Telnet is very easy to use. You simply type `telnet`, press the space bar
to create a space, type the name of the computer you want to enter,
and press Enter. Here's a telnet address to try for practice:

```
telnet locis.loc.gov
```

You'll find yourself connected to the Library of Congress Information System. By following the directions on each screen, you'll have access to the Library of Congress book catalog, federal legislation, copyright information, and more. You could even search for authors with your family name and locate ones to whom you might be related.

Federal job openings and Census Bureau data or topics from aerospace to weather can be accessed by telnet at this address using marvel as the login:

        telnet marvel.loc.gov

This has a 15-port limit. The same information can be reached through gopher at marvel.loc.gov.

Unfortunately, government data is still largely decentralized on the Internet and requires some searching to find what you need. FedWorld was established in 1993 to provide a single gateway to more than 100 government agencies. As of this writing, FedWorld is overburdened, and it is difficult to get a connection. You can try to reach FedWorld by telnet with these addresses:

        fedworld.gov

or

        fedworld.doc.gov

FedWorld is available also by modem at 703-321-8020 (1200 to 9600 bps). You can also try to reach the Federal Job Opportunity Board by telnet at this address:

        fjob.mail.opm.gov (198.78.46.10)

or by modem at this number:

        912-757-3100

One service available through telnet is the Career Connection's Online Information System H.E.A.R.T. (Human Resources Electronic Advertising and Recruiting Tool).

New college graduates and entry-level job seekers should try this address:

        telnet college.career.com (198.207.167.3)

Others can try the following:

```
telnet career.com (198.207.167.1)
```

This menu-driven system is supported by member companies to enable them to reach the most qualified candidates for advertised positions. This service is free to job seekers.

You can search for positions by geographic location or job title. You can also apply for jobs through this system. You'll be asked to register and select a password so that a private e-mail and profile account can be created for you.

Career Connections can also be reached by modem at 415-903-5840 (2400 bps) or 415-903-5815 (14,400 bps), or by sending an e-mail message to this address:

```
postmaster@career.com
```

Other telnet addresses include:

`cap.gwu.edu`	National Capitol Area Public Acces Network login: `guest` password: `visitor`
`econ.tucson.az.us`	Tucson login: `econ`
`window.texas.gov`	Access to several Texas state agencies including the Texas Employment Commission

Finding Job Information Through Gophers

Gopher is an application that allows you to browse and search documents. It was developed at the University of Minnesota and named after its mascot—the Golden Gopher. It's simple to understand and easy to use. Imagine a tree. You scale the trunk to the lower branches and choose to climb one of the branches. You then reach another group of branches and choose to continue along one of the branches available.

This is exactly what a gopher does. The first gopher screen gives you a menu of choices, and you pick one. The new screen then gives you a new set of choices. You select one, and that new screen gives you some more choices. You'll see gopher paths indicated by those choices in a line with slashes (/). For example: Extension Service USDA Information/USDA and Other Federal Agency Information/Job Openings in the Federal Government. The first phrase is the selection you made on the first screen; the next is your selection from the second screen, etc.

Perhaps the only problem some people encounter is getting lost in the tree; that is, they want to jump from branch to branch in the tree. You can't do that in a gopher. You must go back down the tree until you find a new branch that can take you to another part of the tree.

There are gopher sites all over the world. It's recommended that you choose one close to you. Here are a few examples:

Hostname	IP Number	Login Id	Location
cat.ohiolink.edu	130.108.120.25	gopher	North America
consultant.micro.umn.edu	134.84.132.4	gopher	North America
gopher.msu.edu	135.8.2.61	gopher	North America
gopher.uiuc.edu	128.174.33.160	gopher	North America
gopher.uwp.edu	131.210.1.13	gopher	North America
panda.uiowa.edu	128.255.40.201	panda	North America
seymour.md.gov	128.8.10.46	gopher	North America
info.anu.edu.au	150.203.84.20	info	Australia
tolten.puc.cl	146.155.1.16	gopher	South America
gan.ncc.go.jp	160.190.10.1	gopher	Japan

A longer list of public gopher sites can be retrieved from the file, "Special Internet Connections" by Scott Yanoff. For information on where to find this list finger:

> yanoff@csd4.csd.uwm.edu

Let's work through an example together. Enter this:

> gopher.uiuc.edu

You'll see the Root gopher server screen (see fig. 3.1).

It's the gopher at the University of Illinois at Urbana-Champaign. The cursor has been moved using the arrow keys to option 11—Other Gopher and Information Servers.

After you choose this option, you see the Other Gopher and Information Servers screens (see fig. 3.2).

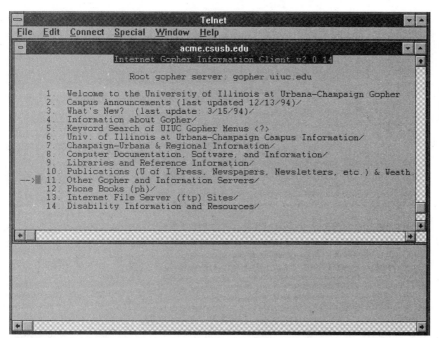

Fig. 3.1. *Internet Gopher Information Client v2.0.14. The Root gopher server: gopher.uiuc.edu screen.*

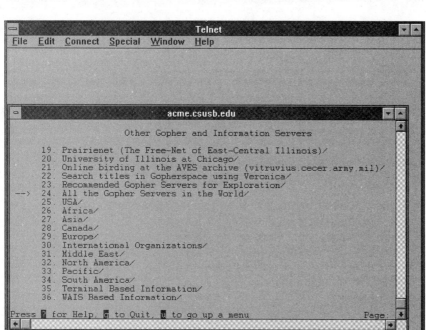

Fig. 3.2. *The Other Gopher and Information Servers screen.*

If you move the cursor to option 24—All the Gopher Servers in the World—and choose this option, you soon see the All the Gopher Servers in the World screen (see fig. 3.3).

The cursor now has been moved to option 7—ACADEME THIS WEEK from the publication the *Chronicle of Higher Education.*

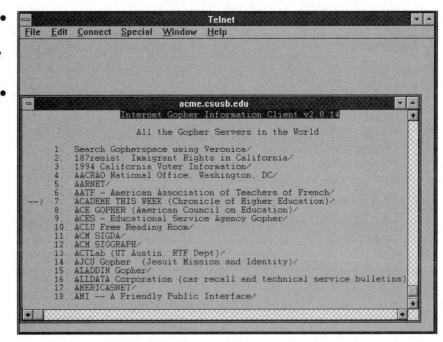

Fig. 3.3. *The All the Gopher Servers in the World screen.*

If you choose option 7, you see the ACADEME THIS WEEK (Chronicle of Higher Education) screen (see fig. 3.4).

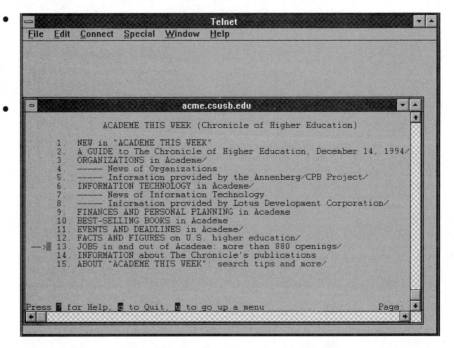

Fig. 3.4. *The ACA-DEME THIS WEEK (Chronicle of Higher Education) screen.*

In figure 3.4 the cursor is at option 13—JOBS in and out of Academe: more than 880 openings.

Should you choose option 13, you see the Jobs in and out of Academe: more than 880 openings screen (see fig. 3.5).

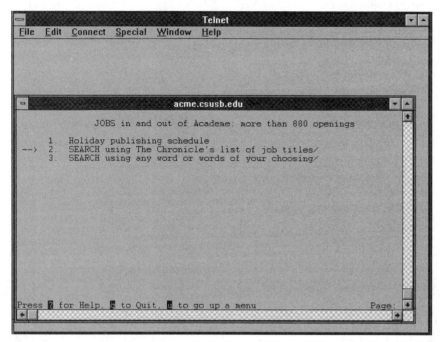

Fig. 3.5. *The Jobs in and out of Academe: more than 880 openings screen.*

The cursor in figure 3.5 is at option 2–SEARCH using The Chronicle's list of job titles. If you choose this option, you see the SEARCH using The Chronicle's list of job titles screen (see fig. 3.6).

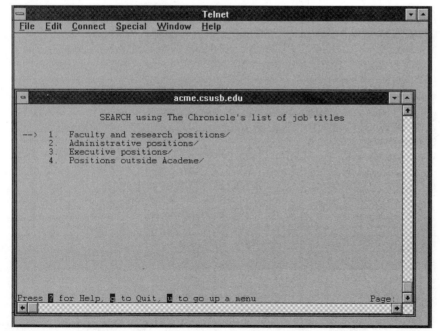

Fig. 3.6. *The SEARCH using The Chronicle's list of job titles screen.*

In figure 3.6 the cursor is beside option 1—Faculty and research positions. If you choose this option, you see the Faculty and research positions screen (see fig. 3.7).

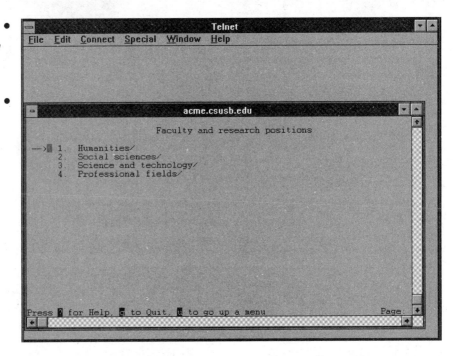

Fig. 3.7. *The Faculty and research positions screen.*

The cursor in figure 3.7 is at option 1—Humanities. Choose this option, and you see the Humanities screen (see fig. 3.8).

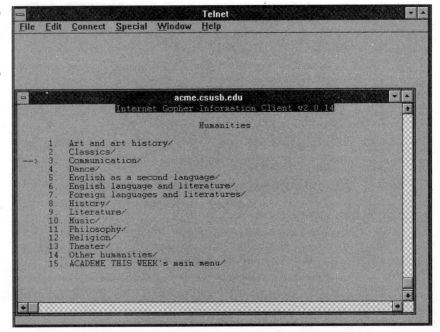

Fig. 3.8. *The Humanities screen.*

If you move the cursor in the Humanities screen to option 3—Communication and choose this option, you soon see the Communication screen (see fig. 3.9).

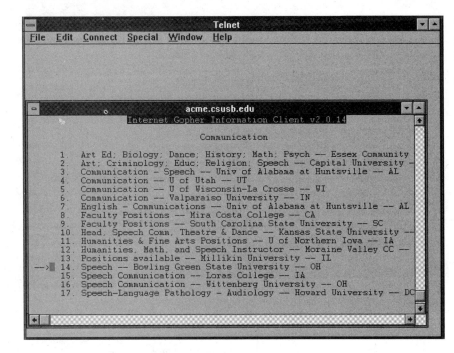

Fig. 3.9. *The Communication screen.*

In figure 3.9 the cursor has been moved to option 14—Speech — Bowling Green State University — OH. If you choose this option, you finally get to the job announcement. You see the first of two screens that describe this particular Speech position (see fig. 3.10).

You can go through the list of All the Gophers in the World to find interesting information of all kinds, but here are some gophers with employment listings:

gopher chronicle.merit.edu	Academe This Week (The *Chronicle of Higher Education*)
gopher cwis.usc.edu	Gopher Jewels from the University of Southern California
gopher.dartcms1. dartmouth.edu	Federal job openings from the Office of Personnel Management
gopher e-math.ams.com	American Mathematical Society
gopher esusda.gov or zeus.esuda.gov	Federal job openings

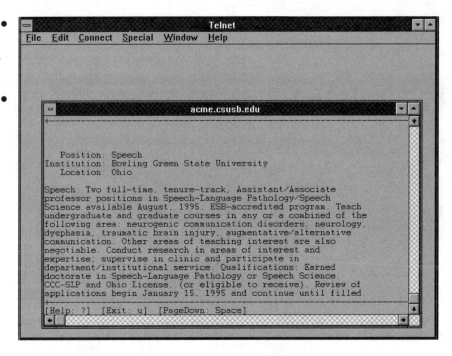

Fig. 3.10. *The first screen describing the Speech position.*

● ● ● ● ● ● ● ● ●

gopher garnet.msen.com	OnLine Career Center (Msen, Inc.)
gopher msen.com	Msen, Inc. main server
gopher gizmo.freenet. columbus.oh.us	Columbus, Ohio Freenet Ohio state jobs
gopher gopher.indiana.edu	Indiana University (For international information use path: The University: Information Services/University Life/International Center/International Career EmploymentNetwork)
gopher gopher.mountain.net	A wide variety of information for West Virginia
gopher nightingale.con. utk.edu	Nursing positions
gopher gopher.usdoj.gov	Jobs for attorneys from the U.S. Department of Justice
gopher gopher.utdallas.edu	University of Texas-Dallas

```
gopher                  American Physiological Association
gopher.uth.tmc.edu
3300

gopher                  U.S. Department of Justice and
justice 2.usdoj.gov     Inspection General's Offices


gopher                  Library of Congress employment
marvel.loc.gov          opportunities

gopher millkern.com     Federal, state, and universities with
                        job listings from Millkern Communi-
                        cations

gopher                  Rice University and pointers to
riceinfo.rice.edu       many more employment listings

gopher stis.nsf.gov     National Science Foundation

gopher                  University of Texas-Austin Central
gopher.utexas.edu       Gopher; job listings from universi-
                        ties and government agencies

gopher                  Academic Position Network
wcni.cis.umn.edu:11111
```

Finding Job Information Through Veronica

On some gopher main menus, you see the option Veronica, which was developed at the University of Nevada, Reno, and is an acronym for Very Easy Rodent Oriented Network Information Computerized Archives.

If it is available, you can request it to search the menus of all known gophers in the world for a keyword. The result is presented as a gopher menu.

There's no end to the job vacancy announcements on the Internet! Now you know how to find them. In the next chapter, we'll discuss simple ways to search the whole Internet for specific information about careers and employers.

CHAPTER 4

Using Internet Databases

Every guidance and job counselor stresses the importance of learning as much as possible about the company to which you're planning to apply. They refer you to libraries to look up such things as companies' annual reports.

Forget that. Using the Internet today is like browsing through a seemingly endless amount of information from the world's governments, corporations, universities, libraries, and individuals. In the preceding chapter, you learned how to use telnet and gopher. In this chapter we'll introduce you to more advanced ways to find information, sample locations to look for information on employers and careers, and ways to move that information to your own computer.

Using Archie

Archie (the name was derived from the word *archive*) was developed at the McGill University (Montreal) School of Computer Science. Archie servers maintain lists of stored files at every known public archive site. An archie search will give you the location of files; it will not give you the document itself. We'll explain how to do that later.

There are public archie sites all over the world. Pick one that's close to you.

Location	Archie Server Name
U.S. Southeast	`archie.sura.net`
U.S. West	`archie.unl.edu`
U.S. Northeast	`archie.rutgers.edu`

Location	Archie Server Name
New York	`archie.ans.net`
Australia	`archie.au`
UK/Ireland	`archie.doc.ic.ac.uk`
Europe	`archie.funet.fi`

Let's try the McGill server. Telnet to this address:

> `archie.sura.net`

and login as `archie`. Remember, you can always enter help to get a list of the commands. If you enter the following:

> `prog jobs`

you'll see screens flash before you with information that looks like that in figure 4.1.

Fig. 4.1. Result of an archie search.

```
Host mc.lcs.mit.edu          (18.111.0.179)
Last updated 03:55      5 Nov 1994

Location: /its/ai/tar
    FILE  -r--r--r--     1993 bytes  19:00   6 Dec 1989  jobs.xmail.Z

Location: /its/ai/devon
    FILE  -r--r--r--     2557 bytes  19:00  30 Mar 1989 jobs.x-mail.Z
jobs.xmailk.z

Location: /its/ai/ray
    FILE  -r--r--r--    41463 bytes  18:00   3 Oct 1988  jobs.babyl.Z

Location: /its/ai/sys2
    FILE  -r--r--r--     4556 bytes  19:00  31 Mar 1985  ts.jobs

Location: /its/ai/sysen1
    FILE  -r--r--r--     6164 bytes  19:00  31 Mar 1985  jobs.87
```

Remember to use your Scroll Lock key to freeze and unfreeze your screen.

In the preceding example the file name is on the far right. Next to it are the date and time the file was created, and next to that is the size of the file in bytes. You can easily fill up your disk space by transferring too many files. Delete files you don't need, or learn how to compress them.

On the far left at top, "Host" is the site, and "Location" is the name of the directory. You'll need this information to get a copy by file transfer protocol (ftp) discussed below.

If you don't have telnet, you can send an e-mail message to this address:

```
archie@nearest archie serve
```

Enter only the word **help** in the message. You'll get information back on the commands you can use. You'll use the next section to actually get a copy of the file itself.

Using File Transfers

File transfer (from *ftp*, or *file transfer protocol*) simply means the act of moving a file from one computer to another. Files can be text, software, photographs, or even digital music. Actually, file transfer is one of the most common uses of the Internet. Many organizations connected to the Internet provide publicly accessible files and allow you to copy those files to your computer by ftp.

The very first thing you need to learn in order to use ftp is the difference between two types of files: ASCII (American Standard Code for Information Interchange) and binary. An *ASCII* file is a simple text file only. It contains no formatting codes, such as tabs, underlining, etc. A *binary* file, however, does contain all the internal codes for formatting.

When you transfer an ASCII file between computers that store information differently, ASCII automatically adjusts the file during the transfer so that the file on the receiving end will be in text. A binary file is transferred as is with no changes. Some network packages come with programs that can convert from one format to another after the file has been received.

To use ftp, you first need the host name. In the preceding example, you'd enter this:

```
ftp mc.lcs.mit.edu
```

Next, you need a login name and password. For publicly accessible files, you login as **anonymous** or **ftp** and use your e-mail address as a password; or, if that is not accepted, try this:

```
guest
```

At the first ftp prompt, tell the host computer to use either ASCII (by entering **ascii**) or binary (by entering **binary**). The response to ASCII will be an A; the response to binary will be an I.

At the next ftp prompt, enter this:

```
cd </the/path/name>
```

To list the files in the directory, enter `ls`. To download a file, enter `get <filename>`. For example, when you login to the host, `mc.lcs.mit.edu`, you'd enter `cd` and the following location:

```
cd /its/ai/tar
```

Sometimes you'll have to do it in steps, such as the following steps:

```
cd its

cd ai

cd tar
```

Ftp is case-sensitive, so remember to enter lowercase words in lowercase letters and uppercase words in capitals. The host computer will let you know if you have been successful.

Now, you're ready to ask for the file. Sometimes you can see what files are at your directory location by entering this:

```
dir
```

If you already know the name of the file you want, simply enter its name, such as in this example:

```
get ts.jobs
```

Again, the host computer will let you know if you have been successful by a message such as "transfer complete." This means that the file is now on your computer for you to access and read.

If your system requires you to rename files, simply do that at the get command, as in the following example:

```
get ts.jobs newname.txt
```

The file would then be named on your computer as `newname.txt` and not as `ts.jobs`.

You'll notice that some files end in the letter Z or in ZIP. That means the file has been compressed. To be able to read that file, you'll first have to uncompress it with a utility file like PKUNZIP.EXE.

Ftp takes a little practice, but it's well worth it. There's a gold mine of information out there for you to bring home free!

If your access to the Internet doesn't include ftp, you can still use it. Some Internet hosts provide ftp by e-mail service. One at Princeton University is this:

```
bitftp@pucc.princeton.edu
```

But first send a help message to verify that the host can send messages to you.

Using WAIS

WAIS (pronounced "ways"), or Wide Area Information Service, allows you to search databases using keywords. Unlike archie and Veronica, WAIS looks through the contents of documents, not just titles. WAIS currently has more than 500 sources to search.

If your site does not have WAIS, you can telnet to public WAIS at this address:

```
quake.think.com
```

and login with the following:

```
wais
```

You'll be asked to supply keywords separated by a space, such as in the following example:

```
Indiana jobs
```

Don't use the word *and* because WAIS will look for that word too! WAIS will search and then show you the sources it has found. The first source listed will be the one that meets your criteria most closely. WAIS takes a little practice, but you can master it. When you find exactly what you want on WAIS, you can have it mailed to you by entering the following:

```
m
```

WAIS will prompt you for your e-mail address.

Using World Wide Web

You've finally reached the section that takes the pain out of finding information in the Internet. Now there is World Wide Web (WWW), an organizing system within the Internet that makes it easy to establish links between computers, and programs, such as Lynx and Mosaic, which are known as "browsers" that present information in the familiar point-and-click format.

Lynx is a widely used Internet search tool, but it displays only text. Mosaic presents information something like a magazine page with lists, icons, and images. Certain words are highlighted in blue. Simply clicking on a blue word provides you with information from wherever it's located. You don't need to find it and retrieve it yourself.

Mosaic also displays graphs and maps and plays audio and video. The computer language that Mosaic is based on is called *HTML*, or hypertext markup language. It is so simple that users are creating their own "home pages" or Web sites.

WWW was developed in Switzerland in 1989 as a way for physicists to share their work and access information. WWW has been expanded as a way to retrieve documents and even images, sound, and animation.

If your site does not have WWW, you can telnet to public browsers at any one of these addresses:

> info.cern.ch
>
> www.njit.edu
>
> ukanaix.cc.ukans.edu
>
> fatty.law.cornell.edu

If requested, login as www.

Web sites are identified by their Universal Resource Locator known as URL. To become familiar with WWW, try accessing some WWW sites.

If you can receive World Wide Web graphics, use the following address for information about "Career Mosaic," a site some large corporations use to post jobs:

> http://www.careermosaic.com

For photos of the First Family, a visual tour of the White House, and a meow from Socks the cat, try this:

> http://www.whitehouse.gov

Unlike many Web sites, the Whitehouse Web asks users to specify whether they need or prefer a text-only Web page.

For NASA Information Services, enter the following:

> http://hypatia.gsfc.nasa.gov

Particularly impressive is the Small Business Administration's Web page. To access it, enter this:

> `http://www.sbaonline.sba.gov`

Perhaps one of the most interesting Web sites is San Francisco's Exploratorium. Enter the following:

> `http://www.exploratorium.edu`

If you're interested in paleontology, try the Web site at Berkeley by entering this:

> `http://ucmp1.berkeley.edu`

Not job-related, but for information about new Disney movies, try the following Disney WWW address called the Buena Vista Pictures Web:

> `http://bvp.wdp.com`

Major corporations use Web sites to post jobs. For example, Thinking Machines Corporation offers job information through a Mosaic server accessible by this address:

> `http://www.think.com`

Web sites are increasing daily. There is a list server that sends out daily updates. To subscribe, send e-mail to: `majordomo@is.internic.net.` Leave the subject blank and enter `subscribe net-happenings-digest` as the message.

There is one site for finding http addresses:

> `http://webcrawler.cs.washington.edu`

If you don't have access to WWW yet, you can still Web pages by e-mail. CERN, the European research group that developed the Web, will provide pages by e-mail. If you know the Universal Resource Locator, send a message to this address:

> `LISTPROC@WWWO.CERN.CH`

In the body of the message, enter the Universal Resource Locator, such as the following:

> `www http://www.exploratorium.edu`

You'll receive up to 5,000 lines by e-mail. Of course, if you wanted to jump to another Web page, you'd have to send another request to CERN.

Examples of Information Available

Job information is available from commercial online services; from departments, agencies, and branches of the federal government; and through state government office listings. The following sections indicate more areas to explore and more sources to try.

Commercial Online Services

The commercial online services make a great deal of material easily available for members to access. For example, America Online's Career Center provides the following:

- Articles on issues important to career development

- Employer Contacts Database Information on thousands of employers and potential employment opportunities

- Career Guidance Services exercises and database with thousands of career options to determine a career direction

- Occupational Profiles Database Information on more than 700 occupations

- Career Resource Library and Employment Agency Database

- Hoover's Handbook detailed analyses of 500 U.S. corporations

- Business and Economic News updated throughout each day.

Federal Government Resources

Excellent starting points for finding basic government information on the Internet are these:

```
gopher sunsite.unc.edu

telnet info.umd.edu

gopher gopher.ns.doe.gov
```

The last one on this list is the Department of Energy gopher. To get to a list of federal bulletin boards, follow this path:

```
Federal Government Information/General Informa-
tion Resources/Federal Bulletin Boards (list).
```

Access the U.S. Department of Labor's *Occupational Outlook Handbook* (which includes the *Dictionary of Occupational Titles* codes) and *U.S. Industrial Outlook* by using this:

```
gopher umslvma.umsl.edu
```

Use path: `University of Missouri-St. Louis/The Library/Government Information`

The 1990 Census Data is available if you try the following entries:

`http://www.census.gov`

or

`telnet info.umd.edu`

`Directory: Educational Resources/United States/ Government/Census-90`

or

`gopher bigcat.missouri.edu`

`Directory: Reference Center/United States and Missouri Census Information/United States Census Data`

or

`gopher sunsite.unc.edu`

`Directory: The UNC-CH Internet Library/Virtual Reference/Census-90`

or

`gopher gopher.ns.doe`

`Directory: Federal Government/Information/Executive Branch/Commerce Department/1990 Census`

The *Commerce Business Daily* is available for a one-day test demonstration if you enter this:

`gopher gopher.netsys.com`

`Directory: Counterpoint Publishing/Demo Access to CBD (1 day; more than one day requires a subscription.)`

The Economic Bulletin Board contains more than 700 daily updated files on current economic and trade information, economic indicators, U.S. treasury auction results, and employment statistics. Try entering the following:

telnet infoslug.ucs.edu

login: **gopher**

Directory: The Researcher/Social Sciences/Economic Bulletin Board

Or try entering this:

gopher gopher.lib.umich.edu

Directory: Social Sciences Resources/Economics/ Economic Bulletin Board

For information about Congress, such as directories and committee assignments, try the following:

gopher gopher.lib.umich.edu

Directory: Social Science Resources/Government and Politics/U.S. Government Resources: Legislative Branch

or this:

gopher info.umd.edu

Directory: Educational Resources/United States/ Government/Congress

And a source on how to get White House information is this:

gopher esusda.gov

Directory: White House and Congress/White House Papers

State Government Resources

For a listing of all state employment offices, enter the following:

```
gopher gopher.dartmouth.edu
```

Use path: Dartmouth College/Career Services/Job
Openings in the Federal Government/Misc. Infor-
mation/All State Employment Offices by state.

Or enter this:

```
gopher esusda.gov
```

Use path: Extension Service USDA Information/USDA
and Other Federal Agency Information/Job Openings in the Federal Government/Misc. Informa-
tion/All State Employment Offices by state.

Keeping Up on the Net

In this chapter, we've gone through the tools you can use to find
information on the Internet. Keep in mind how quickly the Internet
changes. Just in the time this book was in preparation, the World Wide
Web grew many times over.

How can you keep up with the changes? The Internet is largely a
supportive environment. People are willing to help others who need
help. The net is a community. We want you to learn how to use that
community to keep up on the net, as well as to develop a support
group to help you in your job search. In the next chapter, then, we
address using the net for support.

Using Internet Support Groups

During the '90s, California has been decimated by huge losses in the aerospace and defense industries. Mary has worked extensively with many workers who were downsized out of successful careers. At the local Air Force base, a special department known as the Employment Resource Center (ERC) was established to address the reemployment concerns of workers affected by the base closure. Located on base, it became a networking hub for civilian employees and active military personnel. In the center were job postings that included online services, fax machines, word processors for composing resumes, and a State Employment Development Department (EDD) representative who provided placement assistance. Additionally, the ERC conducted special workshops in job search, interviewing, and resume writing, plus a host of other work-related topics. The ERC also conducted on-site classes on how to start a business, pass the California certification test for teachers, and survive life in the civilian world, among others.

There were many ad hoc meetings in the ERC where participants swapped tips as well as success and horror stories. They also passed on valuable information, warned each other about job-hunting pitfalls, shared leads on jobs and training opportunities, and generally supported one another through a traumatic transition period.

At state EDD offices around California, there are special networking groups called Experience Unlimited or the Professional Experience Network, in which persons work together to try to get back to work. These are unemployed people from the professional sector with contacts in different industries at various levels. These individuals, too, have access to job listings, fax machines, word processors, and special workshops through EDD.

Here again, the constant business being informally conducted involves networking with each other and acting as a support group for all the members. When someone gets a lead on a job that's not relevant, the individual passes it along to the other members. When they hear of a special program or training opportunity, they post it on the announcement board. When one member is feeling depressed or has had a particularly bad job-hunting experience, the other members rally around to help the person through it.

The Need for Support

Searching for work is hard. It is a time of frustration, anxiety, high hopes, and low self-esteem. People often take comfort in just knowing that others are going through the same thing. Frequently, job seekers who have been looking for work unsuccessfully for some time will ask hesitantly whether something is wrong with them. When Mary tells them that—because of the current economy, many others have been looking even longer—these individuals immediately feel better. Shared misery is somehow easier to bear. That's why job seekers often form support groups. There are the informal ones, such as the networking contacts you make among your family, friends, and business acquaintances, and the formal ones, such as the ERC and Experience Unlimited. You can seek advice, job leads, and consolation from them.

A Supportive Net

There is such a support group available to you over the Internet. There are people out there who have stories to tell you, both good and bad, about their job search and employment experiences. We decided to do a little canvassing on the net to learn some of those stories for you.

We posted a message to a number of employment newsgroups and asked people to share their horror and success stories about Internet job hunting. The response was overwhelming. People contacted us from all over the country and the world.

Like other aspects of Internet culture, we found our correspondents to be generous with their information; supportive of each other as job seekers; and, for the most part, very willing to help. We were chided a couple of times for posting our survey wherever the business of finding jobs was going on—whether in a resume group, jobs group, or purely a discussion group. We got scolded for not adhering strictly to the usage guidelines of some particular group. But we were never flamed, or criticized with abusive language.

In those few instances when we were corrected, we still sensed that the Internet "neighbors" were once again looking out for one another.

A rich resource of wisdom is out there. People are eager to show you the ropes, and we have compiled several of their responses in this section. The replies we received fall into roughly three categories: success stories, horror stories or warnings, and bizarre stories.

Success Stories

Responses in this category ranged from simple praise for electronic job hunting to suggestions for changes to the system to tales of outright success at finding a job on the net. One remarkable applicant tells of how he created a multimedia resume that generated an incredible 500 responses! We heard stories of how people had been searching for a job for several months and then found one over the net in a matter of weeks.

In many cases, the applicant was in the final stage of waiting for word on a job. In a couple of cases, people e-mailed the good news that they had been hired after the survey was completed. Here are some examples of success stories :

• •

From: David Coleman Oct 27, 94 07:36:35 am EDT
76114.3607@compuserve.com
To: Mary Beth Nemnich <mnemnich@acme.csusb.edu>
Subject: online job search

I recently started looking for work online. Perhaps some of my info will be of use for your book. . . .

I can share with you several ways that I have been using online services in my job search. I started my job search electronically about four months ago. Most people who solicit resumes online do so in the ASCII text format. I wanted to be unique, so I designed a multimedia computer version of my resume.

I had seen some electronic publications in the Windows .HLP format, and I liked what I saw. I bought a book on designing HLP files for Windows and taught myself how to do it.

The multimedia interactive version of my resume includes graphics, sounds, and a voice message. My multimedia resume is in the Windows .HLP format and requires Windows 3.1 to view and hear.

I have uploaded my interactive resume to several appropriate forums in CompuServe and other online services. So far, my multimedia resume has been downloaded by well over 500 individuals.

I also have been targeting various companies and executives online! Using business databases available on CompuServe and America Online, I find out the name of key executives at various companies. Then I do a member directory search to see if the executives have an e-mail address. If they have an e-mail address, I then send them an electronic cover letter and a copy of my digital resume.

I have also been accessing various "Help Wanted" online databases on the Internet, America Online, and private bulletin boards. . . .

My background is in the entertainment industry in marketing and promotion. I have been looking to associate myself with a company that is pioneering new forms of entertainment . . . software companies, multimedia companies, CD-ROM companies, online entertainment, etc.

I have gotten all kinds of e-mail feedback in response to my resume. I have received at least 15 phone calls about possible employment. I am confident that using an electronic resume and online services will eventually help me nail down fruitful employment.

David Coleman

• •

Wed 26 Oct 1994 10:07:15 +0600
To: mnemnich@acme.csusb.edu (Mary Beth Nemnich)
Subject: Re: HORROR STORIES JOBS

Greetings!

Well, I have a success story for you. I decided to check the job listings on a whim back in April or May and found a listing for a job right in my hometown with a very nice company. I sent a cover letter and a text copy of my resume, and I've been working in the position for 5 months!

The only complaint I have about the job postings is that some of these employment agencies post the same 800 articles every couple of days, and it is really tough to wade through them. It might be nice if they would break down the postings by geographical area, but that probably won't happen too soon. So for now my friends have a lot more work looking for their jobs. . . .

Best of luck with your research!

• •

From: Richard Brown   Oct 26, 94 12:08:28 pm
Date: Wed Oct 26 12:08:28 1994
To: mnemnich@acme.csusb.edu
Subject: [miscjobs.offered] HORROR STORIES JOBS

Actually, my only story about job hunting on the net is good. I started reading miscjobs.offered, checked in with the career.com (online career center) daily, and subscribed to the optimist mailing list. Within one month, I had 3 job offers, and contacted a company in the exact location I wanted to work in, who is now MAKING a position for me.

• •

● ●

From: Patrick McBride   Date: Wed, 26 Oct 1994 11:29:25 -0400
To: mnemnich@acme.csusb.edu
Subject: HORROR STORIES JOBS
Organization: via CompuServe Information Service

Hi:

I have posted my resume on the Internet in several places during the last few months.
My biggest problem is not having a full Internet account. I am using AOL and
CompuServe until I discover a wider access service.

But on to your major question:

A) I have had calls and contacts with employers as far away as Sidney, Australia,
wanting to hire Americans.

B) I have either contacted or been contacted by more employers in my field than I had
in 8 months on my own.

I still do not have the career position I want but already this week I have had contact
with two potentials who seem good.

Anyone looking for employment should use the internet . . . It greatly increases one's
chance of finding work.

Good Luck!

● ●

Date: Fri, 28 Oct 94 14:56 GMT
Subject: Re: Job hunting
To: mnemnich@acme.csusb.edu

I am a contract software engineer, working for a major credit card company. I always
look for contracts using uk.jobs.wanted and the CIX contract/vacancies topic. I haven't
found one this way yet,but I've only had three contracts so far.

BTW, CIX, as you are probably aware, is a UK-based conferencing system with about
7,000 subscribers, like a domestic CompuServe. It has, as you can see, a USENET
gateway.

In a previous contract I held, I suggested placing ads on CIX. Two people were hired as
a direct result. (One of them was fired, but that was because he was unwilling rather
than incapable.)

For computer vacancies, it is an excellent medium. I am *amazed* that more agencies do
not place their ads on conferences. For other industries, generally forget it. If you are
preparing a study, it would be a contribution to the medium to place it in the appropriate
newsgroup afterwards.

Gideon Rogers

● ●

• •

Date: Wed, 26 Oct 94 18:46:00 +0100
To: mnemnich@acme.csusb.edu
Subject: Re: HORROR STORIES JOBS

Gentlepeople

On the plus side, companies that give you multiple technical grillings over the phone before leaping (2 or 3 interviews) have been very GOOD places. It's not always pleasant to go through, but in my opinion they are showing a real sense of commitment to the contracts they sign. This says good things about the organization, and they also have a decent sense of what you can and cannot do before you arrive. So there are fewer unpleasant surprises on both sides.

• •

From: a Bay Area Jobseeker Date: Mon, 31 Oct 1994 06:42:38 -0800
To: mnemnich@acme.csusb.edu
Subject: Re: HORROR STORIES JOBS

I've found my last three jobs over the Internet. I was laid off from one of the three, when the company fell prey to the California recession and the up-and-downness of tech companies in the Bay area. But the current one is all right, and I'm still occasionally looking for that perfect job. The first job was a contract job, which lasted for a year. As I want to work in Internet-related jobs, I suppose this is the only way to go!

• •

From: Jon Thackray   Subject: Re: HORROR STORIES JOBS
To: mnemnich@acme.csusb.edu
Date: Tue, 1 Nov 1994 22:31:55 +0100 (GMT)

In article <38ki9p$4ie@news.csus.edu> you write: We are looking for success and horror stories from employers and job seekers about your experiences with job finding and recruitment.

I found one easily via here. See e-mail address below. . . .
This was via an agency advertising here.

Jon

Cambridge, England   ><>

• •

From: Dan Newcombe   Oct 27, 94 09:14:55 am
To: mnemnich@acme.csusb.edu (Mary Beth Nemnich)
Subject: Re: HORROR STORIES JOBS
Date: Thu, 27 Oct 1994 09:14:55 UNDEFINED

Well, I'll call this one odd or different. My senior year of college I had sent out quite a few resumes trying to get a job. I was amassing a good deal of "Thanks for your interest, we have you on file" letters (in other words, "Don't call us, we'll call you").

The last week or two before graduation, I sent out a few pieces of e-mail to a couple of colleges in Georgia asking if they allowed guest accounts that people could dial into. I figured, "Hey, why not? The college I went to did." I got a reply back from one saying no, they don't do that but they do have a job opening which I may be interested in.

So, I replied and got the details and found out the application deadline was two days after I would have moved back. And since my computer was already packed, I couldn't print off a resume till after I moved.

My parents, who had come up for graduation, brought me a newspaper clip of the same job opening that I had been conversing about via e-mail. I graduated and then drove 3 days down the east coast.

When I got there, I hooked everything up, printed the resume, and dropped it off the next morning. I came in for an interview the following Monday. I was the first one interviewed, and was told that it would probably be the middle of the following week before I heard anything. The next monday, at 9 a.m. I got a call with an offer for the job.

Almost everyone says I defied all logic because I got the first job I interviewed for, it was only 2 weeks after graduation, and I was the first person interviewed (usually a bad place to be.)

Dan Newcombe

● ●

From: Andrew Snow   Date: Tue, 1 Nov 1994 10:08:03
To: Mary Beth Nemnich <mnemnich@acme.csusb.edu>
Subject: Re: HORROR STORIES JOBS

Hi,

I'm a contractor, so I don't know if this is appropriate, but I met my most recent contract through a posting on uk.jobs.offerd.

It was a truly excellent way of transacting business . . . no middlemen, no waiting for an interview . . . just e-mail a CV (resume) and fix up a meeting.
Oh, is this a horror story or one of joy?? Absolute joy . . . the place is great, the work excellent, and the people easy going . . . what more could anyone ask for?

Regards,

Andrew Snow
UK

● ●

• •

From: Weston Beal Date: Wed, 26 Oct 1994 09:23:25 +0800
To: mnemnich@acme.csusb.edu
Subject: Re: HORROR STORIES JOBS

When I was in my last year of college, I scanned the job.offered groups every day, looking for anything in RF or microwave. I sent my resume by e-mail to anyone who mentioned RF.
One day I received a phone call from a manager at a Microsystems company who was putting together a group to do signal integrity (RF effects in digital circuits) support for engineering. We talked on the phone. I went to California for an interview, and the next week I got a very good offer from the company. It was my first and last onsite interview. I took the job.

Regards

• •

Horror Stories or Warnings

Our respondents also had some gripes about the way things sometimes work out there. There is widespread dissatisfaction with opportunistic headhunters, for example. The feeling abounds that these recruiters will say or do anything to get a client placed, true or not. One respondent detailed his experience with being made to look like "God" so that a headhunter could collect his fee. This distrust of fee-based placement services also reflects the belief that the Internet should be a noncommercial service.

There were several messages containing a single word: the name of an organization or company. We can not reproduce those here, obviously, but we can tell you that there are several companies that try to recruit people to their multilevel marketing or pyramid-type businesses. We even noted a chain letter being advertised in a jobs newsgroup. Respondents were furious that this type of posting should be there, cluttering up a listing of bona fide job offers. Worse, these "scammers," as one job seeker termed them, were found everywhere, in every group.

This has fostered suspicion among job hunters. We received several wary replies to our survey: "What do you need it for?"; "Send me more details so I can tell if you're on the level"; and "I have a story, but I want to know how you're planning to use it." In subsequent replies, we were careful to point out that we were "neither headhunters nor salespeople."

We heard a few times that people were glad "somebody is looking into this." We were also asked to notify the respondents when our work was finished. They were happy to participate to help others avoid or at least recognize similar pitfalls. Here are their stories:

● ●

Date: Thu 27 Oct 1994 09:47:01 -0500
To: mnemnich@acme.csusb.edu
Subject: Re: HORROR STORIES JOBS

Horror stories:
1. Folks trying to get free consulting by "interviewing": How would you solve >THIS< network problem?
2. Headhunters illegally excluding folks over 40, determined by "What year did you get your B.S.?"
3. Folks interviewing for jobs already filled but organization says "X" number of people must be interviewed.

● ●

From: Mountain View, CA   Date: Wed, 26 Oct 1994 10:09:16 PDT
To: mnemnich@acme.csusb.edu
Subject: Horror Story

In reply to your request for stories of horror, joy, and the bizarre, I submit the following. I consider it a horror story, but you may just consider it bizarre. It all happened in the last week, and writing this has helped me muddle through it.

I replied to a job posting in ba.jobs.contract which stated that the applicant had to possess strong or good capabilities in 14 skills' areas. That was remarkable. I had nine of the skills, so, since I knew they weren't going to find someone with all 14, I thought I'd submit my resume.

The person posting the listing was a headhunter, and I was called and told I had a good resume for the position. They agreed that nobody would have the 14 skills—they said the client was trying to hire God—but it sure would be nice if I could show a nodding familiarity with the other five, all of which concerned facets of UNIX system programming of which I knew nothing. So he interviewed me, looking for anything in my past that even sounded as if I had experience in that area. Failing to find anything, he said, "Well you'll have a week before they'll interview you, so read books on the subject." Since all I would need is a nodding familiarity, I thought this was O.K.

The next day, the headhunter's partner called and said that the client really wanted to interview me the next day. I was told that my original resume had been submitted, so I felt very comfortable about that. But then he amended his comment, saying that the information given to the client consisted of the resume plus the results of the first phone call. He alluded to a new resume. I said I wanted to see it ASAP, but he couldn't produce it. It was not until 9:30 that night that I saw the resume that had been submitted. I had become God.

It said that I had in-depth experience in UNIX systems programming plus a wealth of other proficiencies which had either been fabricated or amplified beyond recognition. The interview was at 1 p.m. the next day.

The original headhunter called to discuss the resume and I told him it was ludicrous and I wouldn't interview. What proceeded was a 90 minute haggling session in which I was pressuring him to remove or tone down big chunks of the resume and to resubmit it. One of the many fabrications was that because my resume listed only the years of my employment and the client required months to be listed, he invented the months I started and ended work at various jobs. But my favorite of all arose because he said that the end of the e-mail transmission with my resume had been garbled. This wiped out my graduate degree and all he could read was MS . . . garbled . . . UC Berkeley. He could read that I had received a BS in aeronautical and astronautical engineering from the University of Illinois, but he extrapolated to determine my degree was from Berkeley. He also gave me a graduate degree in aeronautical engineering. That was interesting because, not only did I not have the degree, there is no college of aeronautical engineering at Berkeley. Minor point, I guess.

I was told that a new, toned down and corrected resmne would be submitted first thing in the morning. That satisfied my requirements, (I did need the job, after all). The next morning I crammed like crazy to acquire a nodding familiarity with UNIX systems programming. I wouldn't be able to brush up on the other nine skills, some of which I hadn't used in a couple of years. But that would just have to do and I went to the interview.

Well of course the new resume hadn't been submitted and they must have expected me to descend from a cloud. Actually, the whole issue of UNIX systems programming was quickly brushed aside by the manager who said it wasn't a very important part of the job. The whole interview focused on exactly "one" of the 14 skills and, of course, it was one I hadn't used in a couple of years and so I didn't demonstrate terrific proficiency.

The headhunter said that the client was pleased with me, but I know how I did and it wasn't stellar. I found comfort in the fact that at least no one else would be as poorly prepared as I was, given that the God job posting is all anyone would have had to go by and who could prepare for that? WRONG!

The next morning I revisited bajobs.contract and saw what had to be the same job posted by another headhunter which now listed only three needed skills. I called the headhunter and asked how it was that their job description could be so radically different from the other one. I was told that they had a full-time employee with a strong technical background who was assigned to that client (a big company) and that he was able to talk to the hiring manager and get all of the details. Great. So, I called the first headhunter to find out what they had done to get the information and he said they had taken the hiring manager to lunch and asked about the required skills. When the manager listed the 14 skills, the headhunters said, 'You're not going to find anyone like that." The manager stuck to his requirements. Evidently, he has since changed his mind. Another headhunter is now posting the concise job description.

I will be stupefied if I get an offer for this position, but I have acquired a nodding familiarity with UNIX systems programming, so it's not a total loss, right?

• •

From: Carlos Robinson   Date: Wed, 26 Oct 94 13:49:31 PDT
To: mnemnich@acme.csusb.edu (Mary Beth Nemnich)
Subject: Re: HORROR STORIES JOBS

One horror story is that these headhunters say they have plenty of jobs and System Administration personnel, but you find out that they only have 2 or 3 System Admin's and no jobs. I have found that most don't even know the computer business and are only salespeople trying to make $$$.

Carlos

● ●

From: Brian Lee   Date: Wed, 26 Oct 1994 18:07:01 -0400 (EDT)
Subject: (fwd) HORROR STORIES JOBS (fwd)
To: mnemnich@acme.csusb.edu

The headhunters won't stop!!! They call all day and even nights and weekends. They are like flies around a . . . of . . . .

● ●

From: Allen Hill   Date: Wed, 26 Oct 1994 14:20:34 -0500
To: mnemnich@acme.csusb.edu
Subject: re: internet job hunting

I don't have any bizarre story to tell but I can relate my experiences. I've been job hunting on the Internet for about 2 months now and it is the first time I've used the Internet for that purpose. I've decided to confine my job search to just using the Internet. I've been somewhat successful: I've interviewed and received a couple of job offers, but haven't found what I'm looking for yet.

The following are some random thoughts:

One thing I find annoying is when someone posts a job but won't take your resume via e-mail. Why use the Internet if you're not going to take e-mail?

Subject headers are VERY important. Since misc.jobs.offered typically has 500+ jobs posted per day, you've got to have some method for weeding out the nonapplicable postings. I use xrn, which displays the subject headers nicely, I can scan those headers rapidly.

The subject headers vary greatly in content. Since I use subject headers, I depend on them for providing the keywords that tell me what skills the job needs and where the job is located. Both pieces of information are critical and usually the job location is left out.

Most postings seem to come from contracting/recruiting firms. I've contacted several of them—some are more interested/friendly than others.

Like all newsgroups, there are always postings from scammers who promote their bogus businesses. I filter these by refusing to look at any ad that doesn't have the key info listed in the subject.

What misc.jobs.offerred needs most is standardization:
1) standard subject format; and
2) it would be nice to have a standard resume format

Allen Hill (Mr. Hill is an AIX programmer.)

● ●

From: Todd Sharp Date: Sat, 29 Oct 94 12:15:24 -0500
To: mnemnich@acme.csusb.edu (Mary Beth Nemnich)
Subject: Re: HORROR STORIES JOBS

Ms. Mary Nemnich,

Can't say that I have any horror stories, just that if you're not looking for a computer science job, I wouldn't look. I've pretty much given up, and I have an MSME. I'd hate to be a nontech looking for a job.

Todd Sharp

From: Dr. mike   Date: Fri, 28 Oct 94 12:46:18 CDT
To: mnemnich@acme.csusb.edu (Mary Beth Nemnich)
Subject: Re: HORROR STORIES JOBS

Ok, here's one:

Last year I saw an ad in misc.jobs.offered for a DSP programmer and sent 'em an ASCII version of my resume. They called me up a few days later and talked with me about the job. It entailed pure software, so I suggested I could do it in my basement. After a week or so they called again and said I was number one on the list of people who could do the job, but they really prefered to have a local person (I'm in Chicago, they were in Boston). I suggested a trade, my software skills for the hardware this was to run on. They said they'd think about it and then called (or e-mailed, I don't remember) that they had hired the local guy. Well that's cool, so I sort of forgot about it.

A few months later, around the beginning of November they called me up again. They decided they really needed my DSP skills so I asked them to send me copies of the DSP chip manuals in the apple. They did. I analyzed the problem and figured the solution would be tight, but I could maybe make things go faster with the DSP chip than with the 68040. They said fine, we'll send you a computer.

The deal was that I would produce a usable code by Jan 1 . . . 6 weeks max. I figured I could get it done, and if not, I'd have tons of fun and would be able to put it on my resume. I was looking to work as a consultant and this would be my first real paying job as one. (I've done lots of stuff on the side for friends and for fun, but never solved a problem for money before.)

I got a top-of-the-line computer a week later than they said I'd get it. Then I feverishly learned the new processor, the operating system, and the interface to their software. After 3 weeks of manic days and nights, I started sending code back to the company. It didn't work, of course, but I began to understand their problem better.

There were tons of minor problems, but by the end of December it was pretty clear that the DSP chip was no faster than the 040. I suggested that I send the computer back and call the deal over. They said that they'd extend the deadline to mid-January. Well, that was nice, it gave me a chance to make things work, but it still wasn't going to make their code run faster.

I actually got that to work o.k. and much of the debugging done by mid-February. But now, it seemed hopeless. There were still lots of bugs and it looked like the computer manufacturer was not going to support the equipment. I figured I'd try to send the computer back. "No, we want you to keep it, finish debugging, and give us two more routines," came the reply.

Well, at the beginning of April I got an e-mail saying that they'd send me $500 for the effort I put in if I'd please send back the computer. I told them to meet me in court. I still have the computer and all the software and haven't heard a word from them since. I'm now a consultant for hire, so I did o.k. The other side lost time and money, but they cut their losses pretty small and had to put up with a major company's goof.

Patience, persistence, truth.
Dr. mike

● ●

From: Mike Golobay   Date: Thu 27 Oct 1994 08:50:45 -0700
To: mnemnich@acme.csusb.edu
Subject: Re: HORROR STORIES JOBS

My company is currently doing the same thing. I have been on the net for a little over a year and know my way around fairly well, so I was "volunteered" to give it a try. Our first attempt was to try to satisfy our needs for APL/2 programmers ASAP (yesterday!). I hunted around in /usr/lib/news/newsgroups for the newsgroups that looked like they involved jobs and then tried to find a FAQ for those groups on rtfrn.mit.edu. No FAQs could be located. So, I cross-posted the job requirements to all applicable looking newsgroups since we are to relocate anyone qualified. Hate mail continues to trickle in. Angry people pounding their electronic fist on the other side of my screen hating me for posting a Dallas job in an Austin newsgroup. Scorching flames from some irate person in L.A. who thought it was serious enough to notify the postmaster of my site, etc., addendum infinitum.

I was able to get some good information from the flames and chose to ignore some of the rest. Yes, we will probably continue to post Dallas openings in Austin newsgroups.

It sure would be great if we could all benefit from each other's experimentation.

● ●

From: Paul Le Vine   Date: Thu, 27 Oct 1994 16:35:22 +0500
To: mnemnich@acme.csusb.edu
Subject: Re: HORROR STORIES JOBS

O.K. Here is my job seeking problem. I am a senior at Syracuse University, and I have been sending my resume all over the place through e-mail and keep getting calls interested in me "immediately." I clearly put on my resume that I will be graduating in May of '95, but these people responding fail to read it carefully. What can I do about this problem?

● ●

• •

From: a Bay Area Employer Date: Mon, 31 Oct 1994 11:10:23 -0800
To: mnemnich@acme.csusb.edu (Mary Beth Nemnich)
Subject: Re: HORROR STORIES JOBS

While it is changing daily, a few years ago the majority of people on the net were connected to a university. We posted 3 positions and, being a defense company, were very explicit about citizenship requirements. We were flooded with resumes from students who were citizens of eastern Europe, Russia, or mainland China. It also seemed clear that since it cost nothing for students to access the net, it was easy to send out canned resumes. In some resumes it was apparent that they did not have access to a good word processor.

• •

From: Steve Clark Date: Tue, 1 Nov 94 09:13:33 pst
To: mnemnich@acme.csusb.edu
Subject: Horror Stories

An addition to your horror/warning story file.

I am a newly graduated human resources specialist who uses the net to look for open recruiting positions. One user of the Delphi service in the states had posted an open invitation for recruiter applications. I e-mailed the guy, outlining my education and experience. I received an enthusiastic reponse saying I was the kind of person he was looking for. He wanted my address, so he could mail me a video tape that would outline the business and give more details.

The video arrived, and I popped it in my VCR, expecting to hear about a contract recruiting job. The offer was actually to sell weight loss and fitness products door-to-door in my city! It had absolutely nothing to do with recruitment at all. I telephoned the guy and told him not to waste my time, and mailed the video back, postage due.

Because he has my address, I have been receiving more offers about this opportunity about once a week. I have sent every one back postage due.

I am more careful now in applying for net jobs.

Steve Clark

• •

From: A Louisiana job seeker   Date: Wed, 26 Oct 1994 00:07:57 -0500
To: mnemnich@acme.csusb.edu
Subject: Re: HORROR STORIES JOBS

Sir,

I am glad to know that somebody is looking into this. I have found about 20 job banks and have yet to find out how effective they are. Could you please post your listing to me when you have completed your study? Thanks in advance.

• •

(This job seeker asked that he not be identified so as not to harm his job seeking efforts. He said, "I don't wish to be seen in a bad light. It is sort of funny. When looking for a job, you have to straddle a line between being different enough to be noticed but not so different as to be shunned. A person who could master this would probably find employment in any economy.")

Bizarre Stories

This category was interesting. Just as in face-to-face job seeking, people sometimes encounter situations that leave them shaking their heads in amazement or confusion. Mary has heard stories like this for years. There was the employer who told a woman applying for a home health aide position that she would be required to get into the shower with him undressed in order to help him with his bathing! Or, the applicant who removed her teeth every time she went to interviews so that she wouldn't get hired and could stay on public assistance.

The Internet neighborhood is just like any other. It contains its share of characters. Here are three examples we could print:

• •

From: Hawaii   Thu, 13 Oct 1994 17:01:59

I recently had an interview with a national contracting firm. At the end of the interview, I was asked to have my picture taken. When I asked for an explanation, I was told this was standard practice and it helped them remember their contractors. They also used it so when several contractors would be sent to the same job, they could show them the pictures so they would know who else they would be working with.

I have never experienced anything like this before. I was so thrown, I let them take the picture. I am now wondering if I should have and if it is legal for them to require a picture to be taken. They made it seem as if not taking the picture would limit my chances for the job.

The company is very respected with over 30 offices, and the jobs are technical and pay very well. I just don't know why they need a picture.

Has anyone ever experienced this before, or have any comments on it?

• •

From: "Bill"   Date: Wed, 26 Oct 1994 06:15:34 -0700
To: mnemnich@acme.csusb.edu (Mary Beth Nemnich)
Subject: Re: HORROR STORIES JOBS

My story is about a year ago, I responded to an ad for a project manager/engineer to work on a contract basis with a local employer (SF East Bay Area). When I was interviewed, the woman who interviewed me made it clear that there were other duties involved because her husband was disabled. The interview went downhill from there. The more she talked that way, the more nervous I got, and the more I talked about my wife and family. (I am single.) I didn't get the job, and have a different outlook on sexual discrimination now.

"Bill"

• •

● ●

From: Denise Chaffin

Mary and Fred:

Okay, here is my horror story. I recruited a woman for a client of mine. She was a perfect fit for my client's job. The position was for a programmer analyst.

My initial contact with her was through the net. I had three phone discussions with her before flying her out for an interview. She was professional over the phone and knew programming technology well. She had a very deep voice, which at first was puzzling but, what the heck, many people have strange voices.

Well to my surprise and that of my client's, when we brought this woman out for an interview, she turned out to be a man who had recently been transformed into a woman. She looked like a woman for the most part, but since transsexual alterations apparently take time, she still had a five o'clock shadow by noon and a masculine voice and hands! She applied makeup better than most women, though!

● ●

One thing we found to be true time and again is that Internet users are more than happy to help each other. Unlike many other real world venues, these folks will respond to you if you write them. In the case of the applicant who was photographed, for example, she turned to her support group for answers and advice, and they came through for her. It is the perception that they are all linked by a common interest—some would say passion—in the Internet that makes net users so accessible to each other.

It is also probably because they all inhabit the same "world," a world unlike the outside one. It may be because the Internet world is so different that people don't feel constrained to act in the same ways that they do in the "real" one. Whatever the reason, people are more open to communication with others on the net. They are "there" for each other.

Real-time Chat

There are many places online where you can meet, get advice, and discuss career issues in real-time. In real-time interactive comunication, another person can see on their screen the words you are typing as you type them. The BBS and commercial online services have places for members to meet and discuss career-related issues.

On the Internet, the best known and most interactive tool is talk. To use talk, you need to know the other person's e-mail address, and that person needs to be online at the same time as you. For example, when Mary wants to chat with Fred, she simply enters:

```
talk fjandt@acme.csusb.edu
```

Fred then enters **talk** followed by Mary's e-mail address. When the real-time conversation begins, you'll see a split screen, with one person talking on the top half, and the other person talking on the bottom half.

Unfortunately, talk is not universally available yet. It can be not only fun but also a valuable way to get advice and support from other job seekers.

Also available on the Internet for conversation is Internet Relay Chat (IRC). IRC has many channels of live chat, which anyone can join at any time. To be frank, most IRC use today is recreational and often sophomoric, but we do know people who have made valuable contacts on the IRC.

If your system already has an IRC client installed, it is a simple matter to join an interactive conversation. At the main prompt, just enter **irc** followed by a nickname of your choosing, up to nine letters long. For example:

```
irc mary
```

The first screen on IRC usually contains information about your local client, such as how many channels are active and warnings and advice for its use.

To use IRC, you will need to type your commands at the cursor. All commands on IRC start with / (slash mark) . To get a list of all current IRC channels, type /**list** at the cursor. This will give you a rapidly scrolling list of channels. To get a closer look at them, hit the pause key. Each listing shows the name of the channel, the topic, and the number of users currently online. To choose a channel, enter /**join** and the name of the channel. You can then enter the conversation by typing your comments at the cursor. To change channels, enter /**join** and the name of the new channel.

A very useful command in IRC is /**help**. Use this command to get information on how to use IRC. To quit IRC, the command is /**quit**. If you don't have a local IRC server already installed on your system, you can telnet to a public IRC server. For information on how to connect with current servers (those change frequently so you need the most updated list) go to the newsgroup **alt.irc.**

As you tackle the grueling job of finding a job, remember that, with electronic job search, it is not the lonely business you have been used to. You are not alone. You now have a support group that numbers in the millions. Now, doesn't that make you feel better?

The Basics of Electronic Resumes

What if you were to receive some 50 to 100 letters per week? Let's say that you already knew the general ideas that were to be covered in each letter and that only the details would vary. How likely would you be to pore over every single one of them? Wouldn't it be more likely that you would skim through them to find the one that looked most interesting and give that letter your full attention first? This scenario adequately describes a weekly task of most human resource professionals: reading resumes.

In the labor market of the '90s, the flood of resumes threatens to bury most human resource managers. Now, thanks to the Internet, there is another source of resumes assailing personnel representatives. Employment bulletin boards, online resume services, and e-mail have added to the crush of paper resumes waiting in the in-basket. Human resource managers look for the most expedient way to get through the "stack" to find the people they want to talk to. This chapter is devoted to getting you into the "keep" pile.

In general, the rules for writing a winning traditional paper resume apply also to electronic resumes. But some special problems do arise when you translate resumes to the electronic medium. These require our close attention. In the following pages, you will learn how to adapt the rules of paper resumes to the electronic medium. Tips on how to make paper resumes attractive and professional will be applied to the electronic variety. Because employers receive hundreds of resumes through e-mail (one service we explored posted more than 1,000 for California alone!), yours must be more competitive than ever.

Resume ABCs

Three basic factors should serve as guiding principles so that you can prepare any resume properly. We call them the "ABCs" of resume preparation. Simply, a resume should be attractive, brief, and clear.

The first factor, *attractiveness*, captures employers' attention and invites them to read on. The second factor, *brevity*, keeps employers interested enough to finish reading. The third, *clarity*, enables employers to conclude whether you have what they want. In this chapter, we examine all three factors and apply them to the electronic resume.

Making Resumes Attractive

In written resumes, one of the most readily apparent indicators of attractiveness is the paper itself. You should give time and thought to selecting paper that is the proper weight and shade. The same is true for choosing the color of ink that will complement your paper choice. For example, a resume printed with burgundy ink on dove (pale gray) paper makes a more distinctive impression than regular black type on white bond paper. Likewise, navy ink on pale blue parchment is elegant and crisp. There are even some new papers that contain artistic borders on one or more sides. Ecru paper, bordered in mahogany marble with brown ink, would surely stand out in a crowd of black-on-whites.

With electronic resumes, however, these appearance factors are eliminated. The "paper" is all the same—a computer screen. Additionally, as a rule, no special fonts or inks are available to you. Thus, you need to concentrate on those aspects of appearance you can control.

One of these is called the "lie" of the resume. By this, we don't mean that you should stretch the truth of your background! The "lie" of a resume refers to its arrangement on the page, or for our purposes, the screen.

This arrangement is key in getting the employer to read your resume. If a resume is too wordy, covered with print, and has very little screen showing through, an employer will deem it too time-consuming to read. Consider again that this person has many more of these to plow through. The best resumes, then, are spare, with good spacing between the body of the resume and the headings, and with decent margins. Now, let's look at how to arrange the resume itself, to give it a readable and attractive lie.

ASCII. The problem with formatted electronic resumes is that they must be sent in ASCII. This acronym stands for American Standard Code for Information Interchange. ASCII is a text file only, meaning that it does not contain pictures, special fonts, programs, or any of the other bells and whistles available to you on a word processor. Especially problematic for us is that ASCII does not contain the codes to make specially formatted documents. When the resume arrives on the employer's screen, the resume is no longer formatted. Instead, it is totally left-aligned and arranged in a haphazard manner.

Accordingly, when typing your resume in ASCII, you will need to space painstakingly everything as you type it, and then save it. If you don't, when you upload your resume to send it, it will not look as professional as a properly formatted resume. Furthermore, it will be confusing to read. *Note:* See section titled "Using an Interactive Multimedia Resume" for more on special resume formatting.

Headings. The easiest kind of resume to read has headings on the left separated by at least five spaces from the body of the resume. Employers like this style of resume because this format is easy to scan for information. For example, if an employer is looking specifically for the educational background of an applicant, it is simple to scan the left headings for "Education" and quickly locate the desired information. Employers appreciate this kind of format in electronic resumes as well.

Some resumes have the headings centered above the appropriate sections. In paper resumes, which should usually be no more than a page in length, space is at a premium. Without a fair amount of spacing—say at least two expansive lines—between headings and sections, headings are more difficult to find and thus more frustrating to employers. (These are people you haven't even met yet. Now is certainly not a good time to frustrate them.) With electronic resumes, space is not such a crucial factor. But it still requires a bit more looking on the part of the employer to find the needed heading if it is centered above the section. It is preferable to set your headings off to the left of the body of the resume.

On paper resumes, headings should be in boldface to make them easier to read. With a variety of fonts available through word processors, the headings can also be in a different size or style than the body. The idea is to make the heading stand out. However, you don't have the luxury of fonts in ASCII. So, the best way to make your headings eye-catching is to put them in all caps.

Making Resumes Brief

All employers have had the unpleasant experience of wading through a resume that is several pages long. On paper, this is simply inexcusable. The general rule is that a resume should not exceed one page in length. Longer resumes are not only daunting to read, they are considered pretentious by most employers. How to fit all of their experience into one concise page is troubling to many job seekers. This is an area in which the electronic resume has some advantages over the paper resume.

Employers are accustomed to paging through several screens while reading their e-mail. This is quite different from shuffling a sheaf of papers mailed by a job seeker. It is generally understood that a full page of type will not fit on a computer screen. Thus, a resume that fills several screens is not considered as breaking the "one page" rule. You have a bit more latitude in the computer medium. However, even here, you need to be careful. A resume that rambles on for six or seven screens will be as annoying to an employer as a paper resume that goes on for two or three pages. So, you will still need to edit your experience. Here are some tips.

Prioritize your experience. Limit your job experiences to those that are most important or relevant to the job for which you are applying. Rank them in order, from most to least important. Focus on those skills that you know will be most significant to the prospective employer.

Use bullets. Full sentences eat up space. It is much more expedient to use *bullets*–short statements that summarize your experience. For example, consider the following excerpt from an auto mechanic's resume:

> I have repaired and rebuilt all types of cars, both foreign and domestic. I can do all phases of auto repair from simple tune-ups right to complete engine rebuilds. I have all my own tools, including both standard and metric. I have all kinds of manuals and my own rollaway. I have had lots of experience in repairing Nissan and Toyota models. I am certified for headlight adjustment and smog inspections and repair.

This bit of experience takes many lines of precious space to communicate. It is wordy and also breaks another rule of proper resume etiquette: it uses personal pronouns. Bullets, along with the elimination of personal pronouns, would take fewer lines to say the same thing:

- Full service from simple tune-ups to complete rebuilds on all makes and models, foreign and domestic

- Full set of tools, standard/metric; manuals; rollaway

- Nissan and Toyota specialist, including electronic systems; smog and headlamp certified

This applicant could even add two more experience bullets and still use less space than it took in sentences. Additionally, the look is cleaner, and bullets are easier and faster to read.

Limit the scope of previous jobs. There are two factors to consider here. First, resumes should never go back more than 10 years. Depending on your field, some experience is stale after a mere five years. Employers are simply not interested in ancient history. Second, you should include only work history that is significant to the position for which you are applying. If you are an administrative office assistant, for example, your experience as a house painter during college is simply not relevant to the employer. It is helpful if you title your work history section "Significant Experience," rather than "Experience."

This lets the employer know that you plan to concentrate only on those things in your background that relate directly to the desired position.

Never list references on your resume. Unless you are specifically asked by the employer to provide references, do not list them on your resume. Generally, references are checked only when the employer is interested in hiring you. To add them to an unsolicited resume not only wastes valuable space, but also unnecessarily invades the privacy of your friends and business associates.

Edit ruthlessly, choose judiciously, write frugally. Keep it brief!

Making Resumes Clear

Have you ever known someone who tries to build you a clock whenever you ask them what time it is? The person ends up giving you so much useless information that you practically forget what it was you asked for in the first place. This is a common problem in resume writing. Employers want you to tell them in the clearest, most comprehensible terms what it is you did and exactly what you want. Too many job seekers end up getting bogged down in jargon, acronyms, or vague and inappropriate language. Here are some suggestions on how to clarify your information.

Jargon. This is in-house, job-related language that people use as a sort of "shorthand" to describe different duties, activities, or responsibilities at work. Bureaucracies are especially good at using jargon, but all companies use it to a certain extent. Some positions or job-related activities occur in various industries but are called by different names. Thus, the jargon used to describe them can vary widely.

Consider this example. A person who checks product quality can be known as a quality control technician, a quality assurance evaluator, a production checker, a quality tech, a process control supervisor, a line inspector, or a quality examiner. Imagine the confusion when you describe yourself as a PCS (production control supervisor) to an employer who uses quality control technicians (QCTs). Just because your former company knew what a PCS was, doesn't mean your future company will.

Even something as mundane as an interoffice memo can become confusing when referred to in company jargon. Memos are known variously as "buck slips," "sheets," even "snowflakes!" Some companies refer to quality control inspections as "surveillances." However, most people associate surveillances with law enforcement.

Applicants who have served a lengthy period of time in the military have a particularly hard time freeing their resumes of jargon. When, for example, they want to reflect time spent in a temporary assignment, former military personnel often refer to it as "TDY." This acronym stands for temporary duty. When they are moved permanently, they call it "PCS" (permanent change of station). To an employer firmly rooted in the civilian world of employment, it is gobbledygook to read, "PCS to Guam" followed by a job description on a resume. These applicants often have difficulty translating military language to civilian terms as well. For instance, people don't in the business world "command" or "lead." They supervise or manage.

It is absolutely essential that you communicate clearly on a resume. Once you have written your job descriptions, have two people completely unfamiliar with your profession read them. If they encounter something that they don't understand, you have most likely fallen into a jargon trap. Is there another term to describe the word you used? Perhaps it can be explained, rather than named. Find a way around it. Confused employers everywhere will thank you.

Language. Keep the language of your resume crisp and professional, but allow your own sense of style to show through. Job seekers frequently believe that resumes should be like the job application, only without lines on the page. The result is a lackluster, dry recitation of facts, with no hint of the applicant as a person. However, the fact is that a resume is meant to be much more than a work history. The primary function of a resume should be to capture the employer's attention. It is often the first look an employer has of an applicant. Consider, then, how you want it to represent you.

When preparing an electronic resume, you want to strike a balance between language that is too rigid and language that is inappropriately informal. Apply the basic rules of proper grammar and spelling. Avoid slang and familiarity. Describe your duties in professional, understandable language, but choose language that is more colorful when describing personal and professional strengths. The busy personnel manager who must read a ton of e-mail resumes will appreciate it.

Selling by Subject Line

A real bonus in sending resumes by e-mail is the all-important, but frequently overlooked, subject line. Too many applicants throw an opportunity away by writing "Resume," "Resume for registered nurse," or something equally mundane for the subject. When an employer scans hundreds of resumes listed by subject line, the catchy ones get looked at first.

You can do a few things with the subject line to catch an employer's attention. One idea is to put your subject in capital letters, or you can surround it with asterisks. You could also use angle brackets (> <) as arrows pointing to your subject line. Use adjectives. Put spaces and back slash marks between titles or terms. Be bold! Use attention-getting words such as "talented," "innovative," "ambitious," and "creative."

Look at some actual examples from the MSEN gopher:

```
WRITER / MANAGER / ANALYST / V. QUALIFIED / CURIOUS
TALENTED, GIFTED, AMBITIOUS COMPUTER SCIENTIST
=============TOP SALES POSITION WANTED=============
******>>>>CREATIVE FREELANCE PHOTOGRAPHER<<<<******
INNOVATIVE P.R. PROFESSIONAL>>>>>PROVEN TRACK RECORD
```

Compare those with these:

```
entry level psych research position
Systems/software
Management
proj. 1dr/rdbms/client-server/imaging (whatever
that means!)
```

A creative subject line grabs the employer's attention and invites the individual to look at your resume. Use it with flair! Become a standout in that endless field of boring one-liners. You'll get noticed. But, be careful—nothing too funny, and never off-color.

Now that you know the general rules for writing a resume, it's time to start building one that will get you that interview.

Making a Resume

When creating a paper resume, there is a certain order in which the information is arranged. Typically, the heading goes first: name, address, and phone number. Next, comes the "Position Objective." This is where you tell the employer in specific terms what you are looking for. Then, some resumes use a "Summary" paragraph, in which you briefly describe your experience.

This is followed by "Experience" and "Education" sections. These two headings can switch places, depending on what you have to offer. For example, if you have recently received your degree in engineering, this is your most valuable asset and should go first. However, if you have fifteen years experience as an engineer, plus a degree, you should lead off with your experience. The areas following experience and education can also vary. Some common headings are "Military Service," "Publications," "Community Service," "Activities," "Specialized Training," and "Awards/Honors." Most resumes conclude with "References furnished on request." This last line is not really necessary because most employers assume that permission to contact references will be given at the appropriate time. You might want to save that space for something more important.

This standard paper format must be manipulated a bit for electronic resumes. Remember that the first few lines on the employer's computer screen will be taken up with the header—your return address, date/time, etc. So, if you begin with your name, address, and phone number, it may be all the employer sees on page one. This is not a strong incentive to read on. Or, the employer may get your heading plus a fragment of what comes next, which doesn't create a professional first impression. Let's examine some actual resumes taken from the Internet.

Sample Resumes

Sample Resume 1 - Supervisor, Oil Industry

Baton Rouge, LA

Career Summary

Twenty-three years experience in steel structural engineering, planning, fabrication, installation, pre-commissioning, and commissioning primarily in the onshore and offshore petrochemical industry and heavy engineering.

Experience

Hook-up Superintendent: McDermott International, Inc., Dubai, United Arab Emirates. Responsible for overall operations, bid submission, and administration of the Offshore Hook-up Operations Department activities for all projects in the Middle East area, Arabian Gulf, Arabian Sea, and the Bay of Bengal. Recent projects include:

ONGCL India- Installation/hook-up and precommissioning of four wellhead platforms and modifications to five existing complexes to accept well fluids from the new installations.

GUPCO Egypt- Installation/hook-up and precommissioning of a gas compression platform and tie-in of a new bridge to the existing production platform.

DPC Dubai- Modification to an existing gas compression platform to include a new compressor train and its associated process skids which required necessary process, instrument, and electrical integration.

IOOC Iran- Demolition, removal, installation/hook-up, and commissioning of production complexes in Nasr and Salman offshore oil fields.

CPC Sharjah- Installation/hook-up and commissioning of a production platform with demolition and upgrading of the existing platforms to integrate control from the new facility located in Murbarak Field.

Hook-up Supervisor: McDermott international, Inc., Dubai, United Arab Emirates. Responsible for offshore installation/hook-up and precommissioning of various projects including:

QGPC Qatar- Installation/hook-up and precommissioning of gas lift modification to seven well head platforms and gas flowline modifications and tie-ins at the main production complex.

QGPC Qatar- Onshore fabrication and offshore installation of seven modules comprising the utilities topsides complex for the North Field Development Project.

ONGC India- Eight four-pile wellhead platforms in Bombay High and South Bassein Fields.

DPC Dubai- Six-pile gas lift platform in South-West Fateh Field.
Bunduq Abu Dhabi- Two dock extensions and two test separators on WHP-D & E platform in Bunduq Field.

Instrument/Electrical Supervisor: McDermott International, Dubai, United Arab Emirates. Responsible for labor resources, construction, precommissioning, and start-up assistance of various major projects including:

Aramco Saudi Arabia - Fabrication of three six-pile tie-in platforms, and modifications to fifteen wellhead platforms in Berri Field.

ONGC India - Fabrication and installation of two four-pile jackets and temporary decks in Bombay High field.

DPC Dubai - Fabrication and installation of five offshore platforms in Falah, Fateh and S.W. Fields and precommissioning of a gas lift, water flood, and living quarters in S.W. Fateh Field.

Gulf RAK - Fabrication and installation of three platforms in Gulf RAK Field. Construction, commissioning, and start-up of an onshore gas/oil separation, storage and LPG facility in Khor Khwair.

Instrument Supervisor: Saia Electric, Baton Rouge, Louisiana. Supervision of major instrumentation upgrades including installation of pneumatic and electronic instruments, field calabration, and loop checking in various operating plants for Exxon Chemical.

Field Engineer/Piping Supervisor: Daniels Construction/H.E. Wiess, Inc., Baton Rouge, Louisiana. Pipe inspection, civil layout, blue print "As Builting," testing and coordinating of personnel for modifications to various units in Exxon Chemical. Fabrication and installation associated with a new loading facility installed for Rubicon on the Mississippi River.

Piping/Structural Inspector/Supervisor: Payne & Keller, Baton Rouge, Louisiana. Pipe and structural inspection related to the construction of an additional chemical facility for Ciba Geigy Chemicals. Coordination of labor and equipment for fabrication and installation, and planning and scheduling on various chemical projects.

Draftsman/Surveyor; Bovay Engineering, Baton Rouge, Louisiana. Civil and pipe drafting and surveying for city and state drainage and road improvement programs. Map detailing utilizing ink on mylar for various Louisiana cities under contract.

Civil Draftsman: Albert Switzer and Associates, Baton Rouge, Louisiana. Layout of civil cross sections, highway right-of-way drafting, and predesign/feasibility surveys.

Education

Mechanical Engineering - Two years, Louisiana State University, Baton Rouge, Louisiana.

Industrial Technology - One semester, Southeastern University, Hammond, Louisiana.

Piping Drafting & Design - January 1974 to June 1974, Barnard & Burk, Baton Rouge, Louisiana.

Advanced Instrumentation (Calibration) - AFL-CIO, Baton Rouge, Louisiana.

Certification/Training

Able Bodied Seaman Certification - U.S. Coast Guard
ff2S Safety Training-
Sea Survial Course 1992-
Total Quality Management-
Time Management-
Communication Skills-
Quality Auditor Training-
CPR & First Aid-
Computer Training in Lotus 1-2-3, WordPerfect 5.1 and Freelance-
Decision Making-

Firms

1981-1994   *(Applicant had listed several companies here by date)*
1980-1981
1978-1980
1974-1978
1972-1974
1970-1972

PROBLEMS:

1. Resume is too long, taking eight screens.

2. Too much detail is given in job history.

3. Not necessary to break out every job site where applicant worked.

4. Applicant uses gender-specific titles (for example, "Draftsman").

5. Headings are hard to find.

6. Not all training listed is relevant.

7. "Stale" experience (more than 10 years old).

8. No objective—applicant can do several things.

Sample Resume 2 - Systems Engineer

```
<!DOCTYPE HTML SYSTEM "html.dtd">
<HTML>
<HEAD>
<TITLE>Resume: </TITLE>
</HEAD>

<BODY>

<Hl>Resume of (Name)</Hl>
<PRE>
NAME                              Marital Status - Married
ADDRESS                           Born - November 24, 1956
OKLAHOMA 74033                    Health - Excellent
PHONE
<ADDRESS>e-mail</ADDRESS>
</PRE><HR>
<Hl>Jobs Interested In</HI>

Jobs that I would be interested in would be part-time contract work
where I can telecommute via Internet from my home in Oklahoma.<HR>

<Hl>Career Summary</Hl>
<H2>August 3, 1987 thru the present</H2>
<H5>Systems Engineer with (COMPANY NAME)</H5>
Duties include project lead for internals area of software for
real-time monitor and control of the Wiltel fiber-optic network. This includes
some systems programming as well as real-time systems design
and programming and included coordinating the efforts of members of
the project team.<P>
Served as project lead for design and development of a system for
collection of call data from telephony switches; Northern Telecom's
DMS250s. This system collects data from the switch as the calls are
completed, and each record is decoded and processed on a real-time
basis, and then distributed to client applications such as Fraud
Detection, Rating and Operational Measurement.<P>
Also involved in modifications and enhancements to a real-time SCADA
system that was purchased for controlling Williams Pipeline's pipeline
network. I wrote software to handle communications between the
application and the remote equipment for a satellite link. Also
designed and developed a system to track product through the pipeline
to various locations, and determine ETA for each product.

<H5>Software</H5>
C, Fortran Datatrieve, Language Sensitive Editor, CMS, MMS, DECnet,
Motif, OpenWindows, CDD, VAX/VMS, Unix, lemacs, Mosaic, HTML.

<H5>Hardware</H5>
IBM RS/6000, VAXcluster, VAXstations, I own a VAXstation 4000 and a
VAXstation 2000, both running VMS.

<H5>Organizations</H5>
Chairman of (Local Users Group)
Was on the National LUG Council of DECUS. Active in the Site Management special
interest group for many years. I have also made technical
presentations before audiences at DECUS' national symposia.<HR>

<H2>March 1, 1987 thru July 31, 1987</H2>

<H5>System Manager with (COMPANY NAME)</H5>
I was in charge of systems programming, performance tuning, and system
updates to the VAXclustor.
<H5>Software</H5>
Fortran, C, Cobol, Macro assembler, Pascal, 20/20, DECcalc, DBMS, CMS,
Datatrieve, CDD and WPS-Plus.

<H5>Hardware</H5>
VAXcluster (VAX 11/780-5 and a VAX 8600). I also configured an extra
node for the cluster before I left, so that they could add a VAX 8700
to the cluster.<HR>
```

```
<H2>November 1, 1983 thru February 4, 1987</H2>
<H5>Programmer/Analyst with the (COLLEGE NAME)</H5>
My duties were not restricted to those of the typical
programmer/analyst. I was also a supervisor as well, and reported
directly to the president of the college. I configured, justified,
and acquired a VAX 11/780 and a microPDP 11/73. Did the annual budget
and contracts for the department.<P>
My responsibilities included hiring and training of programmers and
operators, purchasing of supplies and equipment, and of systems
generation and software updates, performance tuning, etc.
<H5>Software</H5>
VAX Basic, POISE, Datatrieve, RMS, C-Calc, DECword, WPS-Plus, Lotus,
RSTS, VMS, SPPS, and SPSSGRAPHICS.
<H5>Hardware</H5>
VAX 11/780, PDP 11/45, PDP 11/44, PDP 11/73, and DECmate 11.
<H5>Applications</H5>
Implementation of Financial Accounting, Financial Aid, Student
Billing, Payroll, Student Registration integrated systems.
Modifications to these systems. Migrated several systems from PDP to
VAX. Wrote Engineering Maintenance application; also Course Grading,
Test Question Library, Reference Material Catalog, Inventory, Student
Load, Print Server, and utilities. Maintenance programming to all
systems on PDP and VAX, including the school library system.<HR>

<H2>May 1983 thru October 1983</H2>
<H5>Prograrnmer/Analyst with (COMPANY NAME)</H5>
In charge of all accounts for client companies using the DIBS
software.

<H5>Software</H5>
DIBS, Dibol, RSTS, RT-11, and a little bit of MCBA.
<H5>Hardware</H5>
PDP 11/24, PDP 11/23, and PDP 8s.<P>
I left the company because I felt that it was unstable. This view was
correct and they have since existed under various names and lawsuits.
They are no longer a DEC OEM.<HR>      (YIKES!!!)
```

```
<H2>November 1978 thru May 1983</H2>
<E5>Programmer/Analyst with (COMPANY NAME)</H5>
My responsibilities were the Accounting and Inventory systems. Wrote
system utilities.  Performed systems generations and software upgrades
to the operating systems RSTS and VMS.

<H5>Software</HS>
VMS, RSTS, Basic, DCL, and TOLAS software.
<H5>Hardware</H5>
VAX 11/780, PDP 11/45, and PDP 11/70.<HR>

<H2>May 1977 thru August 1978</H2>
<H5>Contract programmer for the (University NAME)</H5>

Worked on a project funded by a research grant. Developed a graphical
data entry system for music generation on the Tektronix graphics
units. Wrote in Fortran and some assembler on the Xerox Sigma VI and
an Interdata 70.<HR>

<H2>1973 thru 1974</H2>
<H5>Programmer</H5>
Assisted in development of a database information system for the
membership of the (NATIONAL ORGANIZATION)<HR>

<H1>Education</H1>
<PRE>
High School     Tulsa Central          1972 through 1974
University       University of Tulsa    1974 through 1976
                 Major: Computer Science
College          Tulsa Junior College   1977 through present
</PRE><HR>
Attended IBM's <B>"AIX Programming"</B> course, which taught how to
write C programs under IBM's version of Unix.<P>
Attended IBM's <B>"AIX Korn Shell Programming"</B>,
ISM's <B>"AIX Internals"</B> courses.<P>
```

```
Attended DEC's <B>"RSTS/E and VAX/VMS Compatibility"</B>,
<B>"VAX/VMS Real-Time Applications"</B> courses.<P>
Attended DECUS's <B>"VAX/VMS System Performance"</B> seminar.<P>
Instructed programming in Fortran one night a week for high school
students while I was a senior in high school and my first two years
of college.<HR>

<HI>Programming Languages</Hl>
C, Basic, Fortran, PL/1, Cobol, Algol, Pascal, apl, Gotran, Dibol,
dBase and Assembler.<HR>

<Hl>Publications</Hl>
I have been published in <B>"VAX Professional"</B> magazine and in
<B>"Proceedings"</B>, both being refereed papers. I have also given
numerous presentations at the DECUS national symposia.
<HR>

<Hl>References Upon Request</Hl>

</BODY>
</HTML>
```

PROBLEMS:

1. Too long—took nine screens to transmit.

2. Excessively wordy.

3. Personal information (age, marital status, etc.) should NEVER appear on resume.

4. Uses personal pronouns.

5. Word processing codes for such things as bolding, paragraph, and carriage return appear in text.

6. Should not list high school, if attended college.

7. Defames former employer (see "YIKES!!!").

Sample Resume 3 - Engineer

```
                           Subject:                        Time: 4:43 PM
OFFICE MEMO                EE/MBA-Engineering Mgr.-NJ      Date: 11/3/94
Please see the below!

NAME
ADDRESS
PHONE

SUMMARY
Engineering Professional with 15 years of increasing responsibility in
electronic design, test and product development.  Broad based experience with
business activities from proposals to production.

PROFESSIONAL EXPERIENCE
(COMPANY NAME) Ringwood, NJ (1990 - 1994)
Primary U.S. Manufacturer of automated burn-in and lifetest equipment for the
laser diode industry.



                    Engineering Manager
                    Responsible for product design and development, resource planning
                    and
                    developing engineering procedures.
                         o    Led a team of engineers to develop innovative solutions for
                    diode
                    testing
                    requirements.  Responsible                for the design and imple-
                    mentation of
                    systems used in the burn-in and lifetesting of lasers and LEDs.
                              o         Successfully managed a high-performance test system
                    development
                    project which became  the company's main product line.
                              o         Contibuted to technical proposals, scheduled
                    projects as
                    required, led
                    design reviews,                     transferred technology to manufactur-
```

```
ing,
maintained

document control, supervised system    and customer acceptance testing.

(COMPANY NAME) Princeton, NJ (1979-1990)
A leading edge technology contract research organization

Associate Member Technical Staff
Responsible for the design of test electronics supporting a laser diode
development group.
          o         Designed multi-channel laser drivers used in the world's
first 10 channel laser diode optical
recording system.  Developed life test equipment for individually addressed
multi-element
                laser diode arrays.
          Responsible for disc testing and evaluation for optical recording
development programs
                funded by the government and internal sources.
Participated in the design of a laser diode characterization system.
o         Designed controllers, stabilization circuitry and high speed, high
                current drivers used in 200 and 500 Mbit/s LAN systems.
EDUCATION
Seton Hall University - Paul Stillman School of Business
          MBA, December 1988.

Rutgers University - College of Engineering
          BSEE (with honors), May 1979.
          Honor Societies: Tau Beta Pi, Eta Kappa Nu
```

```
AWARDS
1988    David Sarnoff Research Center Outstanding Achievement Award
        for "the development of new fiber-optic systems and sub-systems."

1987    RCA Laboratories Outstanding Achievement Award for "the development
and first successful demonstration of multi-channel optical recording using
a monolithic array of                         diode lasers."

MISCELLANEOUS
One Patent
Co-authored 3 papers
Professional Membership: IEEE
```

PROBLEMS:

1. No objective stated.

2. Failed to allow for 80-character-per-line feature of e-mail.

3. Needs to cite publications and patent held.

PLUS:

4. Summarized company profile for each position.

Sample Resume 4 - Software Engineer

Dear Hiring Manager:

    I write to express my interest in obtaining a challenging software
engineering position involving software analysis, design and/or programming,
where my exploration and problem-solving skills will contribute to a solution
to your company's technical problems. I have enclosed a copy of my resume for
your consideration.

    I have over 5 years of software engineering experience and earned my
Bachelor of Science degree in Computer Science with two specialty areas:
Analysis/Design and DataBase. Some of my skills include software analysis
and design, programming in ANSI C under Windows 3.1, UNIX and AmigaDOS,
testing, planning, database, and technical writing. I can work alone as
well as with a team and am dedicated, detail-oriented, organized, responsible, trustworthy, and enthusiastic about ANSI C, MS Windows and UNIX.

    Currently, I am in the market for a new position because on Tuesday,
May 17, my ex-employer laid off about 20 to 25 percent of its workforce,
including me, from the Sunnyvale office because of a quarterly loss which
caused a change in product plans.

    I would welcome an opportunity to discuss my qualifications with you
and to answer any questions that you may have.

                    Thank you.
Enclosure: Recruiter/Head Hunter Terms, Resume
Retruiter/Head Hunter Terms:

    I will be happy to send you my name and phone number if you
agree to the following conditions:
      - We have a nonexclusive relationship.

      - You will contact me before you talk to each of your clients
        about me.
      - If I see a job advertisement or hear of a job lead, then I
        can send my resume to the company without contacting you.

      - When I leave a message, via fax, phone or e-mail, for you then
        you will respond within 48 business hours after receiving the
        message. I will do the same.

    Name, street address, and phone number to be released via e-mail.

              Sunnyvale, CA

OBJECTIVE:

    Challenging software engineering position involving software analysis,
design and/or programming, where my exploration and problem-solving
skills will contribute to a solution of your technical problems.

SKILLS SUMMARY:

    Languages, Data Base Packages/Languages, and Other Software:

XDP AD Windows 4GL	ANSI C	Pascal
Informix Turbo/Online	dBASE III PLUS	FoxBASE
Unify/Accell		
MS Word for Windows	MS Visual C++ Pro	Time Line for Windows

    Operating Systems:

Windows 3.1	MS-DOS 5.0/6.0/6.2	UNIX
AmigaDOS		

```
Computer Systems:
-----------------
 386/486 PCs             Sun 4            Amiga 3000
```

EXPERIENCE:

(COMPANY NAME) Software Division
  Sunnyvale, CA
7/91 - 5/94

Software Engineer
----

* Developed a "Date and Time Entry Field (Edit Control) Behavior"
  functional specification.

* Excelled at a Windows 3.1 SDK Programming class through UCSC
  Extension which covered text output, scrolling, keyboard and mouse
  input, menus and accelerators, memory management, child window
  controls, dialog boxes, icons, cursors and bitmaps, and GDI.

* As the testing technical lead for XDP Application Designer (AD)
  Windows 4GL, developed system microplans, test plans, test case
  specifications, and managed a group of 7 testers. Earned a
  "Commitment, Courage, Quality" award.

* Developed XDP AD Windows 4GL document imaging (scanning, storing
  and retrieving) programs.

* Completed the "Improving the Software Testing Process" course.

(COMPANY NAME) Mountain View, CA   3/90 - 3/91

Software Engineer
----
* Developed ANSI C coding standards for use in software projects.

* Completed an Object-Oriented Analysis and Design course.

* Researched and developed a UNIX Tools Summary.
* Evaluated Atherton Technology's Project SoftBoard.

(COMPANY NAME) Sacramento, CA   1/89 - 8/89

Product Engineer (Co-op)
----

* Ported Unify, Accell/IDS and Accell/CP to different hardware
  platforms running UNIX.

* Installed UNIX on various computers.

(COMPANY NAME) Sacramento, CA   2/88 - 1/89

Software Developer (University Senior Project)
----

* As part of a team, proposed, managed, analyzed, designed,
  implemented, tested, and delivered a patient/clinician tracking
  and report generating data base system by observing the Waterfall
  Software Development Life-cycle.

(COMPANY NAME) Sacramento, CA   7/88 - 8/88

Computer Programmer

```
  * Supported users, analyzed users' needs, and implemented resultant
    revisions in the 52-Track Personnel System.

(COMPANY NAME) Sacramento, CA        7/87 - 3/88

Software Developer (Co-op)
--------------------------

  * Analyzed needs, designed and implemented the Vegetation Control
    System which plans the material applications on the state's
    highways and freeways. Integrated a bulletin board system to
    collect data from each district.

(UNIVERSITY NAME) Sacramento, CA                  9/86 - 5/87

Computer Lab Supervisor and Tutor
----------------------------------

  * Tutored students in Logo, Pascal, FORTRAN77, BASIC and Data
    Structures.

  * Supervised up to 30 students.

EDUCATION:
  Bachelor of Science, Computer Science.
    Specialties: Analysis/Design and Data Base.
  California State University, Sacramento. December 1989.

  GPA - Specialties: 3.68 Overall: 3.35
```

COMMENTS:

This "resume" is actually a cover letter and resume together, a totally acceptable way of applying. An interesting feature of this package, however, is the note to "headhunters" who may see this applicant's resume. Remember that the employer will see this, too. It would be a good idea to delete the message to the headhunter when replying direct to an employer by e-mail.

Resume format is good. If deleting cover letter, needs a summary paragraph and heading.

Sample Resume 5 - Engineer

Gary L. Lee
306 Shady Drive   Inman, SC 29349   (803)578-8805

SUMMARY Dynamic engineer with progressive, innovative approach to the engineering function. Possess excellent communication skills with the innate
ability to bring complex issues to completion while utilizing
employee involvement techniques to ensure that all parties share in the
successful completion of the project. Unusual strengths in OSHA,
environmental health issues and regulations.

EXPERIENCE 1990-Present   (COMPANY NAME)   Spartanburg, SC $40
million company specializing in the manufacture and packing of sewing notions,
employing 220 people in the Spartanburg Plant. Subsidiary of
Prym Germany, a $500 million manufacturer of diversified products
employing 5000 people worldwide.

  Engineering Manager   Responsible for all engineering functions
including safety, EPA, OSHA, and SCDHEC compliance for the Spartanburg facility. Operations include high speed stamping and assembly, plating, toolroom
function, maintenance function, and a variety of packaging
techniques.

  *Designed and built with the involvement of employees a high speed
packing machine which   reduced the number of people required to produce
the same product from 12 to 4. This resulted in a labor savings of
$250,000 per year and enabled a $2.5 million contract for sewing notions
to be maintained with Wal-Mart.

  *Introduced and developed the Borazon Grinding Wheel concept in the
manufacturing area, resulting in increased productivity, reduced downtime and
savings of $250,000 per year.

  *Worked in concert with the Employee Safety Committee to establish
safety procedures which resulted in a savings of $100,000 per year on the
Workers Compensation Premium as well as established OSHA, EPA, and
SCDHEC programs which successfully passed these agencies' inspections.

  *Evaluated the tooling purchased for manufacturing and reduced the
overall cost for tooling by 50% through re-engineering and competitive bid-
ding.

1989-1990 (COMPANY NAME) Cheraw, SC

  Plant 5 Plant Manager   Responsible for a 75 person plant which
warehoused $40 million of raw material and manufactured $4.5 million of
tooling for all 5 INA plants. Operations included a slitter and phosphate coat
line.

  *Established procedures which increased the amount of finished tooling
produced by the Plant 5 toolroom by 30%.

  *Developed a slitter and phosphate line which reduced the cost of raw
material for bearing manufacture by 30%.

  *Installed a Bar Code System which reduced the warehouse manning and
inventory cost by $70,000/year.

1985-1989 (COMPANY NAME) Caldwell and Bridgeport, OH
Engineering Manager (Caldwell 1986-1989) Responsible for all plant
engineering and 16 Engineers and 28 Toolmakers engaged in Manufacturing
Engineering, Industrial Engineering, CAD/CAM Tool Design, Computer
Services, and Tool Room activities. Processes included high speed
stamping, CNC machining, grinding, casting, and plating. Reported to Plant
Manager.

  *Directed all engineering changes associated with $2.9 million plant
expansion and reorganization maintaining perfect delivery record.

  *Designed, developed and introduced Laser Welding Workstation with
sophisticated patentable, Vision System which allowed the penetration of
a $10 million market.

  *Heavily involved in the obtaining of the Ford Q1 award which resulted
in an immediate increase in business of $3-4 million.

Engineering Manager (1985-1986)

  *Converted conventional manufacturing to Just-In-Time cells eliminating 75
positions.

  *Coordinated installation and start-up of $500,000 waste treat system
to meet EPA fluid discharge requirements.

1980-1985 Brenco, Inc., Petersburg, Va.

  Manager, Product and Manufacturing Engineering

  *Introduced SPC resulting in contract with Ford Motor Company

1979-1980 (COMPANY NAME) Glasgow, Ky.

```
      Manufacturing- Grinding
1971-1979 Timken Company, Bucyrus and Canton, Oh.
   Assistant Plant Engineer   Product and Tool Design Engineer
Education University of Akron, Akron, Ohio   BS Mechanical Engineering

Technology
Personal Married, 1 child
Interests Golf, Family activities
```

PROBLEMS:

1. No separation between sections.

2. Headings impossible to find.

3. Excessively wordy.

4. Arrangement out of order.

5. Personal information included—for example, marital status.

6. Stale experience.

Sample Resume 6 - Mechanical Engineer

```
                                        (NAME)
                                        (ADDRESS)
Street
                                Ontario, K8A 1V3
                                Home: (000) 000-0000
                            Work: (000) 000-0000
                            Email:
```

Education University of Toronto, Master's of Applied Science, Mechanical
Engineering;
                        expected May 1995, Toronto, Ontario.

                Technical University of Nova Scotia, Bachelor of
Mechanical Engineering
                        (with Distinction); May 1993, Halifax, Nova
Scotia.
                Saint Mary's University, Bachelor of Science and Diploma
in Engineering;
                        May 1990, Halifax, Nova Scotia.

Awards   o Association of Professional Engineers of Nova
Scotia Award for Best
                        Departmental Senior Design Project (1993).
                o Norcen Energy Resources Scholarship (1992). Value:
$1000.
                o Sexton Scholar (1990-92). Cumulative average above 85%
at TUNS.
                o Presidential Scholarship (1987-88). Value: $5000.
                o Parrsboro Regional High School Scholarship (1987-88).
Value: $1000.
Computer   Micros: IBM PC, Apple Macintosh
Skills   Systems: Windows, DOS, X-Windows, UNIX, VMS
                        Software: LabVIEW, SmartCAM, LaTeX, Auto CAD, most
spreadsheets and
                                word-processors
                        Languages: FORTRAN, BASIC

Related
Experience
May 1994 -   (COMPANY NAME) Research Attached Staff,
present   Chalk River, Ontario.
                   o Currently running an experimental project to examine the
effect of support
                            geometry and tube excitation on damping and
retting-wear work-rate of
                            multispan heat exchanger tubes.

            o Member of a team designing a new temperature-controlled
multispan test rig.

1993   (GOVERNMENT AGENCY) Research Assistant,
Dartmouth, Nova Scotia.
    (summer)   Performed validation study of proposed submarine
force-predicting software.
                    o Recommended implementation of software at DND Research
lab.
                    o Co-authored DND Technical Memorandum to present results.

1992 - 1993 Senior Design Project Team Member, (CO.NAME) Halifax, Nova
Scotia.
    (2 sessions)   o Part of a team that utilized LabVIEW, a computerized
control and data
                            acquisition system, to design lab

experiments for a Mechanical Engineering
                    undergraduate course at TUNS.
                    o Completed project and successfully incorporated system
that academic year.
                    o Final mark assigned: 90%. Won Award.

1992   (GOVERNMENT AGENCY) Research Assistant,
Dartmouth, Nova Scotia.
    (summer)   o Created post-processor software for DND Research lab
to display results from
                        existing modeling program.
                    o Co-authored DND Technical Communication as a user's
manual.
1991   (COMPANY NAME) Junior Assistant, Halifax, Nova
Scotia.
    (summer)   o Part-time at engineering/architecture consulting firm.
                    o Performed drawing mark-ups, calculation checks,
proposal preparation,
                        drawing copies, deliveries and other office
duties.

Other
Experience
1994   University of Toronto Teaching Assistant, Toronto, Ontario.
    (1 session)   o Instructed undergraduate Fluids class and marked weekly
assignments.

1991 - 1993   Technical University of Nova Scotia Student Lounge,
Halifax, Nova Scotia.
                    o Served as Saturday night bartender during 1991-92 year.
                    o Promoted to Staff and Facilities Supervisor for 1992-93.
Hired and trained new
                        staff, managed day-to-day lounge operations.
                    o Served as Acting Manager during spring of 1993. Managed
finances, bookings,
        and made Student Union reports.

1988   Saint Mary's University Teaching Assistant, Halifax, Nova

Scotia.
    (1 session)   o Instructed weekly computer lab for undergraduate
Design/Graphics course.

Activities   o Member of High School Visitation program for
Engineering (1991-92).
                    o Member of TUNS Mechanical Engineering Society (1990-93).
                    o Member of MENSA Canada since 1991.
                    o Secretary of SMU Engineering Society (1989-90).
                    o Member of SMU Engineering Society (1987-90).
                    o Enjoy skiing, writing, music, reading, traveling.

References   Available upon request.

- -

PROBLEMS:

1. Failed to allow for number of characters per line (80) as they will appear
    in e-mail, giving a haphazard, scattered appearance to text.

2. Resume is not readable.

3. Headings are hard to find and arranged out of order.

Sample Resume 7—Public Relations Specialist

Notice the name centered at the top bracketed with asterisks to add interest. Then, it leads off with an attention-grabbing summary paragraph. This gives employers a first look at the job seeker and invites them to read on. The opening can be followed by a traditional resume format, beginning on the next screen. Consider this sample:

```
            ************************************
                         J. B. Seeker
                   Public Relations Specialist
            ************************************

SUMMARY:       Talented PR professional with more than 15
               years of experience and a proven track record
               in building strong company image and community
               relations. Excellent writing skills.
               Motivational speaker. Creative problem-solver.
               Adept at press relations and advertising. M.A.
               degree.

                   J. B. Seeker
                   4231 Success Lane
                   Excell, CA 91116
                   (909) 555-4285
                   jseeker@igc.apc.org

OBJECTIVE:     Challenging position as PR director for a progressive company
               with an eye on the future.

SIGNIFICANT
EXPERIENCE:
1987-Present   PUBLIC RELATIONS MANAGER
               The Westbrook Group, Palm Springs, CA

               * Managed staff of PR and Advertising
                 professionals, developing PR program that
                 increased visibility and acceptance of
                 company programs

               * Directed advertising dept. Wrote and edited
                 copy, designed advertising campaigns

               * Interfaced with television, radio and print
                 media, building strong contacts and positive
                 relations

               * Represented company as featured speaker and
                 ambassador at various community and
                 charitable functions

1983-87        PUBLIC RELATIONS REPRESENTATIVE

               Eagle Manufacturing, San Francisco, CA

               * Designed successful PR campaigns for company
                 products and services

               * Acted as media liason. Offical spokesperson
                 during labor crisis

               * Promoted good will as company representative
                 through community contacts

               * Developed in-house training programs

               * Designed company brochure and point-of-
                 purchase materials
```

```
EDUCATION:     Master of Arts, Public Relations
               University of San Francisco

               Bachelor of Arts, Communication Studies
               University of California, San Diego

PERSONAL
STATEMENT:     Creative and innovative. Cutting-edge
               approach to public relations. Energetic and
               loyal company advocate with a healthy
               understanding of the bottom line.
```

This resume was prepared and formatted in ASCII. Transmission took a total of five screens, which follow:

```
           ************************************
                       J. B. Seeker
                  Public Relations Specialist
           ************************************

SUMMARY:       Talented PR professional with more than 15
               years' experience and a proven track record
               in building strong company image and community
               relations. Excellent writing skills.
               Motivational speaker. Creative problem solver.
               Adept at press relations and advertising. M.A.
               degree.

64 lines more (30%). Press <space> for more, 'I' to return.
Alt-Z FOR HELP3 VT100 3 FDX 3 19200 N81 3 LOG CLOSED 3 PRINT OFF 3 ON-LINE
```

```
                       J. B. Seeker
                       4231 Success Lane
                       Excell, CA 91116
                       (909) 555-4285
                       jseeker@igc.apc.org

OBJECTIVE:     Challenging position as PR director for a
               progressive company with an eye on the future.

SIGNIFICANT
EXPERIENCE:

1987-Present PUBLIC RELATIONS MANAGER
               The Westbrook Group, Palm Springs, CA

               * Managed staff of PR and Advertising
                 professionals, developing PR program that
                 increased visibility and acceptance of
44 lines more (52%). Press <space> for more, 'I' to return.
Alt-Z FOR HELP3 VT100 3 FDX 3 19200 N81 3 LOG CLOSED 3 PRINT OFF 3 ON-LINE
```

```
                    increased visibility and acceptance of
                    company programs

                 *  Directed advertising dept. Wrote and edited
                    copy, designed advertising campaigns

                 *  Interfaced with television, radio and print
                    media, building strong contacts and positive
                    relations

                 *  Represented company as featured speaker and
                    ambassador at various community and
                    charitable functions

1983-87          PUBLIC RELATIONS REPRESENTATIVE

                 Eagle Manufacturing, San Francisco, CA

                 *  Designed successful PR campaigns for company
                    products and services

24 lines more (73%). Press <space> for more, 'i' to return.
Alt-Z FOR HELP3 VT100 3 FDX 3 19200 N81 3 LOG CLOSED 3 PRINT OFF 3 ON-LINE
```

```
                 *  Acted as media liason. Offical spokesperson
                    during labor crisis

                 *  Promoted good will as company representative
                    through community contacts

                 *  Developed in-house training programs

                 *  Designed company brochure and point-of-
                    purchase materials

EDUCATION:       Master of Arts, Public Relations
                 University of San Francisco

                 Bachelor of Arts, Communication Studies
                 University of California, San Diego

PERSONAL
STATEMENT:       Creative and innovative. Cutting-edge
4 lines more (95%). Press <space> for more, 'i' to return.
Alt-Z FOR HELP3 VT100 3 FDX 3 19200 N81 3 LOG CLOSED 3 PRINT OFF 3 ON-LINE
```

```
STATEMENT:       Creative and innovative. Cutting-edge
                 approach to public relations. Energetic and
                 loyal company advocate with a healthy
                 understanding of the bottom line.




Command ('i' to return to index):
Alt-Z FOR HELP3 VT100 3 FDX 3 19200 N81 3 LOG CLOSED 3 PRINT OFF 3 ON-LINE
```

Sample Electronic Resume Format

Now let's look at a complete sample of an electronic resume format:

```
*************************************
*               NAME                *
*************************************
```

SUMMARY:
* Strong, short opening paragraph.
* Identify your profession.
* Highlight 3 or 4 of your job strengths.
* Invite employer to read on.

```
             Name
            Address
      City, State, Zip,
   Phone (H) Phone (msg)
```

POSITION OBJECTIVE:
State a specific goal. Gives resume direction.

SIGNIFICANT EXPERIENCE:

(Dates go here)

List jobs that support Objective.
Position Title
Name & Location of Company
* Put each job description in "bullet" form to save space.
* Work in reverse order.
* List most important duties.
* Do not use personal pronouns.

EDUCATION:
Name & Location of College/University
Type of Degree and Major
Honors, if appropriate.
Certain, applicable coursework, if required.

Optional Headings:

MILITARY SERVICE
Branch. Dates. Rank/Job.

SPECIALIZED TRAINING
Job-related, not covered in Education.

PUBLICATIONS
Name of publication. Title. Date.

HONORS/AWARDS
Job-related most helpful.

PERSONAL STATEMENT:
* List personal qualities that reflect fitness for employment.

* Make an assertive statement of your job-related strengths.

REFERENCES:
This information is optional; employers assume references will be supplied. Never list reference information on resume.

```
             Name
      E-Mail Address
```

Using an Interactive Multimedia Resume

Previously, we discussed the nuisance of having to compose a winning resume when faced with the limitations of ASCII. We encountered a job seeker who had done some extraordinary things with his resume, utilizing the newest software and a creative spirit. David Coleman is a regional promotions manager in the music industry. He has had some exposure to interactive publications like magazines and was inspired to apply this technology to his resume. He created an interactive, multimedia resume that has been downloaded by more than 500 employers!

David said that, although he wanted a professional-looking multimedia resume, he didn't want to exceed the limits of any potential employer's computer. Most employers might not have a sound card, for instance, or a particular program to run a high-tech resume (computer firms excepted, of course). The fact is, you could go all the way to the high end of the spectrum and produce a CD-ROM, but if an employer cannot look at it, what good is it?

David isn't a computer programmer, so he bought a couple of books and a few programs and "played around with them." He wanted to design something that would reach the largest audience by keeping it uncomplicated or as he put it, "the most simple common denominator." He felt the easiest format would be in Windows Help with a Windows speaker driver included. Using this, anyone running Windows 3.0 or higher could view and hear all parts of his multimedia resume. He used an 8-bit sound card instead of a 16-bit to keep the file smaller, and a scanner to add pictures. Lastly, he used a self-extracting installation program that would install the program on an employer's hard drive.

To experience David's resume, you click on different icons and highlighted sections. Each icon has its own sound effect, and there are also photographs and music. The multimedia resume ends with a recording of David's voice summing up his qualifications.

He provided us with a disk and we have reprinted some of it here. Keep in mind that the real experience lies in the interactive nature of his resume. But you can get a clear idea of what the future of electronic resumes will look like.

Resume of David Coleman

Click on any icons or GREEN TEXT to navigate through the resume

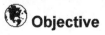 **Objective**

 **Qualifications**

 **Achievements**

 **Experience**

 **Computer skills**

 **Personal**

 Click to hear a message from David Coleman

Objective

I am a fifteen year marketing and promotion veteran in the entertainment industry seeking a challenging position utilizing my skills in management, advertising, promotions, marketing, sales and public relations. I am seeking new employment opportunities in the industries of multi-media, interactive television, video, film, cable, broadcast, software, virtual reality, on-line services, entertainment and other forms of media.

 Return to Main Menu

Achievements

 **Market Development and Sales**

 **Advertising and Promotions**

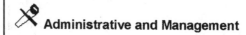 **Administrative and Management**

 **Customer Relations**

 Return to Main Menu

Computer Skills

Multi-media presentation design
(Winner of the 1994 Compuserve/Geffen Records Multimedia Contest)

DOS, Windows and Unix

Wordprocessing

Desktop Publishing

Novell Networks

Computer bulletin board design & operations

 Return to Main Menu

Qualifications

Directing/Supervising	Promotion	Communicating
Media Utilization	Marketing	Motivating
Public Relations	Sales	Management
Demographic Research	Inventory Control	Problem Solving
Computer Utilization	Pricing/Purchasing	Image Development

 Return to Main Menu

Experience

Use the scroll bar on the right side of this window to move the information up or down

Regional Marketing & Promotion Manager   1992
  EMI Records Group, Atlanta, GA

Southeast Regional Promotion Manager   1989 - 1992
  MCA Records, Atlanta, GA

Midwest Regional Promotion Manager   1987 - 1989
  Arista Records, Kansas City, MO

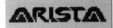

Local Promotion Manager   1986 - 1987
  Arista Records, Charlotte, NC

Personal

David Coleman
4180 Triple Creek Court
Atlanta, GA 30319
(404) 936 - 9131 (voice)
76114,3607 (Compuserve)
DavidC179@aol.com (Internet)

I am married with two children and in excellent health.
References are available upon request.

👉 **Return to Main Menu**

Using Unique Techniques
We found the following unique resume format in `uk.jobs`.

```
Sun, 16 Oct 1994
Subject: Physicist Available for R&D Work
```

Here is the sort of position I am looking for. As the subject heading suggests, my objective is to follow a career in
R&D.

An IDEAL position would be:

```
F     Full of real opportunities to broaden my expertise,
A     At the cutting edge of technology,
N     Not in a hostile working environment,
T     Taxing on the brain cells rather than the nerves,
A     Appropriately well-paid,
S     Satisfying,
T     Tremendously exciting,
I     Immune to chronic downsizing exercises,
C     Challenging.
```

It sounds fantastic enough to be a mere fantasy. If you
think you can help it turn to reality, even in part, then
contact me at. . . .

P.S. If this approach does not work, I guess I will have to
revert to my boring old method of posting a resume with a
hyperpolite letter (the one that starts with "Dear Prospective Employer. . . .")

Using a "catchy" or "cute" format can be risky and is usually frowned on in real-world recruiting. However, things are different in the culture of the Internet. We wanted to know what employer reaction was to this resume. Our respondent told us that he'd received many responses, mostly positive, but that he'd been chided in two cases for behavior unbecoming a scientist. "It seems that people want their scientists to be serious," he said. However, when he returned to his standard resume format, he received only 20 percent of the response he got with his less conventional one.

The following objective caught our eye. According to its author, it did the same with several employers and he was eventually hired:

```
Objective
I intend to coerce the world into making sense, one
object at a time. This is an obsession of sorts. A
crusade against VCRs that blink twelve o'clock when
it's three-thirty; a protest against one-way streets
and their "no left-hand turn" signs; a revolt against
screeching modems with cryptic legends on their faces
and no visible volume controls.
```

This applicant also wrote a different subject line:

```
"Human Interface Designer for lease"
```

Getting an Employer's Attention

These techniques are unusual, but acceptable in certain fields. We submit them to illustrate the variety of styles and approaches out there, not as examples of how your resume should look.

Now all that remains is to bring your resume to the attention of an employer. You want to approach these people in a professional manner and distinguish yourself through your subsequent contacts with them. In the next chapter, you learn the rules governing proper communication behavior on the net.

C H A P T E R

7

Internet Job–Hunting "Netiquette"

Most job seekers wouldn't dream of dropping in unannounced on an employer in the middle of a business day and expect an audience. Yet, through the miracle of e-mail, such casual interfaces are now entirely possible. When employers access the "new mail" message and find your resume there, you have effectively "gotten in" to see them. If you were fortunate enough to get a busy employer's undivided attention you would not take liberties with this important person. You would be extremely mindful of your behavior during your interview. However, because of the unique culture of the Internet, people often make mistakes in etiquette and conduct when electronic job seeking that they might not otherwise make in person.

Conversation on the net, "chat" if you will, is highly informal. People use nicknames and feel free to speak very candidly to others "out there" in cyberspace. This is due largely to the anonymity factor in computer-mediated communication. The thinking is "They can't see me, they don't know me, and they can't find me." There is something remarkably freeing in knowing that. So, people tend to let down their guard and say and do things they wouldn't ordinarily say or do in conversation. Be aware, though, that the same rules of etiquette governing face-to-face job hunting also apply in the electronic labor market. Remember that the employer is evaluating you from the first word on your subject line to the last statement on your resume. You are not there to give those all-important nonverbal cues to the employer. All they have of you is written words on a screen. Those words, in effect, become you. So, you would do well to give some serious thought to how you want them to represent you.

Suppose a total stranger approached you on the street, slapped you on the back, and called you by your name as though he or she had known you intimately for years. Then, this same person proceeded to ask you for a big favor involving money. This person finished by saying he or she would be calling you soon. Language directed to employers that is too informal is a serious breach of job-hunting etiquette. It is akin to slapping an employer on the back when you don't even know him or her. Employers don't like it one bit.

General Rules

In the real world of work, manners are expected. If an applicant is too familiar, the employer will be turned off. Such behavior is presumptuous. Even though you may think that the dynamics of your relationship with an employer are different by virtue of your contact taking place in cyberspace, you must remember that the basic power structure remains the same. Certain behavior is expected of you. Here are some rules of etiquette for electronic job seeking:

- **Never address the employer by first name.** "Ms. Jones:" or "Dear Mr. Brown:" is appropriate. NEVER "Hi, Joan."

- **Always use your full name when signing correspondence.** Using only your first name presumes intimacy.

- **Watch return addresses.** A few of the net resumes we checked out had "clever" names. We found a "Smart Guy" and a "Wise Guy," for example. Consider the effect these nicknames have on employers. They are being provided with a first impression based on these seemingly insignificant "clues." They wonder, "Is this guy maybe too 'smart' for our organization?" It is a risk better not taken. Use your own name.

- **Never e-mail a resume "for a friend."** We noted several subject notations that said this very thing. This is the same thing as taking a friend along to an interview or calling a company for someone else "just for information"—practices employers loathe. If you must send resumes or correspondence by someone else's access, have that person forward it for you. Your name and identifying information will appear on the resume or letter itself. The employer will figure out that this is where you can be reached.

  Along these same lines, if you accessed your employer through a resume service that the employer paid for, do not share this referral with other job seekers. Employers pay for the privilege of having the service screen for them. You have been approved and are expected. Your friend has not and is not.

- **Avoid slang expressions.** "I'll get back to you" is rude. "I will contact you again at the end of next week" is more appropriate.

■ **Forget about using "smileys," or "emoticons," those facial expressions made by using punctuation marks :-).** They are used to add expression, emotion, and feeling to written statements. If an employer sends one to you, that's an invitation to be more informal. Otherwise, they are inappropriately casual.

■ **Write in complete sentences.** People communicating electronically tend to use a type of verbal shorthand, i.e., "Available after next week. Thanks for attention." Take the bit of extra time and keystrokes it takes to respond properly.

■ **Never presume on the employer's time.** Always ask if what you propose is convenient. "I would like to arrange an interview at your earliest convenience," not "Give me a buzz so we can talk" or "I'll be expecting your call."

■ **Don't make demands.** For example, don't tell employers to respond to you by a certain date. "I haven't even met this person yet, and they're ordering me around," says Kimberly, a human resource interviewer with a national retail chain. "It is better to make polite requests, rather than aggressive demands. Manners really count in e-mail messages." Let employers set the agenda. It's their call.

■ **Never assume employers are waiting breathlessly for you to come along and "save" their company.** A little humility goes much further than a lot of bravado.

■ **Don't inundate the employer with a string of messages.** Once you have sent your resume, you may follow up at well-paced intervals—about every three to five days. Remember, this person is receiving hundreds of these things. Give them a little time to get back to you.

■ **Don't assume that the employer will remember you.** In subsequent messages, it will be necessary to reference your prior correspondence, the kind of work you do, and any communication or instructions the employer may have sent you. Julie, a supervisor in a large HMO says, "I get these message fragments and have a hard time trying to figure out what the person is referencing, what we had previously discussed. It really helps if I have a copy of at least part of our prior message. That way, I can put our conversation and the applicant in context." And always identify yourself clearly, with both names, in every message.

■ **Check your e-mail several times a day, every day.** If you let your messages sit for several days, you may risk losing a job opportunity or alienating a potential employer. Things move pretty fast in the Internet world. You need to keep pace.

- **Never keep employers waiting.** Answer your e-mail messages promptly. You know how it feels to watch for that "new mail" message. Most people wouldn't dream of ignoring a phone call from an employer; they answer it right away. Yet they tend to let their e-mail in-basket pile up. Or, they read their messages and don't answer them until later. Keep on top of your mail. It's only polite.

- **Be polite and observe proper manners.** "Thank-you" is a completely legitimate phrase. The time it takes an employer to read an e-mail and respond is just as valuable as any face-to-face encounter.

- **Be friendly, but not too familiar.** Adopt a professional, yet cordial writing style. These people are human beings just like you. They are interested in you. Be careful, though, about crossing the line. Don't ask personal questions, and never volunteer personal information about yourself.

- **You need to strike the right balance.** Be assertive . . . but not aggressive. Enthusiastic . . . but not pushy. Professional . . . but not stiff. Agreeable . . . but not a doormat. Knowledgeable . . . but not a know-it-all. Persistent . . . but not annoying. Above all, be respectful. Don't forget: This person may be your future boss.

Newsgroup Fundamentals

Sometimes you will job search by use of newsgroups. These are conferences devoted to employment-related topics. Some are support groups, where weary job seekers can air their gripes and frustrations about the crummy labor market. But many others are places for actual job and resume postings. Following are some tips for proper behavior on and use of newsgroups.

Follow the Employer's Instructions

READ! Sounds simple, doesn't it? But, when you spot a "perfect job," you may be in such a rush to respond that you miss the all-important message which says, "Please fax or mail resumes." or "No e-mail except messages!!!!!!" (We counted the exclamation points on that one—there were six. Think the employer means business?) If you ignored or missed that message, your resume would not be considered, regardless of your qualifications. The employer reasonably deduces that, if you can't follow simple instructions in the application process, you certainly won't be able to do so on the job. Furthermore, it just plain ticks employers off!

Several announcements said, "Local applicants only," meaning that people outside a specific geographical area would not be considered. The employers probably wanted to avoid relocation expenses. Sometimes it is because they want people familiar with the local sales or labor market. One posting said only in-house applicants would be considered. In this case, the company was a large, international firm with a staff of hundreds. Their employees all over the world could read this message and respond to it, but no outsiders should. When you respond inappropriately, it inconveniences the employer and disappoints you. Read the instructions carefully and follow them!

Follow Newsgroup Usage Instructions

Established newsgroups, such as those that post jobs, frequently have rules governing their use. Often, they will post frequently asked questions (FAQ's) that help new users learn the ropes. Don't be the kid in class that raises his or her hand to ask a question the teacher just answered yesterday. Take the initiative and read the "about the (newsgroup name)" section carefully. Then, play by the rules of the group. If you don't find a FAQ list, then post a short note asking for one. People who have been utilizing the newsgroup for a while get tired of seeing the same questions posted again and again.

Networking

Oops! There's that word. All too often overused in the world of work and job hunting, the networking concept was made for the Internet. While perusing a new newsgroup, that computer whiz you were chatting with last night on the conference sees a posting for a software designer which fits exactly with your qualifications. A quick e-mail and you've accessed a position that you may have missed before. Or, you respond to a job posting and the employer tells you thanks, but you're not for them. By all means, ask for a referral. So often, these people know each other or have heard of other openings within the industry. If they know of something, they'll usually pass it on.

Choose Your Group

Maybe you've been spending all your time in a sort of generic "jobs" group when a different newsgroup exists that serves your particular career or field of interest. Special conferences exist where participants discuss issues pertinent to their specialized discipline or sphere of work. In these exclusive newsgroups, users forward information they have found at other sites on the Internet. Of course this information includes job postings. Here, you will find only those jobs that are relevant and appropriate to your field. We spotted Wayne Greenwood's resume posting for "Human Interface Designer" in the Online Career Center. We sent him a message inquiring about responses to his somewhat unusual resume. He replied: "I did end up finding a job through the Net, but my new employer didn't find me the same way you did. I replied to a posting in the Internet newsgroup comp.human-factors, which is where the snarly interface designer types hang out. . . interviewed with them a couple of times and landed the job."

Surf the net and find your own niche. It's just like moving into a new neighborhood. You have to get out there and make friends—contacts who can help you move forward in your new community. By the same token, if you come across something that isn't suitable for you, pass it on. In the unique culture of the Internet, individual users are, in a sense, part of a "neighborhood," a fraternal community linked together by avid interest in this remarkable form of communication. Much like people in a real-world community, net users watch out for one another. They have to do their "community service." If you help your electronic neighbor "raise a barn" today, the same community will rally round to help you raise yours tomorrow.

Postings Are Public

Remember that what you write is likely to be viewed by many, many people. These can be people who know you or the employer you are trying to target. Keep your postings professional and never publish private e-mail messages.

Writing Tips

In the world of face-to-face interviews, the applicant's appearance— grooming and facial expression—is all important in a chance at the job. Some employers rate the appearance factor as high as 75 percent in determining whether or not the applicant is selected. This is a factor that is easily controlled through intelligent, pertinent grooming choices. In electronic job search, however, your entire appearance is limited to what is written on that screen. Let's take a careful look at how to write on the Internet.

The problem with the written word is that it is static. Once it's on the page and you hit the "send" key, it's there for life. Someone wise once said, "Never put anything in writing!" What lies behind this extreme caveat is the fear that what is written will forever have the potential to come back again and the writer will be held to its content. There is also the fear that, with the written word, no opportunity exists for mediation of the message by the writer. In other words, however the receiver interprets it is how it will be received. We are reminded of the quote: "I am sure that you believe that you understand what it is that you think I said. But I'm not sure you realize that what you heard is not what I meant."

Messages on the net are especially vulnerable to misinterpretation. The receiver can't hear the inflection of voice or discern a chuckle from a sneer. They can't see the raised eyebrow or a roll of the eyes. There is not even handwriting to be analyzed! All that is there are words.

So you must be thoughtful and cautious when constructing your messages. Here are some ideas:

- **Don't e-mail mistakes!** Be sure that your messages are written in complete sentences, using proper grammar, punctuation, and spelling. If writing is not your forte, you might consider composing all messages in your word processor first, where you can spell-check them and, in some cases, even style-check them, before uploading them into e-mail. Some mail systems on the net already have processing functions like these built in.

- **If you don't know, don't guess.** Just as your messages have the potential to be misunderstood by employers, you also can misunderstand theirs. If something comes to you that you just don't "get," message them and ask for clarification. Don't try to bluff your way through a response. Chances are you'll get it wrong and end up looking bad.

- **Avoid being "funny."** A "clever" remark on your end can arrive as impudence on the other. Better to play it straight, unless and until you have established some kind of relationship with the employer through several messages and have a sense of his or her brand of humor.

- **Watch line length.** It is a good idea to limit the length of your sentences to approximately 60 spaces. This is because when your message arrives at the other end, it can be somewhat indented. Different systems "read" sentence length differently, so your neatly composed message can reach its destination looking sloppy. Deliberately return at the end of each sentence, allowing for a neat right margin and no line extension to the end of your screen.

- **Don't use caps lock.** In the language of electronic communication, capitalized words are read as shouting. The only place caps are permissible is in your subject line. Don't forget, there is no way to add emphasis, such as underlining or italicizing yet. Your written sentence must convey meaning by itself. And remember: NO SMILEYS.

- **Watch your tone.** Don't whine or gripe. Employers get plenty of messages that read, in part, "Haven't you come to a decision yet? I have been out of work for more than six months, the bills are due, the car's broken down, the dog's sick . . . ." Or, "This is my third message. When are you going to get back to me?" This is **not** the way to win a job.

- **Write for several readers.** It is often not only the receiver who reads your message. The human resources manager may forward it to the department supervisor who then gives it to the line supervisor. These people can be different genders, ages, and ethnicities. At the very least, they are all individual personalities. Each has a different frame of reference on the job. Your message should be generic enough to be read, understood, and appreciated by all of them.

■ **Stick to the point.** You're here to do business. Get to it. Don't meander all over with irrelevant chat. If you wish to insert a personal note, fine. Just stay focused on your stated purpose—finding a job.

The issue of netiquette has been written about extensively on the net. Articles are frequently excerpted and posted to various newsgroups, forums, and BBSs. The reason is simple: When that many people are sharing the same arena, occasional misunderstandings, conflicts, and mistakes are bound to occur. Chuq Von Rospach has been involved with USENET and the Internet since 1978. He works for Apple on various projects, including Internet tools. We selected an excerpt from an article he wrote, "A Primer on How to Work with the USENET Community," to sum up the importance of netiquette.

A Primer on How to Work with the USENET Community
by Chuq Von Rospach

USENET is a large collection of computers that share data with each other. It is the people on these computers that make USENET worth the effort to read and maintain, and for USENET to function properly those people must be able to interact in productive ways. This document is intended as a guide to using the net in ways that will be pleasant and productive for everyone.

This document is not intended to teach you how to use USENET. Instead, it is a guide to using it politely, effectively, and efficiently.

The easiest way to learn how to use USENET is to watch how others use it. Start reading the news and try to figure out what people are doing and why. After a couple of weeks you will start understanding why certain things are done and what things shouldn't be done. There are documents available describing the technical details of how to use the software. These are different depending on which programs you use to access the news. You can get copies of these from your system administrator. If you do not know who that person is, they can be contacted on most systems by mailing to account "usenet".

Never Forget That the Person on the Other Side Is Human.
Because your interaction with the network is through a computer, it is easy to forget that there are people "out there." Situations arise where emotions erupt into a verbal free-for-all that can lead to hurt feelings.

Please remember that people all over the world are reading your words. Do not attack people if you cannot persuade them with your presentation of the facts. Screaming, cursing, and abusing others only serves to make people think less of you and less willing to help you when you need it.

If you are upset at something or someone, wait until you have had a chance to calm down and think about it. A cup of (decaf!) coffee or a good night's sleep works wonders on your perspective. Hasty words create more problems than they solve. Try not to say anything to others you would not say to them in person in a room full of people.

Don't Blame System Admins for Their Users' Behavior.

Sometimes, you may find it necessary to write to a system administrator about something concerning his or her site. Maybe it is a case of the software not working, or an escaped control message, or maybe one of the users at that site has done something you feel requires comment. No matter how steamed you may be, be polite to the sysadmin., he or she may not have any idea what you are going to say, and may not have any part in the incidents involved. By being civil and temperate, you are more likely to obtain his or her courteous attention and assistance.

Be Careful What You Say about Others.

Please remember: you read netnews; so do (millions of) other people. This group quite possibly includes your boss, your friend's boss, your girlfriend's brother's best friend, and one of your father's beer buddies. Information posted on the net can come back to haunt you or the person you are talking about. Think twice before you post personal information about yourself or others.

Be Brief.

Never say in ten words what you can say in five. Say it succinctly and it will have a greater impact. Remember the longer you make your article, the fewer people who will bother to read it.

Your Postings Reflect upon You—Be Proud of Them.

Most people on USENET will know you only by what you say and how well you say it. They may someday be your coworkers or friends. Take some time to make sure each posting is something that will not embarrass you later. Minimize your spelling errors and make sure that the article is easy to read and understand. Writing is an art and to do it well requires practice. Because much of how people judge you on the net is based on your writing, such time is well spent.

Use Descriptive Titles.

The subject line of an article is there to enable a person with a limited amount of time to decide whether or not to read your article. Tell people what the article is about before they read it. A title like "Car for Sale" to rec.autos does not help as much as "66 MG Midget for sale: Beaverton, OR." Don't expect people to read your article to find out what it is about because many of them won't bother. Some sites truncate the length of the subject line to 40 characters so keep your subjects short and to the point.

Think about Your Audience.
When you post an article, think about the people you are trying to reach. Asking UNIX questions on rec.autos will not reach as many people as you want to reach as if you asked them on comp.unix.questions or comp.unix.internals. Try to get the most appropriate audience for your message, not the widest. If your message is of interest to a limited geographic area—apartments, car sales, meetings, concerts, etc.—restrict the distribution of the message to your local area. Some areas have special newsgroups with geographical limitations, and the recent versions of the news software allow you to limit the distribution of material sent to world-wide newsgroups. Check with your system administrator to see what newsgroups are available and how to use them.

Be familiar with the group you are posting to before you post! You shouldn't post to groups you do not read or groups from which you've only read a few articles—you may not be familiar with the ongoing conventions and themes of the group. One normally does not join a conversation by just walking up and talking. Instead, you listen first and join in if you have something pertinent to contribute.

Be Careful with Humor and Sarcasm.
Without the voice inflections and body language of face-to-face communication, it is easy for a remark meant to be funny to be misinterpreted. Subtle humor tends to get lost, so take steps to make sure that people realize you are trying to be funny.

Only Post a Message Once.
Avoid posting messages to more than one newsgroup unless you are sure it is appropriate. If you do post to multiple newsgroups, do not post to each group separately. Instead, specify all the groups on a single copy of the message. This reduces network overhead and lets people who subscribe to more than one group see the message only once instead of having to wade through each copy.

Summarize What You Are Following-up.
When you are following up someone's article, summarize the parts of the article to which you are responding. This allows readers to appreciate your comments without trying to remember what the original article said. It is also possible for your response to get to some sites before the original article. Summarization is best done by including appropriate quotes from the original article. Do not include the entire article because it will irritate the people who have already seen it. Even if you are responding to the entire article, summarize only the major points you are discussing. When summarizing, summarize!

Use Mail, Don't Post a Follow-up.
One of the biggest problems we have on the network is that when someone asks a question, many people send out identical answers. When this happens, dozens of identical answers pour through the net.

Mail your answer to the person and suggest that they summarize to the network. This way the net will only see a single copy of the answers, no matter how many people answer the question. If you post a question, remind people to send you the answers by mail and at least offer to summarize them to the network.

Read All Follow-ups and Don't Repeat What Has Already Been Said.

Before you submit a follow-up to a message, read the rest of the messages in the newsgroup to see whether someone has already said what you want to say. If someone has, don't repeat it.

Be Careful about Copyrights and Licenses.

Once something is posted on the network, it is probably in the public domain unless you own the appropriate rights (most notably, if you wrote the thing yourself) and you post it with a valid copyright notice; a court would have to decide the specifics and there are arguments for both sides of the issue. Now that the United States has ratified the Berne convention, the issue is even murkier. For all practical purposes, though, assume that you effectively give up the copyright if you don't put in a notice. Of course, the information becomes public, so you mustn't post trade secrets that way. When posting material to the network, keep in mind that UNIX-related material may be restricted by the license you or your company signed with AT&T and be careful not to violate it. You should also be aware that posting movie reviews, song lyrics, or anything else published under copyright could cause you, your company, or members of the net community to be held liable for damages, so we highly recommend caution when using this material.

Cite Appropriate References.

If you are using facts to support a cause, state where they came from. Don't take someone else's ideas and use them as your own. You don't want someone pretending that your ideas are theirs; show them the same respect.

Mark or Rotate Answers and Spoilers.

When you post something which might spoil a surprise for other people—such as a movie review that discusses a detail of the plot—mark it with a warning so that others can skip the message. Another alternative would be to use the "rot13" protocol to encrypt the message so it cannot be read accidentally. When you post a message with a spoiler in it make sure the word "spoiler" is part of the subject line.

Spelling Flames Are Considered Harmful.

Every few months a plague descends on USENET called the spelling flame. It starts out when someone posts an article correcting the spelling or grammar in another article. The immediate result seems to be for everyone on the net to turn into a sixth grade English teacher and pick apart each other's postings for a few weeks. This is not productive and tends to cause people who are friends to get angry with each other. It is important to remember that we all make mistakes, and that many users on the net use English as a second language. There are also a number of people who suffer from dyslexia and who have difficulty noticing their spelling mistakes. If you feel that you must make a comment on the quality of a posting, do so by mail, not on the network.

Don't Overdo Signatures.
Signatures are nice, and many people can have a signature added to their postings automatically by placing it in a file called `$HOME/ .signature`. Don't overdo it. Signatures can tell the world something about you, but keep them short. A signature that is longer than the message itself is considered to be in bad taste. The main purpose of a signature is to help people locate you, not to tell your life story. Every signature should include at least your return address relative to a major, known site on the network and a proper domain-format address. Your system administrator can give this to you. Some news posters attempt to enforce a four line limit on signature files — an amount that should be more than sufficient to provide a return address and attribution.

Limit Line Length and Avoid Control Characters.
Try to keep your text in a generic format. Many (if not most) of the people reading USENET do so from 80-column terminals or from workstations with 80-column terminal windows. Try to keep your lines of text to less than 80 characters for optimal readability. If people quote part of your article in a follow-up, short lines will probably show up better, too. Also realize that there are many, many different forms of terminals in use. If you enter special control characters in your message, it may result in your message being unreadable on some terminal types. For instance, a character sequence that causes reverse video on your screen may result in a keyboard lock and graphics mode on someone else's. You should also try to avoid the use of tabs because they can also be interpreted differently on other terminals.

Summary of Things to Remember:

- Never forget that the person on the other side is human.
- Don't blame system adminstrators for their users' behavior.
- Be careful what you say about others.
- Be brief.
- Be proud of your postings; they reflect on you.
- Use descriptive titles.
- Think about your audience.
- Be careful with humor and sarcasm.
- Post a message only once.
- Rotate material with questionable content.
- Summarize what you are following-up.
- Use mail, don't post a follow-up.

- Read all follow-ups and don't repeat what has already been said.
- Double-check follow-up newsgroups and distributions.
- Be careful about copyrights and licenses.
- Cite appropriate references.
- When summarizing, summarize.
- Mark or rotate answers or spoilers.
- Avoid spelling flames; they are considered harmful.
- Don't overdo signatures.
- Limit line length and avoid control characters.

Just as in any flourishing community, observance of civilities and appropriate behavior keep peaceful coexistence a reality. Practice good manners.

Psychological Aspects of Electronic Job Search

Frustration

Frustration is a standard problem with job search in general. It usually results from the just-missed opportunities, the "one that got away." Applicants often wonder who that other "perfect" person is who is taking all the jobs. It is easy to let feelings of inadequacy creep in. Added to this problem is the fact that, in today's labor market, job seekers are constantly playing a numbers game. *So many* people are looking for work.

On the Internet, frustration is a constant companion. After all, the sheer vastness of the system is daunting. How can one possibly find all there is to find? It is easy to begin to feel like an infinitesimal spec in cyberspace, a mosquito smashed on the information superhighway.

One particularly frustrating problem with job search on the net concerns *pathing*. Pathing refers to the different screens you pass through to reach a desired area. Unless you have some record of how you got there, it is often difficult to find your way back to where you've been. After having spent hours getting there the first time, you don't want to have to try and recreate the route. It's a good idea, then, to make a "map" of the route you have taken. One way you can do this is by jotting down the pathing steps. It is easier, however, to capture your session on disc, which makes a record of every screen you passed through on the way to your destination. You can do this through most communication programs on your personal computer. Simply insert a disc prior to logging on.

Of course, with "information overload," which is often experienced on the Internet, the question is where to look, what to consider, and what to ignore. When it comes to job search, you can control for geographical area, occupation, even wage range. If you are an accountant seeking work in Minnesota, what possible good will it do you to search jobs in the West? Similarly, don't waste your time looking at all the accounting clerk postings, which are clearly below your level of expertise. Remember, too, that you don't want to waste an employer's time by "going fishing" in San Diego when you only want to "reel in" a job in Minneapolis. Focus your attention precisely on what you want.

Side-Tracking/Isolation

One peculiar aspect of the Internet culture is that users—particularly new ones—tend to get "hooked" by the seemingly endless parade of information available. It is not unusual to log on at 6:30 p.m. "just to take a quick look" and find yourself turning off the computer at 2 a.m. Some people get so caught up in the Internet "world," they become isolated after a while, spending days at a time online, chatting with this or that newsgroup, or playing some interactive game. BEWARE. You have a job to do. If you go on the net twice a day, make sure that at least one of those times is dedicated to job search. Promise yourself that you won't get sidetracked by some other seductive activity until you have made at least one productive contact or attempt at getting a job. Then, by all means reward yourself. Go play in Diversity University (an interactive game where you meet different characters as you progress through a mythical college—you can even attend lectures!) or spend some time talking to a job seeker's support group. Just never lose sight of your main mission and purpose for using the Internet. Stay on track and get "hooked" on a job.

In Word Only

As we've mentioned, there are some advantages and disadvantages to the absence of nonverbal cues in electronic communication. Those cues are what your receiver can see and hear when communicating with you face-to-face—such as voice tone and inflection, facial expression, and body language—which influence how they interpret your message. For example, "Nice jacket," said with a snide tone and a roll of the eyes takes on a whole different meaning than the words by themselves. When you are not there to provide interpretation or any nonverbal clues, your message can be construed a number of ways. Following are some characteristics of the applicant not readily apparent in electronic communication.

- **Gender.** When a return address on a message to an employer says simply, "jsmith," it could be anybody. Many female applicants have chosen this option for the initial stages of application—say an e-mail letter of interest to a company—to give themselves a better shot at jobs in nontraditional occupations (jobs typically held by men.) In other cases, the name of the applicant could be either male or female, such as Kelly or Dana or Pat, giving no gender clue to the employer.

By the same token, if no clue is given in the return address of the employer, you also have no idea of the identity of the person on the other end. Say your contact in the company was a woman, though you didn't know it. Michele, who works for a clothing manufacturer, says people responding to her often mistake her name for "Michael."

"When I get messages like, 'I'm looking forward to meeting a manager who takes his interest in fashion design seriously,' I've already formed a negative impression of the candidate." A careless pronoun could cost you a job opportunity.

- **Age.** E-mail messages are not age-specific. Unless the job seeker says something completely obvious like, "I got my experience in bridge-building when I worked for the WPA during the Depression," no way exists for telling the age of the applicant. Be careful, though. One applicant warned us of unscrupulous recruiters who ask, "When did you get your degree?" or similar questions designed to elicit age without asking for it directly.

- **Appearance.** Employers reading your message cannot discern your appearance from words on a screen. They don't know if you are totally bald or have a beard to your chest. They can't tell whether you are sitting at your computer in a business suit or in your underwear. (Actually, they try not to think about that!) Ken, an executive search consultant, calls it a "guessing game." "You can't help but form mental pictures of the person writing to you," he says. "Funny thing is, I've only been close to what the real person looks like a couple of times. I think that helps keep the whole business fair." It is precisely because they can't see you that personal preferences and prejudices of employers don't play as prominent a role in electronic communication as face-to-face. This is a major benefit. In electronic communication, the playing field is level. You can truly be judged by the content of what you have to say, not by how you sound or look while saying it.

- **Anxiety.** A common but troublesome problem with in-person job search is nervousness. With electronic job search, this difficulty is virtually eliminated. There you sit, at a very comfortable distance from the employer, at your own desk, on your own turf. No one is there to accept a sweaty-palmed handshake or hear the quiver in your voice. You are relaxed and confident.

- **Facial Expression.** For many job seekers, merely making eye contact with the employer is difficult, whether out of shyness or nervousness. For others, smiling does not come naturally with strangers in a "forced" situation. Yet, eye contact and facial expression are critically important in face-to-face interviews. Employers are people, just like you. If you don't look them in the eye, they don't trust you; if you don't smile at them, they don't like you. Electronic job search has an advantage here, too. "I just feel like a big phoney, grinning at total strangers," says Albert, a loan processor. "When I 'talk' to them on the Internet, though, I can be friendly in writing. It helps me sort of get to know them before I actually meet them."

- **Speech Patterns.** Employers' prejudicial attitudes toward certain speech patterns can hold otherwise competent applicants back in the selection process. Job seekers who speak in heavily accented English, though they may have excellent credentials otherwise, don't always get a fair shake, usually not making it past the telephone interview. The same is true for individuals with language disabilities who frequently find themselves on the business end of discrimination in the application process.

Dolores, a recruiter with an outplacement firm, told us about one candidate she had difficulty in placing. "He had been an engineer in Cambodia and had found work in a Bay Area firm owned by fellow Cambodians. When the company downsized and he looked for work in other companies, he was faced with major discrimination because of his accent. He worked as a math tutor for the local junior college and his students had no trouble understanding him. We concentrated on his writing skills, had him focus on e-mail applications, and eventually he was placed."

E-mail provides an unbiased forum for these applicants. Here, they may express themselves eloquently in writing, although they may not do as well orally. The employer gets a look at the candidate's credentials, free of prejudice. They are able to judge the applicant based on merit, not on any particular patterns of speech. In electronic job search, everyone sounds the same.

- **Typed vs. Handwritten.** Another definite plus for many Internet users is the keyboard itself. Handwritten correspondence and applications can work against you, whereas all e-mail messages look alike, in terms of writing. Type is type. No judgments there. Additionally, no one is there to watch you laboring over your work application or cover letter. No erasures or unsightly white-out blobs mar your presentation. Your mistakes will never be seen. They will have been conveniently edited out before the employer ever sees them.

All the employers we spoke to were in agreement on one major point: They seemed to feel that the absence of nonverbal cues imposed fairness on the application process and made them better recruiters. Jeannette Daly, a human resources assistant, summed it up, "There is a tremendous advantage to using e-mail for the hiring person because no information about the applicant is evident, other than their qualifications. For example, we can't hear an accent and don't have any idea about how the person looks. We have to judge them on their merits, as it should be. It eliminates bias."

A Whole New Game
Accessibility

The greatest advantage of electronic job search is probably access. You can "get in" to employers in a way that is often impossible in the real world. All you need is an e-mail address. When you locate a job on the net, the contact name given is the name of the one person in that organization who can help you. You don't have to search all over the company until you find the person you must talk to about the job. The scenario in real-world job search goes like this: You target a company that you think—sometimes it's no more than a vague idea—may have need for a person with your skills. You then either make a phone call or go by in person to inquire.

Receptionist: "May I help you?"

Job Seeker: "Yes, I wonder if I could please speak to the person who does the hiring?"

Receptionist: "We're not hiring."

Job Seeker: "Well, who normally does the hiring for data entry operators?"

Receptionist: "We're not hiring."

Job Seeker: "Then, could I fill out a job application, in case a job opens up?"

Receptionist: "WE'RE NOT HIRING."

Make no mistake, the receptionist or operator or assistant is not necessarily privy to what goes on in terms of hiring for every department. There may very well be a job open about which the receptionist knows nothing, but this person's job is to keep you away from the busy managers. Essentially, the receptionist stands between you and the opportunity.

In electronic job search, no gatekeeper—assistant or secretary—must be gotten through first. This has changed the whole game of job hunting, really. The "invisible shield" between you and the employer has been lowered by this very accessible medium.

Speed

Working along with the accessibility factor is speed. You are not relying on conventional mail delivery or on someone else's dependability to get your message to the employer. Thus, turn-around time can be remarkably fast in electronic job search. Remember, too, that you are not limited to certain hours of the day when you try to contact an employer. There is no locked door with an "Open M-F, 8 a.m.-5 p.m." sign on the Internet. You can send your message any time, any day.

Internet Culture

One last important benefit to this new world of job seeking is that you and the employer are meeting on common ground. You are essentially both members of the same club or community. You have each spent time in the fascinating world of the Internet. However, with entry into this new "global village," you take on certain responsibilities. In the parlance of the net, a "lurker" is someone who sits by and reads postings without ever joining in the discussion. But, the Internet experience is participatory. It is incumbent on you to learn all you can about its many uses, and then, jump in! There is room for everyone and your input is welcome.

You will not find a more helpful community. When we were doing research over the Internet, our requests for assistance were **never** refused. Virtually all users who were asked for information or to render an opinion or to allow us to quote them agreed enthusiastically. We were frequently referred to other people and sources for more help. We also found that hierarchy, so prevalent in real-world interactions, is absent from the Internet. A telephone call to a large corporation seeking comment from a highly placed source would likely result in the query being referred to an underling to be "handled." We had equal access to CEOs and unemployed job seekers alike. **We boldly e-mailed where no phone call had gone before** and were pleasantly surprised at the response. Once you have truly interacted with your fellow citizens of the Internet, you will never again understand the "lurker" mentality. You will begin to relish the opportunity to help someone, repay a favor, or pass on a tip or insight to a kindred job seeker. In short, you will take your place as a participating member of the Internet culture.

The Internet Interview

In interviewing, as with other practices in job-hunting, the Internet process once again differs markedly from the face-to-face variety. In the usual sequence of events, your paper resume is received by mail and, if the employer is interested in you, you are contacted and an interview is scheduled. One or two clarifying questions may be asked over the phone at the time your interview appointment is set, but, for the most part, any in-depth questions are held off until the face-to-face interview itself. Let's compare this standard practice with the Internet process.

With electronic interviewing, the sequence is largely the same; that is, you respond to a job opening, submit a resume, and are interviewed. What differs is the manner in which the process takes place. First of all, you will have found the job opening through a newsgroup or online placement service, rather than in a newspaper ad or at an employment agency. Secondly, your resume will be the electronic variety, sent by e-mail to the employer. Finally, you can expect to be interviewed, at least initially, over e-mail. In fact, there will probably be several preliminary interviews by e-mail before you get a face-to-face interview with the employer. Unlike conventional interviewing, there is *always* a preliminary interview with electronic interviewing.

This chapter will examine the electronic interview and help you prepare for dealing with it effectively. You will also be given pointers on telephone interviewing, also a part of the electronic interview. Bear in mind, though, that electronic interviews never supersede the face-to-face kind. Not entirely. You still need to be proficient at answering questions and thinking on your feet when you meet the employer in person. Therefore, the last section in this chapter will help you prepare for that all-important face-to-face meeting with the employer, based on the context of each situation. Now, let's take a look at the e-mail interview.

Electronic Interviewing

When an employer receives your e-mail resume over the Internet, it is screened for basic qualifications. Then, if it is found satisfactory, you will be contacted first by e-mail, before you are called in to interview. Employers do not proceed directly to the interview from the resume because e-mail provides the perfect means for preinterview inquiry. Preinterview screening is almost never done in the world of face-to-face job seeking. The result is that, for many employers, the interview process is long and can involve some disappointing "surprises"—things the employer didn't discover about the applicant until the actual interview.

The Internet preinterview is conducted through a series of e-mail messages between the employer and applicant. Much of the correspondence is for clarification purposes, but a lot of information is gathered about the applicant during these exchanges. For example, suppose you respond to a posting for an administrative assistant position. You e-mail the employer a resume outlining your experiences related to the job. Let's say, however, that the employer is looking for a specific type of desktop publishing experience and you haven't listed it on your resume. It is a fairly simple matter to send you an e-mail asking for clarification. The employer may also decide to ask you for a bit more detail about that last position you held in the university public affairs office. You respond with the requested desktop publishing information and also flesh out your job duties at the university. Additionally, you detail the way in which you used the desktop publishing program to compile the monthly newsletter and student profiles for the student-of-the-quarter awards.

This give and take is exactly what happens in the face-to-face interview. The employer starts with the framework of the resume and then the applicant fills in the details when he or she arrives for the interview. E-mail interviews provide opportunities for you to give more detail than was previously possible *before* the interview, possibly increasing your chances of getting the position. Electronic interviewing can assist both the employer and the job seeker in the recruitment process. For employers, it saves valuable downtime that would be spent in clarification of details before the "meat" of the interview. They also find out whether the applicant is indeed suited for the position in question before going to the expense of bringing the applicant in for a face-to-face interview. For applicants, they know beforehand if the position in question is a good match for their skills and whether or not they are interested in the company or the job.

Exchanges Can Be Conversational and Friendly

Even though e-mail interviews are written, with delays between questions and answers, they are still very much conversational and often informal. Thus, employers and job seekers frequently find out other enlightening things about one another besides only job-related information. For instance, if an applicant inquires about child care centers available in the employer's area, the employer assumes the applicant has a family. Sometimes an inquiry about area museums or galleries can spark a discussion of mutual interest between the employer and applicant. Or, if the employer suggests that bass fishing in Minnesota is great around the time your interview is scheduled, you'd have to be pretty dense not to figure out that fishing is an enjoyable hobby for the employer. (By all means, bring a rod along in your suitcase!)

A common exchange between job seekers and employers pertains to the medium in which they are meeting. E-mail conversations frequently involve discussions about the types of computers and software being used, preference for one program over another, hobbies involving the computer, experiences of the Internet, even computer games. Remember, the employer talking to you is computer savvy. He or she relies on the medium for recruitment and no doubt uses it extensively in other applications. Chances are very good that the employer has a personal computer at home. This is a good opportunity to demonstrate your knowledge and expertise as well as your genuine interest in the world of computers and the Internet.

One of the most obvious things employers can discern about you through e-mail interviews is your writing skills. This can be tricky, especially if you are not the best writer. It's a good idea to compose responses in your word processor first and then upload them into e-mail. Make sure they are spell-checked and grammar-proofed before you send them. Be sure to save them in ASCII first. And remember: Once you hit "send," it's irretrievable. Read everything over at least twice before you e-mail; it's hard to take back written words.

Keep your general attitude positive. Just as with face-to-face interviewing, you should never interject negative statements into your messages. Keep references to former employers positive. Be assertive in discussing your capabilities. Focus on what you have to offer, rather than on any shortcomings you have.

Be unfailingly polite. Keep in mind that this *is* an interview. The employer may have initiated more informal conversation, but you don't want to cross the line between friendly informality and impudence. You're building a first impression here. Present yourself in a courteous, dignified manner.

Declining a Position

Suppose you decide that, after having gotten a more detailed look at the company, this job is not for you. After all, this often happens with employers who decide against calling an applicant in for an interview after several e-mail contacts. You should certainly notify the employer that you have decided to decline the position. Just walking away from your "conversation" is rude and unprofessional. And word does get around in business. E-mail the employer a polite thank-you for considering you and decline any further interviews.

Tips on E-Mail Interviewing

Through e-mail interviews employers get a look at your general manner, writing skills, even your philosophy and attitude toward work and their organization. True, it is all taking place on a computer screen, but make no mistake, you are being interviewed. Many of the same rules that apply to face-to-face interviews apply here. Following are some tips for electronic interviews.

- **Be concise.** Do not give vague answers to direct questions. Help the employer understand fully what it is you do and how hiring you will benefit the organization.

- **Give detail.** It is intensely frustrating to get one-word responses to questions and then be faced with "pulling" information out of the applicant. The employer has contacted you in order to get more detail on some aspect alluded to in your resume. Elaborate. By the same token, you need to be aware when the employer is asking you closed-ended questions, i.e., "Have you worked with Windows applications?" This question calls for a yes/no response. Answer it as though it had been asked open-ended, that is, "What types of word processing packages have you worked with?" Expand on it.

- **One thing at a time.** Sometimes, interviewers will write one question that is dovetailed with another question, for example, "Did you leave your last position to go back to school?" Here, there are really two questions: "Why did you leave your last job?" and "Have you returned to school?" It is up to you to respond to each of these questions individually.

- **Give just enough.** There is really no need to tell the whole story in an e-mail message. Remember, the idea here is to get invited to a face-to-face interview. So, state highlights and always offer to give more information when you meet the employer. **Note:** When it comes to questions of a technical nature, however, in which the employer is asking you to demonstrate knowledge of a particular skill needed to perform the duties of the position, be explicit. If you don't provide this information in the e-mail interview, you won't be invited to a face-to-face one.

- **Give examples.** "The proof of the pudding is in the eating." The best way to convince an employer that you have the needed skills, knowledge, and ability is to cite examples from past job performance demonstrating your experience and qualifications.

The employers we spoke with were enthusiastic about e-mail interviews. They view them as a real boon to the application process. They spoke of a sense of getting a better handle on the applicant through a series of Internet "conversations." Jeannette Daly of Care Management Science Corp. put it this way, "We use Internet messages to delve a little deeper than the resume, to get a better 'feel' for the applicant. We ask things like, 'Do you have this specific experience? When did you work with this or that? Please clarify.' By the time we're at the interview stage (face-to-face) we feel we already know the applicant and have a better understanding of his or her background."

Ms. Daly noted that the majority of correspondence she receives is polite and professional, a point of view echoed by several employers. Andy Ballantyne, Ballantyne Computer Services, added that the tone of the exchange is also important. He, like most employers, is put off by "overconfidence and people who appear to have real ego problems." Sometimes applicants exaggerate in the hopes of making a good impression and beating out the competition. Unfortunately, this is a mistake that can backfire badly. Says Ballantyne, "Don't overblow it and try to make more out of your experience than you really have. The same goes for bragging. Don't do it. Just discuss your background honestly."

Some companies use interactive multimedia programs to conduct their preinterviews. Great Western Bank uses such technology in their recruitments. In their preinterview process, you can be tested electronically for your fitness for a job in banking. This test, which is performed on an interactive CD-ROM, even includes a transaction where you interact with a "virtual customer" on a computer screen! This is a new twist on the hypothetical interview question: "What would you do if . . . ?" Mary Nemnich spoke with Michael Dorn, manager of program development in the training department of Great Western, about the company's electronic prescreening procedures.

> **MN:** Where does your interactive CD-ROM fit into your recruitment process?
>
> **MD:** We use our "applicant assessment aid," as we call it, to accomplish our initial screening for tellers. Usually, an applicant will have filled out an application and undergone a telephone interview prior to assessment. Telephone interviews are very important because bank employees, especially tellers, need good phone skills to field phone calls and assist customers. This initial interview weeds out the bottom 10-15 percent. After that, we call the applicant in to do the interactive program.
>
> **MN:** How does the program work?

MD: It takes about 20 minutes to complete and covers several important areas. First, there is a math and money section that evaluates basic math skills and the ability to count cash. Applicants respond to questions on screen by use of a touch-screen monitor or a mouse.

Next, there is a voice response section where the applicant "speaks" to customers on a computer screen. This part records the applicant's voice and measures sensitivity to customer service. Then, the applicant's voice is recorded again while making a customer sales presentation in which he or she offers other financial services available at the bank.

Lastly, there is the noninteractive section where the applicant hears three employees describing what the job of teller actually entails. It gives the applicant a realistic expectation and understanding of what the job is really like.

MN: How is this preemployment evaluation scored?

MD: Scoring is based on a five-point criteria system. What we have done is to try to remove some of the subjectivity from the selection process. It can often be scored while the applicant waits. There is a recommended score and if the applicant doesn't score above that, it's unlikely he or she will be called back.

MN: Is this service available online?

MD: No, not yet. At this point, the applicant has to be physically located at a Great Western facility in order to complete the program. Currently, we have this program in place at all of our Florida facilities and at about 20 percent of our branches in California. We plan on making it available at all our branches. Eventually, we envision putting all our personnel forms online. It saves an incredible amount of time and duplication of work. [Plans are underway for online capability by 1996.]

MN: What has this electronic capability done to the interview process for your company?

MD: It has really freed up our managers' time because they only need to spend time interviewing those candidates who are most appropriate for the job. You know, there are those who say that there is no human contact anymore — that the interview process has become depersonalized due to advances like these. But the truth is the applicant still has to meet one-on-one with the interviewer to get the job. That has not changed.

Mr. Dorn mentioned the importance of the telephone interview when hiring bank employees. However, the phone interview is a standard part of the electronic interview process for getting **any** type of job. In the following section, you will receive advice on how to succeed in this significant part of the preinterview phase.

The Telephone Interview

Following the e-mail interview stage, a telephone call to the applicant is invariably placed for further clarification. This is not standard procedure in traditional hiring practice. It is much more common with the Internet because the applicant is often remote to the employer. This is a function of the "global marketplace" feature of the Internet, where job seekers can browse for jobs anywhere in the world. So, it is frequently not practical, for the employer or the applicant, to hold face-to-face interviews. Thus, employers make a phone call first.

Telephone interviews present some new problems for job seekers. In this instance, the employer doesn't have nonverbal cues, such as facial expression, body language, or appearance of the applicant. What they do have is your voice, words, and, maybe most importantly, your presentation. The following suggestions may help you succeed in the telephone interview.

Be Prepared

A major problem with phone interviews is that they are rarely scheduled. You can be taken by surprise at any time and be expected to perform well. The solution is to try to prepare in advance for them.

Keep a notebook with job-related information in it near the phone. This should include a current copy of your resume, a list of references, data on the company, and copies of all prior e-mail correspondence with this employer. Mary recommends to all her clients that they keep a file—whether in a loose-leaf binder or file box—of all pertinent job search information, including contacts, dates, notes, and a follow-up suspense file. And KEEP IT UP TO DATE.

Take notes as you talk with the employer. It will help with both the current phone call and future reference.

Practice answering questions. Rehearse a couple of different responses to pat questions. Make some notes of questions you might want to ask employers.

Brush up on your phone manners. Answer by saying "Hello," not "Yeah," or by just barking your name into the receiver.

Involve the family. It is annoying to have children answer the phone and then demand to know, "Who is this?" Teach them to say simply, "Just a moment, please" and get you immediately. Explain to everyone how important it is that you receive all messages if you are not there. Teach everyone how to take a proper message, including the name of the person, company name, and a complete phone number. Leave a message pad and pencil next to the phone.

Put a Professional Message on Your Answering Machine

Skip the tinny background music. No celebrity impersonators. Nothing cute. Say your name or phone number clearly so that employers will know they have reached you and not a wrong number.

If you have voice mail on your computer, put your name first. The employer won't have to wait through a long list of instructions before leaving you a message. You might consider stating, "Please leave your name, phone or fax number, or e-mail address" in your message. It is also a good idea to warn employers to be expecting either voice mail or answering machine on your phone. When you call the employer back, follow these tips:

- **Modulate your voice.** Try to sound enthusiastic. Speak distinctly. Visualize yourself sitting in front of the person to whom you are speaking. You will find yourself sitting up straight, being more focused, and even smiling into the phone.

- **Ask for a face-to-face appointment.** Everyone is better in person than on the phone. If the employer appears ready to end the conversation and hasn't yet scheduled an interview, ask if it might be convenient for you to meet with them in person in the near future.

There is no doubt that the Internet will revolutionize the job-finding process. Jobs are easier than ever to access. All you need to know is where to look. Once you find the opening, you have only to contact the employer electronically to get your foot in the door. Then, e-mail smoothes the way by providing important preinterview glimpses of both the employer and the applicant. But, in the final analysis, it all comes down to two people communicating face-to-face in the interview. David Davidowicz, owner of an online placement service in Boston called Job Finders, had this observation: "The process really hasn't changed all that much. The job seeker still has to sell him or herself to the employer. It still comes down to the employer and applicant, one-on-one in the interview. The Internet just provides more options."

With that in mind, we need to take a careful look at the traditional, face-to-face interview.

The Face-to-Face Interview

This is it. The big moment is at hand. You have navigated the vast highway of cyberspace and located a job. You've managed to make it past a sea of other applicants with a resume that opened the door to an opportunity. Subsequent e-mail interviews with the employer opened the door wider. And now you wait confidently to walk through that door the next morning at the face-to-face interview. Well, perhaps "nervously" better describes your frame of mind as you contemplate the coming appointment. What will the interviewer ask? How will you respond? Have you made the right grooming choices? How will you handle that all-important salary discussion? You wonder what the interviewer will be like, how heavy traffic will be on the way there, whether or not this is really the company for you. At least, we hope that is what's going through your mind before an interview. You should be trying to think ahead, to prepare for every eventuality. Sadly, many job seekers fail to adequately prepare for their interviews. The result is that they fail to get the job or end up in a job that is less than satisfactory. For a successful job interview, preparation is key.

On the other hand, there are those applicants who "overtrain"—read all the books, attend every seminar, and spend so much time in preparation that there remains no spontaneity at all in the interview. These job seekers run the risk of failure because they end up giving rote, canned responses that turn interviewers off. Consider the following scenario: "Tell me," the interviewer asks, "what would you say is your greatest strength?" As the job applicant launches confidently into a response, the interviewer listens with a sigh. This is her sixth interview today and this is the third time she has heard the same response. Not *just about* the same, *exactly* the same. She wonders how she will get past the rote, automaton-like answers to the real person across the desk from her. In fact, she has almost begun to reject applicants on the basis of such a canned response to her questions. Have all job seekers read the same book, gone to the same class, or what? she wonders.

The experience of this interviewer is hardly unique. So many self-help guides are available on interviewing that applicants have begun to take on an "assembly line" appearance. For the most part, the advice is good advice; that is, it would work, in a sterile, generic type of interview. The problem is that no interview fits that pattern. All interviews are individual. Each possesses its own character and tone. Thus, a single, prepared answer can't possibly work for every interview. What is missing is any consideration of the context of each individual interview.

In the following pages, we will take a situational approach to the employment process. You will be encouraged to analyze the context of the particular situation and to weigh the factors evident in each interview before making a decision on how best to respond to questions. Context will also help you realize how to best handle the other components of the employment process, such as grooming.

Context Clues

Any number of factors, or clues, can help you assess the interview context. Some are quite obvious and readily observable in the setting itself. Others require some advance preparation and forethought on your part. The three most helpful components to evaluating the interview situation are:

1. Researching the company;

2. "Reading" the surroundings; and

3. "Sizing up" the interviewer.

We will examine each of these variables in an attempt to get a clear "fix" on the interview context.

Researching the Company

Frequently referred to as "doing homework," this often overlooked step is crucial to a successful interview. Employer research can be accomplished through either formal or informal means. If the company in question is a large public corporation, a great deal of information on it is usually available in the public domain. Several publications that provide information on major corporations are available on the Internet (see Chapter 4) or in the local library. A check of *Dun and Bradstreet's Book of Corporation Management, Standard and Poor's Register,* or *Moody's Industrial Manual* will reveal valuable insights into a company's structure, its financial picture, even, to some extent, its culture.

Business publications, such as *Fortune, Inc., Money,* and *The Wall Street Journal* are all excellent sources for information on corporations. A truly serious job seeker will make it a point to subscribe to at least one business journal and should continue to do so once on a job. These publications often provide data beyond a simple statement of the annual earnings and general financial picture of a company. Here, you can also learn about such things as a company's benefits package, employee perks, and even get an occasional glimpse at that nebulous, hard-to-define commodity—corporate culture.

Inc. magazine publishes its annual "Inc. 100," a ranking of the fastest growing small, public companies. These surveys include valuable personal interviews with the CEOs of the featured companies. *Working Mother* magazine publishes articles profiling companies that are most "family friendly." It spotlights those that have child care arrangements, family health plans, and advancement potential, evaluating them and comparing them to other organizations. The sort of information contained in these and other articles can help you assess the context of an interview by showing you in advance how the company operates and "thinks."

For the smaller or locally owned businesses, other means of research are available to you. Easiest of all is to simply call or write and ask for a brochure or newsletter on the company. Most smaller companies regard such written data as good P.R. for their organization. Many make their annual reports available to the public for the same reason. Another way to learn about a company informally is to become a consumer of the goods or services it provides. Being able to speak knowledgeably about its product goes a long way toward cementing you as the favored candidate.

Finally, an excellent way to research a potential employer is to talk directly to the people who work there. This can be accomplished through an informational interview or simply by chatting with members of the organization. The purpose here is to find out about the workings of the company—their corporate philosophy, the general working environment, even the salary and benefits structure.

Here are some general areas to consider for formulating questions appropriate for an informational interview:

- Description of the kind of work performed—outline of positions within organization

- Types of background necessary to apply. Include degrees, certificates, etc., besides work experience

- Personality traits desirable in employees

- Available career paths and training options

- Most rewarding aspects of job

- Most frustrating or difficult aspects of job

- Best way to do well and advance in organization

- Organization's main competition

- Organization's salary/benefits structure

- Organization's mission statement

The last item is valuable in forming a picture of the company's philosophical base and is essential to gauging the context of the interview.

Face-to-face informational interviews are set up with either the personnel director or the head of the particular department that interests you. They are scheduled, structured periods, usually about 15-20 minutes in length. That's a big chunk out of a busy human resources person's day. Consequently, job seekers often have difficulty in getting an appointment. With the Internet, you can e-mail a brief message to the employer, outlining your purpose and questions. These "interviews" are much more favorably regarded because of the time factor. Also, the threat that the applicant will press for a job, contrary to the stated purpose of gathering information, is nonexistent. Consequently, interviewers feel more comfortable discussing the company from the safe distance the net provides.

In your message, make the employer aware that the purpose of the "interview" is *only* to derive information about the company. You must also remember that the aim here is not to ask for a job, but to find out everything possible about the organization in order to make yourself the best competitor for the job. Employers regard these queries as an expedient means of getting a look at what's "out there" in terms of applicants and also as an inexpensive way of getting good P.R., always a priority with businesses.

The other way to go about informational interviews is with the line staff themselves. If the staff actually serves the public directly, it is a simple matter to approach them as a customer and informally ask what it is like to work for that company. You should make no secret of the fact that you're looking for work and may be considering their organization or a similar one. In fact, you should talk to everyone. Many an opening has been found through networking and passing the word. For example, if someone has a friend with a brother who works for the company of interest to you, that's one way of getting an informational interview with a staff member. Sometimes a phone call to any department in the organization, but preferably to the one that interests you, is sufficient. Just remember to be honest. If you don't state the real reason for the interview up front, such behavior will be remembered later.

Reading the Surroundings

Want to know the lay of the land before the actual interview? Then, by all means, pay a visit to the site. Most companies have an open door to the public. One can drop in as a consumer or curious passerby. Of course, an excellent time to pay a call is at the informational interview itself. However, if you haven't had time to do so beforehand, a brief visit to the site before the scheduled interview time, just to look around, is essential.

Of course, once in the interview itself, an applicant has a chance to really get a feel for the corporation. If one is astute, clues can be picked up that reveal a great deal about the context. Consider the physical layout of the interviewer's office. Is it very orderly, neat as a pin? Somber? Professionally decorated? Poorly lit? A total mess? These factors all dictate behavior based on context. Let's consider some other environmental clues:

- Are the offices discreet rooms with doors or are they separated by low, uniform dividers?

- What is the pace of the visible staff? Brisk? Relaxed? Calm? Frenetic?

- Is there music? What kind?

- What is the decor, such as furniture, paintings on the walls, carpeting? Is there any decor to speak of?

- Are there constant interruptions or is the interview room cloistered?

- How are the employees dressed?

- Look at the parking lot. Are there separate, marked spaces for management and supervision?

- What is the breakroom like? Are there comfortable chairs or tables? Is it neat or cluttered? Clean? Are there magazines or music or some other form of entertainment? What about a bulletin board? If there is one, what sort of information is posted there?

- Is there a time clock?

- Do phones ring constantly or rarely?

- Is there conversation among employees?

- Is there noise, or can you hear the clock ticking?

Some of these clues give rather obvious information. If, for example, the phones ring constantly and the employees tend to run rather than walk, you could fairly surmise that the atmosphere is harried and probably stressful. But, it may require some thought to put these factors together to come up with a more or less cohesive and accurate picture of the organization. For example, the use of uniform height dividers for offices rather than walls generally denotes a company with a "team" philosophy, where all employee input is valued and hierarchy is downplayed. Work spaces are similar to encourage interaction by management and staff. On the other hand, a parking lot with clearly delineated spaces for management and supervision might be indicative of a tight hierarchy within the corporate structure, where supervision is favored and workers know their place. Sometimes an office with a hopelessly anal-retentive demand for order and structure may stifle an individual with a strong need for flexibility and creativity. If, on the other hand, such order appeals to you, you would be well-advised to point out your penchant for the orderly.

So far, we have laid some crucial groundwork in trying to discover the context of an interview situation. It remains for us now to try to get a handle on that all-important person across the desk as the final piece of the context equation.

Sizing Up the Interviewer

It is intrinsic to human nature to take the measure of the people we meet. We do it all the time, automatically. We develop an instinctive way of reading others that is sometimes the saving of us and at other times can prove to be our undoing. It is this instinct that makes us form instant, lifelong relationships with some people or causes us to give a wide berth to others because we get a "funny" feeling about them. With some careful consideration and planning, though, these "feelings" can be honed into a useful tool for gauging the personality and character of interviewers and, by extension, their expectations of potential employees. Let's examine some clues.

- **Their e-mail.** You can tell a lot about your interviewer by his or her e-mail messages. Some are very warm, writing in a conversational style, addressing you by your first name. Others are witty, mixing little jokes and humorous remarks in with job-related questions. Still others get right down to business—no chit-chat or informality. Before you ever meet the interviewer, you begin to form certain "pictures" of the person, based on his or her approach and style. But it still remains for you to check him or her out face-to-face.

- **Their office.** Let's begin with the physical setting of interviewers' offices. Some put a desk the size of a 747 between themselves and you. This is a clear message to you to keep your distance. A straight-backed, rigid chair for the applicant says, "O.K. Let's get to business and then you leave so I can get back to mine." Here, you would be advised to adopt a crisp, businesslike style, with brief, professional answers. And, for heaven's sake, **don't touch that desk!**

  Then, there is the homey, comfortable environment—kids' pictures on the desk, executive "toys" around, soft chairs, and a sofa. There may not even be a desk between the applicant and the interviewer, but rather two chairs grouped around a coffee table. This environment invites more intimacy. It says, "Be yourself. Tell me about who you are so I can get to know you." Here, your manner, though still professional, should be relaxed and open, more personable. It would be a mistake with this employer to sit ramrod straight and give cool, truncated response to the questions.

- **The Interviewers.** Then, of course, you must evaluate the interviewers themselves. As a job applicant, you should be like a sensory sponge, drinking in every detail of the interviewers, processing them in order to figure them out. How is the interviewer dressed? What is his or her hairstyle? What is his or her body language saying? Consider the following suggestions about what to look for in an interviewer:

- What items has he or she chosen to display on the desks or walls? Certificates, pictures, personal memorabilia, awards?

- What does the interviewer do between questions while you are speaking? Look directly at you? Fiddle with items on the desk? Take notes or stare out the window?

   Are shoes shiny, buttons all in place? Or is hair messy, clothing rumpled?

   Does the interviewer smile and make eye contact or does he or she tend to look away and maintain a sober, noncommittal expression?

   Does the interviewer make "chit-chat" or stick strictly to business with rapid fire, closed-ended questions?

- Are you invited to call the interviewer by his or her first name?

- Are you invited to sit down or offered a handshake?

Sometimes, a room is designated the "interview room" and is not the personal work space of the interviewer, so it may not always be possible to draw conclusions about the person based on working environment alone. But, you must always be alert to the personal clues visible on the interviewer. Look for personal style, manner of speech, eye contact, and facial expression. All should help dictate the applicant's behavior. All of them reveal the context of the interview.

Hypothetical Interview Situations

Now, using what we have learned so far, let's set up some hypothetical contexts based on our observations and think about what sort of interview situations they might dictate.

Situation I

Through research, you find that this company was founded by a single individual on a shoestring. The company has grown dramatically and is now a national, public enterprise. The founder and CEO, who is still very much a viable presence in the organization, maintains a hands-on style of leadership. Company perks are many, with employee bonuses given for exceptional performance.

The office building is fairly new, the offices decorated in contemporary style and colors. The working spaces are separated by low, uniform dividers. There is an air of subdued energy, with the employees engaged in busy but not frantic activity. You observe some conversation but no music. Personal accouterments in the work spaces are limited to one or two pictures and some plants, but otherwise, desks and areas are more or less uniform. There are two designated parking spaces in the lot—one for the office manager and one for the employee of the month.

In the informational interview, you learned that this company offers flex-time, an on-site gymnasium, child care assistance, and an incentive program for employees wishing to take college courses. An open door policy exists for every supervisor and manager, all the way to the top of the organization.

The interview is held in a comfortable office which, it is explained, is the office of the interviewer. There are lamps, rather than over-head lighting, plants, a desk in the center of the room, and two club chairs and a coffee table near the window. A full-length mirror hangs on the back of the door, which has been closed for privacy. The interviewer is a woman, extremely well-groomed in a fashionable red business suit. She greets you with a warm smile and handshake, asks you to address her by her first name, and ushers you to the chairs by the window.

Contextual Conclusions

These factors point to a context in which you must make particular choices. To begin with, knowing that the company was started by a self-made entrepreneur, you should emphasize your strengths as a motivated self-starter. The tone of the office suggests that energy, enthusiasm, and ambition must be stressed as personal qualities you possess. It would help tremendously if you could point to examples of outstanding job performance, such as an instance where your efforts resulted in a monetary savings to your former employer, because it has already been determined that this company rewards excellence. Of course, interest in physical fitness would be nice, but what is called for here is a more general sense that you are the sort of person who strives for a "personal best."

Lastly, your grooming should be first-rate. This interviewer takes personal appearance so seriously she has a mirror in the office for periodic checks. Note, however, that the color of suit chosen is far from somber or serious. This is a cue to the applicant that some latitude for personal style and sense of individualism is afforded by this company. (Although you must beware of mirrors placed directly behind the interviewer. This is a "trick" to see if the applicant is easily distracted or self-absorbed. Avoid glancing at your reflection, primping, or looking at your image as you answer questions. Yes, some applicants actually do that! Keep your attention focused on the interviewer.) Next, Let's examine a different interview context for comparison.

Situation II

In this case, your research revealed that the company is a well-established local accounting firm with two branch offices in the same county. A company-supplied brochure emphasizes the firm's stability and reputation. Nothing is said of profit or growth except in very general terms, as the pamphlet is merely an introductory statement to prospective clients. The company president has been appointed by a family board of directors and handles the interviewing himself.

The offices are located in the same building they have occupied for more than 25 years. Colors are dark and carpeting is neutral and worn. Several formal paintings decorate the walls, but no personal effects are visible on any of the employee desks or in their work spaces. There is very little noise, except for the sound of computers, typewriters, and telephones. Office chatter is minimal and conducted in hushed tones. The pace of the workers is subdued.

The interviewer is a man in a dark blue suit and plain navy tie. His clothes are conservative and appear a bit dated. His office contains a large desk, a painting on one wall, and several certificates from community agencies and a business license on the other. His desk holds no personal items. The applicant sits across the desk in a straight-backed mahogany chair, which has been placed about two feet from the interviewer's desk. The employer previously declined your request for an informational interview, so you have spoken to one secretary and the security guard. They tell you that there is very good job security with the company, but it takes a long time to move up. On the way to the interviewer's office, you note that the breakroom is really nothing more than a partitioned area furnished with commercial tables and gray chairs. State labor law regulations and notices of upcoming meetings are posted on the bulletin board. There is a time clock just inside the door.

Contextual Conclusions

Clearly, this data represents a completely different context from the previous interview situation. Free-form answers emphasizing creative thinking ability and ambition are not called for here. What should be stressed is the applicant's desire for long-term employment and company stability. Respect for authority and chain of command plus the personal qualities of dependability and loyalty would be prized in this organization. Because this company has a time clock, punctuality should also be offered as a strength. Answers should be pointed and brief. Grooming called for here is conservative and simple. And don't touch that desk!

Questions in Context

Of course, the interview questions themselves must always be evaluated in terms of the context of an interview. Some of the more commonly asked questions should ideally yield somewhat different responses, depending on the circumstances of each interview. We will look at a few commonly asked interview questions and decide on appropriate answers based on knowledge of self and context.

What is your greatest strength?

Answers to this question require a bit of tailoring from one situation to the next. No pat answer will work every time. With this particular question, the interviewer is looking for two things in your answer. The strength in question could be either **professional** or **personal.** Thus, in formulating a response to this question, you must weigh not only the interview situation itself, but also the type of job being discussed and your own real strengths. Let's consider a couple possibilities for answers.

Professional: In the case of an interview for a highly technical position, a job-related strength—demonstrating expertise in a particular skill—would be the best choice of response. An auto mechanic might say, "Besides being able to do a complete engine rebuild, I can machine valves and do milling to specifications. I am also very strong in electrical systems diagnosis." Here, the applicant has focused on strengths as they relate to performance of the job. Similarly, a bank teller would focus on his or her ability to balance consistently and correctly. A machinist should emphasize the ability to work to tolerance. All of these job-related strengths tell an employer that the applicant isn't just talking. Referring to specific skills not only demonstrates competence but also knowledge of what the position entails. However, there is still the second component of this answer to consider—your personal strengths.

Personal: If an employer were hiring a machine to do the job, a simple recitation of professional strengths would suffice in this answer. But, the fact is, employers hire people, and people come equipped with different strengths as well as weaknesses. It is essential, therefore, that the interviewer reveal the person, not just what that person can do. If you misunderstand this fundamental concept of interviewing and hiring, the game is lost.

Put another way, you may have heard or even said yourself, "Employers hire friends. It's not what you know, it's who you know." Quite right. They do not hire people they don't like or trust, essentially, people they don't "know." Your primary job during the interview, then, is to communicate to the employer who you are. You do this by emphasizing personal qualities that make you a desirable candidate for the job.

One way to understand the importance of your personal qualities as an applicant is to put yourself in the position of the employer. Let's say you wanted to hire someone to clean your house. What if you had to go out on a public street, stop the first person you saw, and ask that person to clean your house. You would give him or her some money and the keys to your home, and send your new employee off. You're thinking, "No way!" Yet, that's exactly what employers do every time they hire someone. They "give the keys" to a stranger and offer that person money to do a job. Just as your first concern would be with the *kind* of person you were sending into your home (letting the cleaning ability take a back seat), so employers are acutely interested in you as a person, not just in what you can do.

Know Your Strengths and How to Communicate Them

The "strengths" question requires some self-knowledge on your part as well as the ability to communicate this to the employer. The auto mechanic in our first example, then, should point out to the interviewer that he or she is not only a competent mechanic but a dependable employee who can be counted on to be at work as scheduled. The bank teller would be wise to emphasize cash-handling ability as well as strong interpersonal skills because tellers are in the public eye. A secretary could stress discretion and the ability to handle multiple tasks. These qualities are all crucial to an employer but are not evident on the surface of things.

Self-awareness and consistency are both important in considering answers to tough questions and interview context. A secretary who stresses neatness as a strength but has a button missing has clearly made a blunder. You should always be sure that your answers reflect reality. In other words, it is better to be honest when listing your personal qualities to an employer.

Be acutely aware of the dynamics at work in the whole process. Let's again consider the applicant at the interview where the phones ring off the hook, harried people bustle around, and the interviewer is continuously interrupted by work. Offering punctuality, say, or interpersonal skills as strengths wouldn't score nearly as many points at that particular interview as offering the ability to work well under pressure.

So, you must be able to select a strength from a whole host of possibilities and then make sure it really applies to you and fits the context of the interview. Here are some suggestions for personal strengths that employers find appealing:

- dependable
- motivated
- good listener
- self-starter
- discreet
- personable
- detail-oriented
- flexible
- punctual
- organized
- loyal

Plus, the ability to:

- work independently
- think creatively
- work well under pressure
- make decisions
- shoulder/delegate responsibility
- work effectively with people at all different levels (*Note:* Never say, "I like to work with people!" Not only is this a cliche, the unspoken response of many employers is "What else would you be working with, aardvarks?")

Remember to evaluate yourself fairly and honestly, and choose your representative qualities wisely. No employer likes to be conned. Now let's look at another common interview question.

What did you like most about your last job?
This question practically directs you to think about the context of the interview. Yet, the answers many applicants give no longer warrant them for consideration by the employer. Some common answers given here are, "Oh, I just loved the people I worked with!" or "I really liked my boss." or "They had good benefits." The first two answers tell the interviewer that the applicant's last company was a neat place to work, so why is he or she here? The last answer indicates that this applicant is out for what he or she can get from the company. Neither answer shows any thoughtfulness in relation to the current context.

Again, it is incumbent on you to think about the company to which you are applying and what the conditions might be like on the job in question. You must then evaluate the components of your last job to see if there is a correlation with this one. Consider the following examples:

On her last job, Debra, as division secretary, was responsible for putting together a departmental newsletter which told about current events as well as outlined unit goals and accomplishments. She now finds herself in an interview for administrative assistant to a department manager. Knowing that she will be responsible for generating and editing a great deal of correspondence, wouldn't she be wise to volunteer that she liked the newsletter aspect of her last job?

Claudia worked for a small operation with only a few people on staff. The employees did virtually everything in the operation. Consequently, Claudia had different assignments every day. She is currently interviewing with an organization that has many departments and a diversified product line. Explaining that she liked the varied job responsibilities and prided herself on being flexible in her last job can only help her secure this new one.

Evaluating Yourself

Finally, a certain amount of self-analysis is essential to interview preparation. Besides a firm idea of the kind of work you want to do, you should have an "ideal" profile in mind of the sort of company for which you want to work. Additionally, you should be well-acquainted with the "product" you will be marketing at the interview, namely, you. Here are some questions you should try to answer about yourself prior to the interview:

- What are my short-term goals? Long-term?

- Am I willing to relocate? Commute? Travel?

- How do my hobbies and outside interests make me a better candidate for this job?

- What factors from my previous job(s) can I use as evidence of my fitness for this job?

- What are my own personal traits that apply to the position in question? (For example, preferences for working alone versus with the public, detail work, supervision, physical work versus cerebral work, need for creativity, structure, firm guidelines, etc.)

- What are my intentions toward this job? Do I plan to stay here and forge a career or use this as a stepping stone in my career path?

- Is the corporate philosophy of this company in line with my own philosophy? (*Note:* This question relates not only to how you perceive the nature of the working relationship of employer to employee but may also involve ethical considerations. For example, Claudia turned down a lucrative career position with an oil company because it had caused an environmental accident.)

- What are my chances for advancement?

- Is there a good match between my skills, knowledge, interests, abilities, and the challenges of this position?

A truly fair and honest assessment of yourself, coupled with an understanding of the context of each interview will result in an encounter with the employer that will be beneficial and satisfying to both of you. By all means, read all the information you can get on interviewing. Take seminars and find out the common questions and responses. Just remember that, like you, each interview is unique and deserving of individual attention as well as respect. All that is left for you now is to:

Get Serious: Apply yourself to this process in a thoughtful and thorough manner.

Get Started: Lay the necessary groundwork. Research the company. Find out all you can.

Get Ready: Dress for the part. Practice. BE PREPARED!

Get Control: Know the territory. Discover the context.

And, above all,

Get That Job!

CHAPTER

9

Advice for College Students

The Internet is a rich resource of job information for college students and recent graduates. Where you look depends on what your career plans are. Perhaps you have decided to stay in education and are searching for jobs at colleges and universities. Maybe you want information on positions for research assistants and teaching assistants. The net has listings for both of these. Some graduates look for work in specific geographical locations. Still others want to confine their job search to a specific discipline—for example, math or science. It is possible to search only those areas. Or, maybe you are still an undergrad and need help focusing on a particular career field. A specific gopher server can help you access that information.

Places to Look

This section gives you some specific sites and directions for online job search, especially for college students. (See Chapter 3 for general job leads in the Internet "classifieds.") This list is only a representative sample. Bear in mind that there are many, many more sites you can mine for jobs.

Entry-Level Jobs

This list is for recent grads with little or no experience. Generally speaking, entry-level refers to people with one to three years experience or recent college grads with no experience. Access this list through newsgroups at:

        misc.jobs.offered.entry

or telnet at

        telnet college.career.com

Jobs in Education

For students who decide they just can't get enough ivy, several sites exist for jobs with colleges and universities.

The *Chronicle of Higher Education* publishes its list of job openings in the gopher: ACADEME THIS WEEK. This comprehensive listing gives jobs in colleges and universities both in the United States and overseas. It is updated with every publication and appears on the Internet the day before it goes to press. To access:

```
gopher chronicle.merit.edu
```

You can also reach ACADEME through "All the Gopher Servers in the World" from your "Other Gopher and Information Servers" item on the primary gopher menu. The *Chronicle* can be searched by geographic location, keywords, or a list of terms provided by the *Chronicle*.

Another listing of jobs in education is available through the Academic Position Network (APN). Listings are included for positions at all levels, not just faculty but staff and administrative as well. As with the *Chronicle*, there is no charge to browse APN. Access at:

```
gopher wcni.cis.umn.edu 11111
```

You can search APN by entering keywords separated by "and" and "or." You can also search by geographic location and college or university.

Teaching or Research Assistantships

Many of the online placement offices of universities list their own research assistant (RA) and teaching assistant (TA) positions. But Rice University in Texas operates a gopher with access to employment listings for a host of other universities. These listings include RAs and TAs for various schools. Also included in the Rice gopher is a listing of college and research library (C&RL) jobs. It is an excellent resource. Access:

```
gopher riceinfo.rice.edu
```

Jobs by Discipline

You may have spent years becoming a specialist in one particular field. It is a relatively simple matter to search Internet jobs by discipline. For instance, you can key in your subject area at places like APN. Here are some other gopher sites.

Math: American Mathematical Society

```
gopher e-math.ams.com
```

Science: National Science Foundation

```
gopher stis.nsf.gov
```

Biology: BIOSCI

gopher net.bio.net

Jobtrak

Jobtrak is a daily posting of jobs available in many college career centers. The placement center prints out a listing of the current jobs and students may refer to or browse Jobtrak offerings online themselves. No fee is charged to students, unless the career center charges.

Online Career Center (OCC)

Online Career Centers is an extensive, free listing of jobs available nationwide with some international jobs posted as well. Various universities and colleges make OCC available to their students. You may search the database by geographical area or keywords. Jobs are in the private and public sectors with openings in health care, manufacturing, education, industry, and government. Organizations pay a fee for membership. Access:

gopher msen.com /
Online Career Center /
browse jobs /

When you enter gopher.msen.com, you will get the main gopher information screen. Then, you will be led by a series of prompts through different screens (see figs. 9.1 through 9.8).

Fig. 9.1. *The main gopher information screen (arrived at by: gopher gopher.msen.com) #16 selected: The Msen Career Center.*

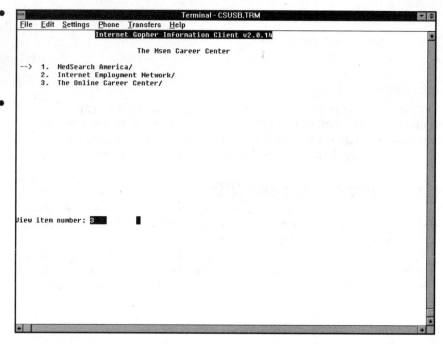

Fig. 9.2. *The Msen Career Center screen, #3 selected for The Online Career Center.*

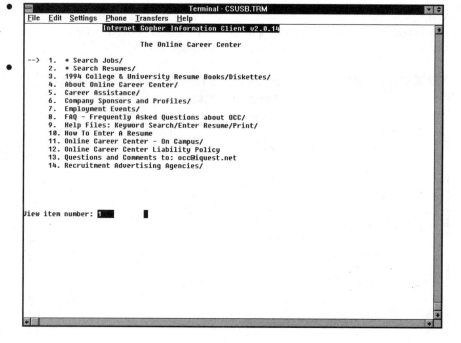

Fig. 9.3. *#1 selected, Search Jobs.*

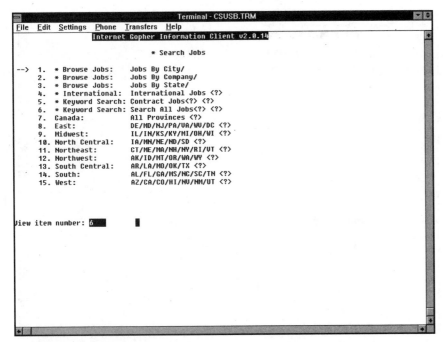

• • • • • • • • •

Fig. 9.4. *Search Jobs screen, #6 selected: Keyword Search: Search All Jobs.*

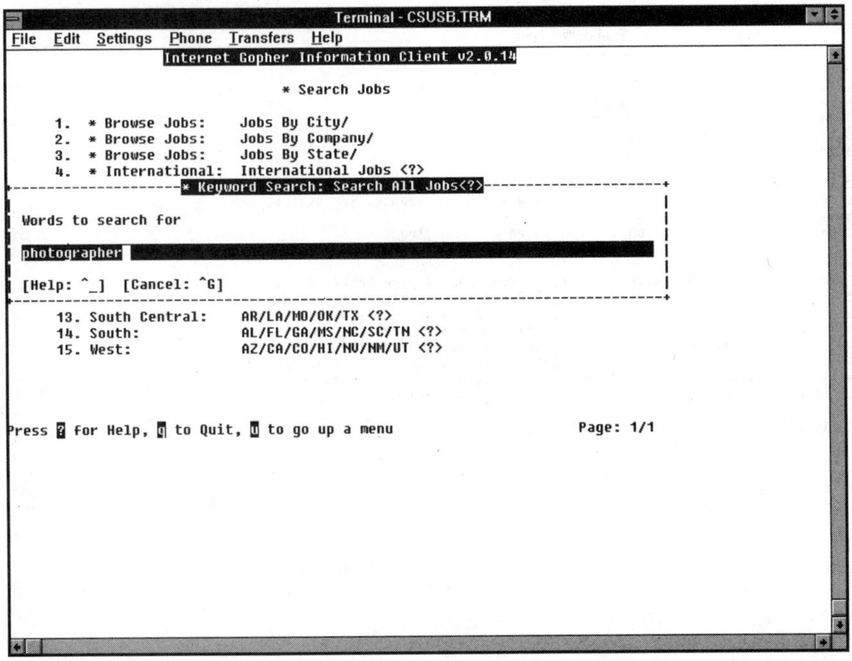

• • • • • • • • •

• • • • • • • • •

Fig. 9.5. *Shows keyword "photographer" entered.*

• • • • • • • • •

Fig. 9.6. *Photography Position selected.*

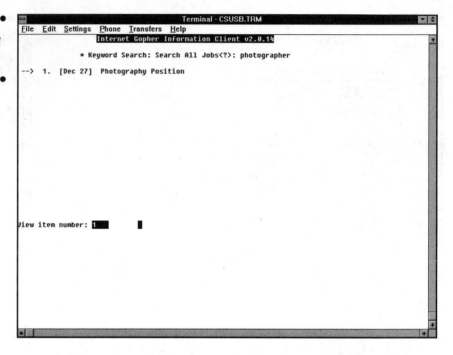

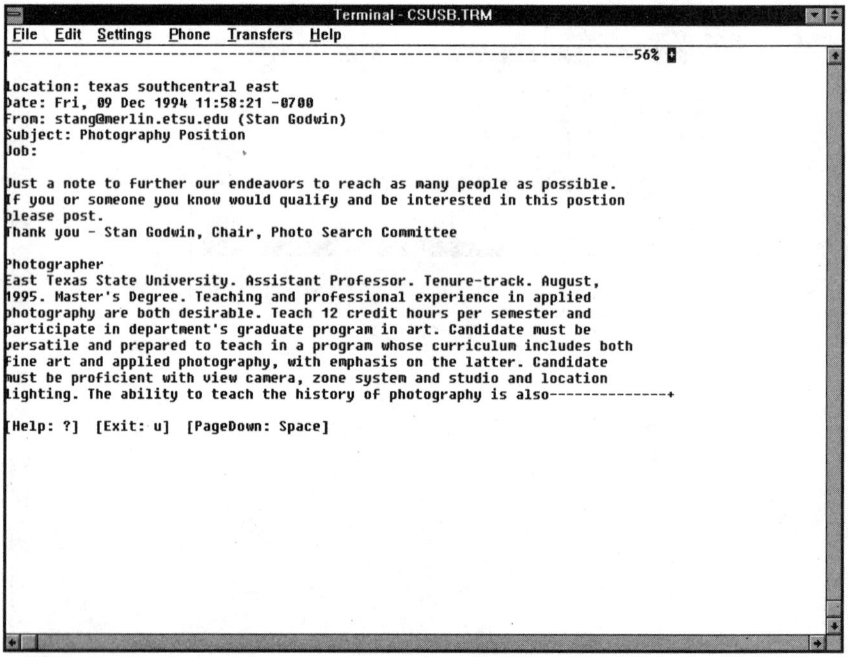

Fig. 9.7. *Job posting for photographer.*

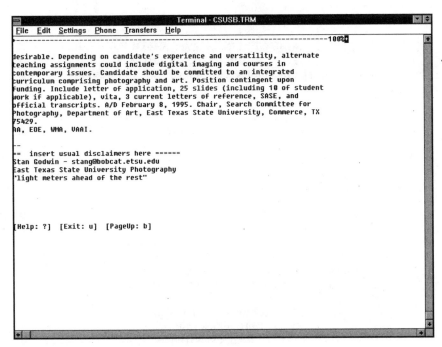

```
┌─────────────────────────────────────────────────────────────────┐
│                      Terminal - CSUSB.TRM                    ▼ ▲  │
├─────────────────────────────────────────────────────────────────┤
│ File  Edit  Settings  Phone  Transfers  Help                      │
├──────────────────────────────────────────────────────100%────────┤
│ desirable. Depending on candidate's experience and versatility, alternate
│ teaching assignments could include digital imaging and courses in
│ contemporary issues. Candidate should be committed to an integrated
│ curriculum comprising photography and art. Position contingent upon
│ funding. Include letter of application, 25 slides (including 10 of student
│ work if applicable), vita, 3 current letters of reference, SASE, and
│ official transcripts. A/D February 8, 1995. Chair, Search Committee for
│ Photography, Department of Art, East Texas State University, Commerce, TX
│ 75429.
│ AA, EOE, WMA, VAAI.
│
│ --
│ == insert usual disclaimers here ======
│ Stan Godwin - stang@bobcat.etsu.edu
│ East Texas State University Photography
│ "light meters ahead of the rest"
│
│
│
│ [Help: ?]  [Exit: u]  [PageUp: b]
│
│
└─────────────────────────────────────────────────────────────────┘
```

Fig 9.8. *Job posting for photographer (continued).*

Besides using the Online Career Center to search for jobs, you may also enter your resume at the OCC.

Following are the guidelines for entering your resume into the OCC database, reprinted as they appear in the msen.com gopher.

How To Enter Your Resume

Make your resume available to thousands of employers across the country through OCC on Internet. The OCC online keyword searchable database is available to all employers who have Internet access. There are no charges for employers to access your resume, and no charge to you if you enter your own resume online.

---------------------------- ATTENTION ----------------------------
IF YOU POST YOUR RESUME BY 5:00 P.M. EST, YOU MAY SEE IT
IN THE OCC DATABASE AFTER 7:00 A.M. EST THE FOLLOWING DAY.
THIS IS A PUBLIC ACCESS DATABASE AND MAY BE ACCESSED BY ANY
INTERNET USER.

You may, at no cost, enter your full-text resume
into the OCC Internet database via email.

- *** Your resume must be in ASCII format. ***

- THE EMAIL "SUBJECT:" LINE SERVES AS YOUR RESUME
"TITLE" — and will be the first
information seen by employers when viewing your resume.

- Your resume will stay in the OCC database for
90 days. To extend your resume beyond 90 days,
you may re-enter it at any time.

- Each e-mail account number is permitted only
one resume at any given time. Therefore, the
most recent resume uploaded will be displayed.

- To change or update your resume, simply
re-enter
it, and the previous one will disappear.

If you DO NOT have Internet access, you may mail your
typed resume (cover letter optional) to:

ONLINE RESUME SERVICE
1713 Hemlock Lane
Plainfield, IN 46168

Your resume will be processed and entered online
into the OCC resume database for six (6) months.

Each resume submitted to ONLINE RESUME SERVICE must
contain a "title line" not to exceed 45 spaces.
Ex: "Chemical Engr/5 Yrs Exp/Oil Industry-NY"

Cost: $10.00   Up to three (3) pages (including
cover letter)

You can access a huge listing of individual college placement centers by using gopher. Begin by typing `gopher` at the prompt. This will bring you to the Root gopher server (see fig. 9.9).. At this screen, select Other Gopher and Information Servers (see fig. 9.10).

At the Other Gopher and Information Servers screen, select "All the Gopher Servers in the World (see fig. 9.11).

It will take some time to retrieve this directory because it is enormous. Once connected, however, you will have access to an extensive alphabetical listing of gopher servers. Among these are many colleges and universities. We have selected the gopher server for Arizona State University so that you may see how to navigate through the screens to get to employment information (see fig. 9.12).

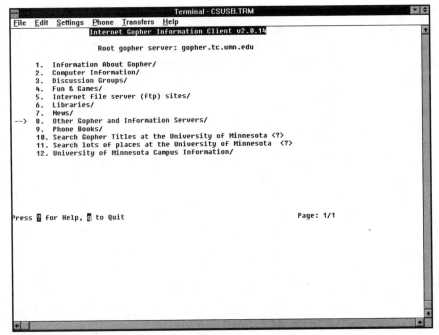

```
┌─────────────────────────────────────────────────────────────────────────┐
│                       Terminal - CSUSB.TRM                          ▼ ♦  │
│ File  Edit  Settings  Phone  Transfers  Help                             │
│            Internet Gopher Information Client v2.0.14                     │
│                                                                          │
│                 Root gopher server: gopher.tc.umn.edu                    │
│                                                                          │
│        1.  Information About Gopher/                                      │
│        2.  Computer Information/                                          │
│        3.  Discussion Groups/                                            │
│        4.  Fun & Games/                                                   │
│        5.  Internet file server (ftp) sites/                             │
│        6.  Libraries/                                                     │
│        7.  News/                                                         │
│   -->  8.  Other Gopher and Information Servers/                          │
│        9.  Phone Books/                                                   │
│       10.  Search Gopher Titles at the University of Minnesota <?>        │
│       11.  Search lots of places at the University of Minnesota  <?>      │
│       12.  University of Minnesota Campus Information/                    │
│                                                                          │
│                                                                          │
│                                                                          │
│ Press ? for Help, q to Quit                       Page: 1/1              │
└─────────────────────────────────────────────────────────────────────────┘
```

Fig. 9.9. *The Root gopher server screen.*

```
┌─────────────────────────────────────────────────────────────────────────┐
│                       Terminal - CSUSB.TRM                          ▼ ♦  │
│ File  Edit  Settings  Phone  Transfers  Help                             │
│            Internet Gopher Information Client v2.0.14                     │
│                                                                          │
│                  Other Gopher and Information Servers                     │
│                                                                          │
│   -->  1.  All the Gopher Servers in the World/                          │
│        2.  Search All the Gopher Servers in the World <?>                │
│        3.  Search titles in Gopherspace using veronica/                  │
│        4.  Africa/                                                       │
│        5.  Asia/                                                         │
│        6.  Europe/                                                       │
│        7.  International Organizations/                                   │
│        8.  Middle East/                                                   │
│        9.  North America/                                                │
│       10.  Pacific/                                                      │
│       11.  Russia/                                                       │
│       12.  South America/                                                │
│       13.  Terminal Based Information/                                    │
│       14.  WAIS Based Information/                                        │
│       15.  Gopher Server Registration <??>                               │
│                                                                          │
│ Press ? for Help, q to Quit, u to go up a menu    Page: 1/1              │
└─────────────────────────────────────────────────────────────────────────┘
```

Fig 9.10. *Other Gopher and Information Servers screen.*

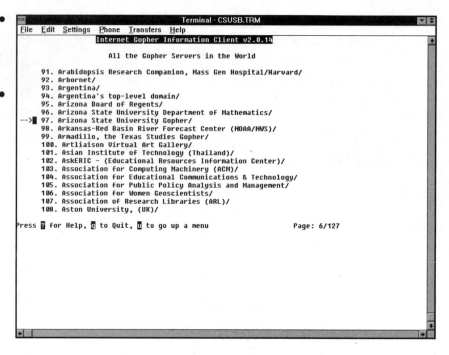

Fig 9.11. *All the Gopher Servers in the World* screen.

Fig 9.11. *All the Gopher Servers in the World* screen.

First, we selected the Arizona State University (ASU) Gopher.

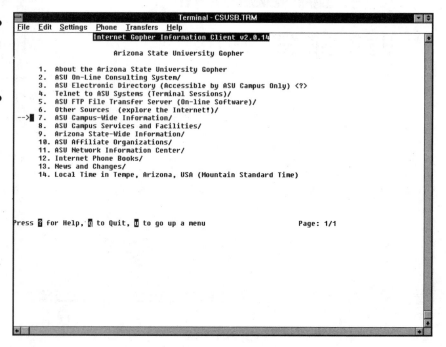

Fig 9.12. *The Arizona State University Gopher* screen.

Then we selected option 7—ASU Campus-Wide Information.

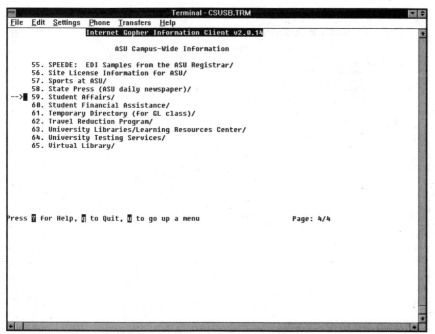

Fig. 9.13. *ASU Campus-Wide Information screen.*

Fig. 9.13. *ASU Campus-Wide Information screen.*

From there we went to option 59—Student Affairs.

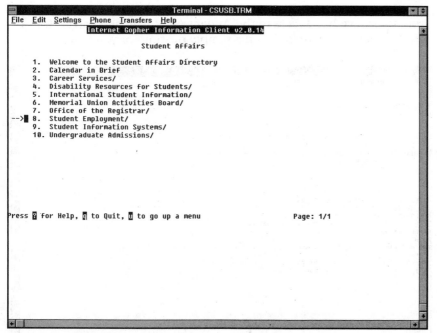

Fig 9.14. *Student Affairs screen.*

At Student Affairs, we chose option 8—Student Employment.

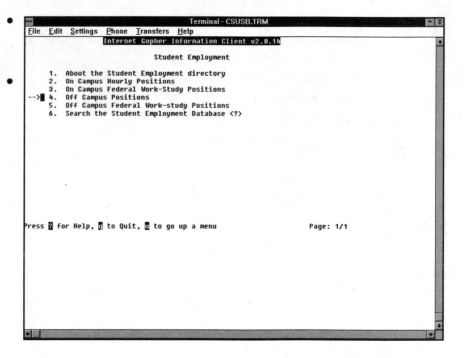

Fig 9.15. *Student Employment screen.*

We then selected option 4—Off-Campus Positions—to get to the job opportunities.

From there, we had access to the student employment database for off-campus jobs. We have included a sample posting for you here.

Fig 9.16. *A job posting from ASU Off-Campus Positions.*

Be aware that not all campus placement offices are open to public perusal. Some of them are limited to currently enrolled students only. Some offer campus placement services for alumni. These may be available to you online. Also, many campus gopher servers have gateways to the Internet and thus other placement services. Check out your own college or university placement office services.

Fee-Based Recruitment Services

Several fee-based recruitment services are available to job seekers online. Many of these do not charge a fee to job seekers, only to the employer. Two of these are Online Opportunities and Job Finders. We have included information from both of them here.

David Davidowicz is proprietor of a fee-based online recruitment and placement service called Job Finders. His service is "100 percent free to applicants." It contains thousands of jobs searchable by keywords. Keywords allow you to control certain criteria and better match you with prospective employers. David spoke with Mary Nemnich about how his service works.

MN: Tell us, if you would, how you work with applicants.

DD: I specialize in placing the listings in areas that job seekers will look. I firmly believe in providing listings to job seekers for free. I try to give them the freshest, most accurate job listings possible, so listings are deleted two weeks after they are posted. The job seekers who use Job Finders get exposure to a well-known, easily accessible commercial employment database of national and worldwide job opportunities. They can also post their resumes through us in the Help Wanted-USA online resume database.

MN: We encountered some dissatisfaction and even suspicion among job seekers with so-called "headhunters." How does Job Finders deal with them?

DD: I will not run listings that appear dishonest or deceptive. I require recruiters to state who pays their fees. I'm very concerned with quality on both sides.

MM: What advice can you give applicants to help them do a better job of electronic job search?

DD: I would like to see more accurate information distributed to applicants. The old school of thinking for resumes of "get their attention with flashy typeset and an ever changing format style" is not the way to job search in the electronic age. Applicants must be concise and to the point listing any specialized experience they possess. The keywords will do the talking, not the flashy paper or typeset. When the smoke clears it all boils down to words anyway. This is a good way to

cut right to the chase. I would also discourage applicants from applying for positions that they are not qualified for.

Posting a resume in any or all of the resume databases out there is a new and exciting concept, not available before the PC hit the street. I am always interested in posting listings on new services. The more, the better.

David Davidowicz can be reached at Job Finders via e-mail at `MAWORCTR@aol.com` or voice at (508) 840-4479.

Online Opportunities

Online Opportunities is a fee-based employment BBS located in Philadelphia that offers a variety of job and career information. Online Opportunities carries more than 8,000 jobs weekly. Ward Christman, executive director of Online Opportunities, provided the following information to job seekers.

Job seekers are becoming frustrated with newsgroups that have gotten so huge over the years that no one has the time to search through all the jobs. My service allows job seekers to pinpoint the right job by entering keywords. For example, if an applicant is an engineer looking for a job in Seattle, they enter `engineer` and `Seattle` as keywords, and only jobs meeting those specifications will be searched. There is a lot less time wasted in looking at jobs that don't fit. Our database of jobs is also maintained. Applicants who dial into the Online Opportunities can view job opportunities which are updated every two weeks.

Additionally, Christman's agency provides applicants access to online resume services. "In addition to viewing employment ads, job seekers can also gain national exposure for their employment credentials by listing their resume in the World Wide Talent Bank," he told us. Inclusion in the talent bank costs $40 for one year and the resume is listed on services such as America Online's Career Center and the Internet's Online Career Center.

Keywording is the secret to the success of the function as well. Says Christman, "Subscribing employers search through the resumes online by entering keywords relevant to the open position. Then the system sorts through the database and brings up only those resumes that match the keywords searched. Again, it saves the applicant from inappropriate referrals."

To enter a resume, applicants may simply dial the BBS and upload the resume directly into the system. Or, the service takes diskettes with resumes in ASCII format. Online Opportunities will also take paper resumes—"as a last resort"—but there is a $5 charge for conversion to digital form.

Online Opportunities provides a host of other services to job seekers. "We want to be a full service BBS," says Christman. "Through Online Opportunities, applicants have access to college, corporate, and recruiter directories; resume writing tips; as well as the services of a professional resume writer; career tips; and much more." He concludes, "The 'Information Highway' isn't just for computer hackers anymore. Millions of other people are using it to find a job!"

After you dial up Online Opportunities' BBS, you will get a series of screens directing you how to search jobs and enter resumes.

Fig. 9.17. *First screen after dial-up to Online Opportunities BBS. Describes service and gives prompt for log-in.*

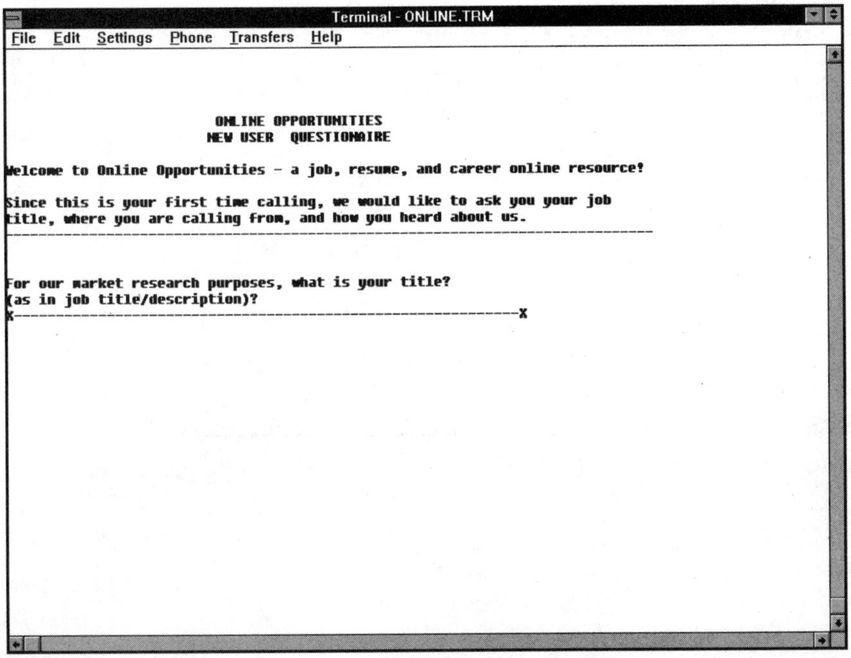

Fig. 9.18. *New User Questionnaire screen.*

Fig. 9.19. *New User screen containing data entered by job seeker.*

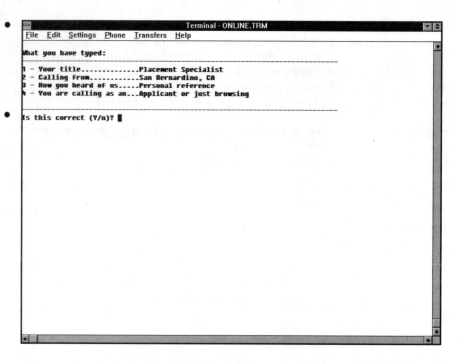

```
                                Terminal - ONLINE.TRM
 File  Edit  Settings  Phone  Transfers  Help

What you have typed:
------------------------------------------------------------------------
1 - Your title.............Placement Specialist
2 - Calling from...........San Bernardino, CA
3 - How you heard of us.....Personal reference
4 - You are calling as an...Applicant or just browsing

------------------------------------------------------------------------
Is this correct (Y/n)? █
```

Fig. 9.20. *Explanation of service with prompt to register.*

```
                                Terminal - ONLINE.TRM
 File  Edit  Settings  Phone  Transfers  Help

Welcome, and thank you for completing our new user questionaire.

As an anonymous guest you will have 40 minutes this call to
look around and get to know us.

If you believe our system will be helpful in your career/job search, please
<R>egister by pressing "R" from the Main Menu.

<R>egistering costs nothing and will allow you to sign on with a personal
account giving you the option to:

    * Upload your resume into any of our resume databases
    * Search the thousands of wantads online
    * Download resume/job/career programs and files
    * Participate in online discussions
    * Allow you to purchase items from our online store
    * Much more!


-Press Any Key-
```

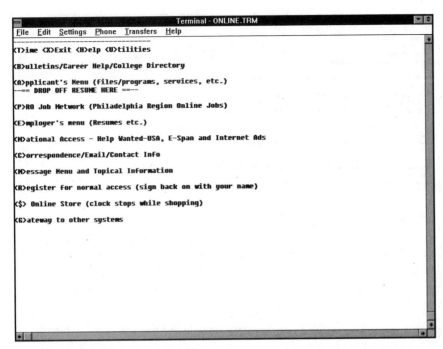

Fig. 9.21. *Main menu of services.*

```
┌─────────────────────────── Terminal - ONLINE.TRM ───────────────────▼─┤
│ File  Edit  Settings  Phone  Transfers  Help                          │
├───────────────────────────────────────────────────────────────────────┤
│ <T>ime <X>Exit <H>elp <U>tilities                                     │
│                                                                        │
│ <B>ulletins/Career Help/College Directory                            │
│                                                                        │
│ <A>pplicant's Menu (files/programs, services, etc.)                  │
│ --== DROP OFF RESUME HERE ==--                                        │
│                                                                        │
│ <P>RO Job Network (Philadelphia Region Online Jobs)                  │
│                                                                        │
│ <E>mployer's menu (Resumes etc.)                                     │
│                                                                        │
│ <N>ational Access - Help Wanted-USA, E-Span and Internet Ads         │
│                                                                        │
│ <C>orrespondence/Email/Contact Info                                  │
│                                                                        │
│ <M>essage Menu and Topical Information                               │
│                                                                        │
│ <R>egister for normal access (sign back on with your name)           │
│                                                                        │
│ <$> Online Store (clock stops while shopping)                        │
│                                                                        │
│ <G>ateway to other systems                                           │
└───────────────────────────────────────────────────────────────────────┘
```

Fig. 9.22. *Applicant Information screen.*

```
┌─────────────────────────── Terminal - ONLINE.TRM ───────────────────▼─┤
│ File  Edit  Settings  Phone  Transfers  Help                          │
├───────────────────────────────────────────────────────────────────────┤
│ The National Online Newspaper                                         │
│                              Subscription Expires: 00-00-00           │
│ <+>Main Menu                                                          │
│                                                                        │
│ <A>pplicant Information                                               │
│ <E>mployer Information                                                │
│                                                                        │
│ <H>elp Wanted-USA NATIONAL wantads                                   │
│ (A demo using last week's ads is available, but is not available to  │
│ anonymous callers - please go to the main menu and choose <R>egister │
│ to sign on with your real name)                                      │
│ <4> USENET Job Newsgroups                                            │
│                                                                        │
│ <W>orld Wide Talent Bank - special offer from Montgomery Newspapers  │
│ <C>ustom Databanks' Search Systems                                   │
│                                                                        │
│ <M>embership subscriptions available in our Online Store            │
│                                                                        │
│ <$> How to become a Help Wanted-USA database reseller for your area │
│                                                                        │
│ <J>ump to the Regional Wantad Menu                                   │
└───────────────────────────────────────────────────────────────────────┘
```

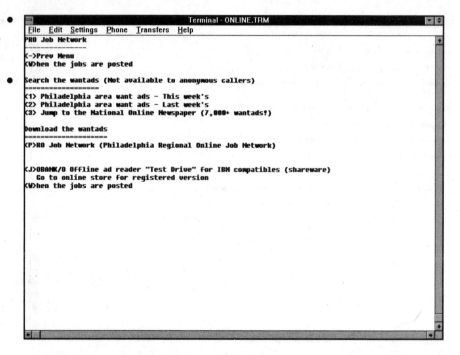

Fig. 9.23. *Applicant Information screen.*

Fig. 9.24. *National Online Newspaper screen.*

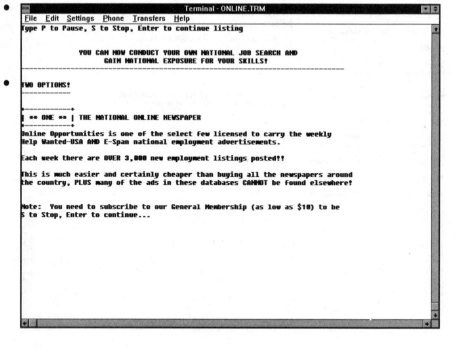

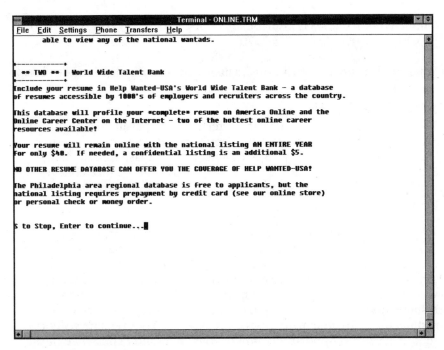

Fig. 9.25. *World Wide Talent Bank resume service screen.*

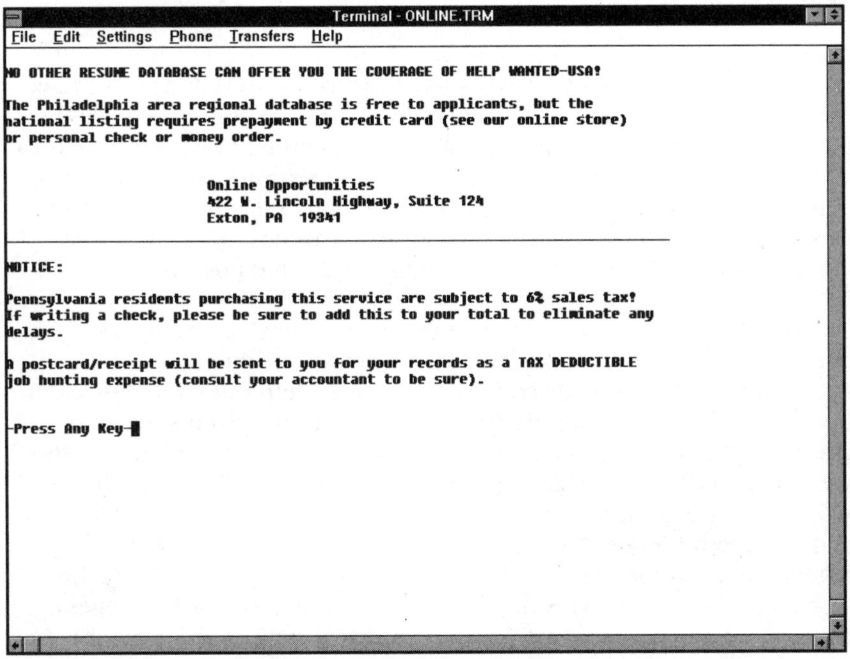

Fig. 9.26. *World Wide Talent Bank resume service screen (continued).*

Online Opportunities is available by phone (610) 873-6811; fax (610) 873-4022; or BBS (610) 873-7170.

You may also contact Ward Christman by e-mail at: `sysop@jobnet.com`

Job Company

The Job Company is a resume and referral service available to students on some California campuses. This company uses a scanner to enter and store resumes from college students in a database free of charge. Searches are then conducted for employers desiring to hire college students. Here, according to John Malone, president of the Job Company, is how it works:

"When you mail or fax your resume to the Job Company, we scan it (just as it is) into our computer. Our system has a special OCR (optical character recognition) program that 'reads' your entire resume. The artificial intelligence feature of our computer enables it to 'understand' what it reads. Our computer then stores all the information on your resume. Every time we get a job opening, our computer reads your resume for a possible match to the job request. Your resume will be sent to every job opportunity where your skills and experience fit the opening.

"We have become an excellent source for companies recruiting college and university students throughout California," says Malone. "We have the ability to run searches on only college resumes for companies that have either cut back on their on-campus recruitment or want access to candidates who are eager to train at a lower salary than many candidates who have 10 or 15 years experience and demand higher salaries." The Job Company is able to conduct searches on any level, so applicants may request either part-time or full-time positions.

The company also provides "resume enhancement" services to students for a fee to help make their resumes more competitive. John Malone explained, "In our continued quest to help our candidates and because many companies are now using scanning systems, we can assist through a feature called 'resume enhancement.' For a fee of $65, we will spend approximately 30 minutes with a candidate supplying words that are computer recognizable and that fit with the candidate's skills and experience. Most scanners will recognize 80 words per resume. If a resume has the wrong format or lacks 'hit' words (John's word for job-related terms that employers use in keyword searches), the resume may never come up for 'human' review. It will probably be buried and eventually purged from the system. We enable our candidates to increase their chances not only on our system, but on any system used by a company the candidate contacts directly."

Malone says that small and large campuses around California are signing up for Job Company services on an ongoing basis. He adds,

"The Job Company measures its effectiveness by how many resumes are retrieved by employers, as compared to how many of these same resumes receive interviews or direct contact. We are averaging an approximate success rate of 90 percent." John Malone may be reached at The Job Company, 3189 Danville Blvd., Alamo, CA 94507, 510-831-6707, e-mail `jgmalone@ix.netcom.com`

Tips for a Successful Student Job Search

When talking to recent college graduates, I am often reminded of the scene in "The Graduate" in which Benjamin's (Dustin Hoffman's character) uncle has one word of advice for his newly graduated nephew: "Plastics." The meaning of that one-word admonition in the '60s was that Benjamin was assured a bright future if he landed a job in the plastics industry.

Unfortunately for today's graduate, no such assurance exists. The job market is tight, industry is depressed, and companies are downsizing. Graduates today must be more competitive than ever to gain an edge in the labor market. This section will provide insights on how to use your college degree and relative inexperience to your advantage.

Realigning Your Resume

Obviously, most recent grads don't have as much job experience as seasoned employees who have been in the labor market instead of school. You might think that this is problematic for writing a competitive resume. But you really only need to rethink the standard resume format and be more creative in job descriptions to write a proper and honest resume which attracts employers.

Education First

For starters, remember that as a recent graduate, you want to lead off with your education. Here, you will not use the standard two-line space which gives only the name and address of the university, degree, and graduation year. Education, after all, is your strongest offering to the employer. Elaborate. Indicate classes you think most closely match the company's needs. Include those special Saturday seminars and extra classes you took to really delve into advertising. Feature the paper you presented at a regional university conference. Discuss the special departmental honors you received. This is your big offering. Give it some attention. The employer will, too.

Part-Time Jobs Are Still Jobs

You may not think that those part-time jobs you held during school have any relevance to your future career, but your employer is interested in them. You merely need to learn how to present them. For example, your experience as second assistant manager at the athletic shoe store, where you were in charge of two high school underachievers, can be mined for important generic job duties and attributes. You handled cash, budgeted, scheduled, controlled inventory, supervised, performed evaluations, opened and closed, served customers, and made sales. You had to be responsible, dependable, accurate, fair, organized, motivated, and adept at customer service and complaint mediation, just to name a few. The same is true for your jobs in restaurants or the college bookstore. Look carefully at each of your part-time student jobs and think about the responsibilities you held. How do they relate to your future job prospects? Can you find something relevant to put on your resume? Employers appreciate this.

Internships and Special Projects

Now, what about the special projects you worked on as a student? Mary recently worked with an engineering student who had participated in two projects for private companies which had gone to his university for help with specific engineering problems. That was work experience, directly related to his job objective. Maybe you held an unpaid internship related to your major? It should go without saying that you include all internships and externships as job experience on your resume. They exist to give undergrads experience in the world of work for which they are preparing.

Your work experience is no less valid than any other job seeker. It is up to you to present it in such a way as to show its relevance to your prospective employer.

Positive Qualities

Too many college students focus on all of the reasons why they won't be selected—which mostly revolve around experience. But employers hire candidates for a variety of reasons, not just experience. In fact, decisions are made every day to hire someone with less experience and better personal qualities rather than more experienced candidates with other problems. Remember, employers want you to tell them why you would make a good candidate for the job. Applicants with experience need only point to examples from their work history that illustrate their fitness for a job. You can do the same thing using your experience as a student. Let's examine some positive qualities of student applicants.

Ability to Work with Deadlines

College students live in a world of schedules—papers due, projects pending, exams coming up. You are responsible for deadlines every day of your student life. Deadlines are also a reality in the work arena. You're good at meeting them. Offer this strength to employers.

Ability to Handle Multiple Tasks

During school, you worked on several projects for different classes simultaneously. "Why do they all want major papers and projects at the same time?" is a common student lament. This can be turned into an advantage in the job interview. Illustrate your ability to keep assignments straight and get everything in on time.

Ability to Achieve Goals
Your entire education revolved around the goal of graduating. You worked toward achieving that goal. You studied your head off to be top of the class. Employers like applicants with goals.

Ability to Work as Part of a Team
Remember those group projects in school that made you groan? It was difficult working with all those different personalities. You sometimes felt that not all members gave equally. In the world of work, you will frequently be part of a team effort. Many employers have adopted the Total Quality Management (TQM) philosophy of management. In TQM, teams work toward solutions of problems. You will already have similar experience from school.

Ability to Adapt
When that class you had to have closed, you somehow made the adjustment and still graduated on time. Your many professors exhibited huge personality differences, yet you managed to work successfully with all of them. You were able to fit your work schedule around your school schedule and survive on less sleep and money. Let's face it. The whole college experience involves adapting to many different conditions and changes.

No Bad Habits to Unlearn
All this time you've viewed your relative inexperience as a handicap, while employers often view it as a plus. Sometimes, seasoned employees want to do things their own way. This can cause real problems on the job. Inexperienced applicants are more easily molded into the company's way of doing things.

Enthusiastic Employees
Recent college grads burst on the work scene, eager to try out the theories they merely studied at school in the real world of the workplace. Employers welcome enthusiasm and energy. It gets the blood of the organization going. Too often, long-term employees are set in their ways, out of ideas, and lack energy. Companies need the infusion of fresh ideas and dynamism of college hires to keep them going.

Knowledge of New Theories
College students get the whole picture when studying a discipline. They are often exposed to the latest theories and schools of thought in their field. Employers like to be in touch with cutting edge information through their employees.

This is where your expertise with the Internet comes in especially handy. Colleges and universities had a real advantage with this new technology because they were among the first organizations to use it.

Two employers we spoke with said they had recently gotten online and were still feeling their way along. One department manager who had a job opening posted in a newsgroup told me he really wasn't the one I wanted to talk to. "This is the first time I've ever recruited for my department over the Internet," he said. "There are a couple other people here who have, but I'm not really knowledgeable or comfortable with it, yet." This is precisely the situation in which you would have an edge as a recent college grad with lots of Internet experience.

Writing Ability

Here's where all those hours spent slaving over a word processor or typewriter pay off. You can write that new policy statement. You can submit that press release. You can edit the in-house newspaper. Writing skills are important in the workplace. Many employees don't have the ability, and yours gives you an edge.

Remember that you will have already had a few chances to demonstrate your writing ability through e-mail correspondence with the employer. Do not throw those opportunities away. Construct your messages intelligently, with great care.

Fact Finding and Information Gathering

College students emerge from school adept at research. You had to be able to see all sides of an issue in order to present your own. Employers like employees who can research the information needed on some particular question and come back with an answer. Your education has prepared you for this.

The primary use of the Internet in colleges and universities is for research. Through the net, you can access libraries throughout the world. You can contact media producers and tap into information databases of all kinds. You can become the research source at work because of your experience on the net. This is a tremendous plus in your favor. Offer it at your interview.

Part of being a successful job seeker is knowing how to make the most of your assets. Examine your career as a student. Look for those things that made you a success at school, then translate them into employment terms.

Avoiding Mistakes

There are several mistakes to avoid as a job seeker. Consider those that follow.

What Can You Do for Me?

Mark, a human resource manager for a computer company, told me about an interview with a recent college grad. The applicant looked good on paper—he had a degree from a prestigious school with good grades. During the interview, though, he wanted to know all the "wrong" things. "He asked me what time he had to be to work in the morning and how long he'd have for breaks and lunch. He also had questions about vacation and sick leave policy. I got the feeling he wanted to know just how much time he'd have to spend actually working. Time off seemed to be more important to him than time spent making contributions to our firm."

This is not your job as summer camp counselor or night clerk at the motel where you could do your homework. This could be your future, your second home, for the next 20 years. The same questions you asked as a student no longer apply. You have to demonstrate real interest in the company and voice your plans for making a contribution to it.

Says Elaine, head of marketing for a manufacturing company, "So often, inexperienced applicants ask me what we can offer them. The real deal is that we want to know what we're getting. I need to be sure that the person across from me will give me full value for the training time and expense I will be investing in him or her. Yes, I plan to offer profit sharing, a company car, and an expense account. But, neither my company nor I plan to do that for 'free.' Time in the interview would be best spent telling me what I'll be receiving in return for a good job with a bright future."

I'm Here to Fix This Place

That same wild-eyed enthusiasm that attracts employers to recent grads can also work against them. Sometimes in their zeal to make a contribution, new hires charge into the job with the attitude that they will make some changes and "rescue" the organization. Employers fear that they will upset the applecart, alienating existing staff, and perhaps valued customers. Don't be too quick to point out flaws of the organization, even if your intentions are good. If you have suggestions, pick your moment carefully. Go through the chain of command. Ask someone who knows the ropes to tell you the proper procedure for making a suggestion.

I Know Everything Already

Debby is an office manager who is responsible for training all new hires. She had the following to say about the know-it-all syndrome. "Perhaps it's pride, but all too often, recent college grads are resentful of being corrected. At first, they are willing to take instruction and appreciative when their mistakes are corrected. After a while, even though they still have a lot to learn, they're not as likely to take constructive criticism willingly." Good employees generally have the attitude that something can always be learned.

Grooming

Okay, when you were king of the "frat" at college, your earring with the omega symbol was a real fashion plus. But human resource managers take a dim view of earrings on male applicants. True, you see some managers sporting gold or diamond studs in the entertainment or information systems industries. However, the fundamental rules for appropriate grooming in the employment interview are virtually the same for every industry across the board. Following are some tips for proper grooming choices.

For Men

Clothing

Degreed professionals are expected to wear a suit and tie to the interview. When you were an undergrad, you could get away with a neat shirt and slacks for the retail job at the mall. Not so, anymore. Your grooming choices are carefully inspected. The amount of care you have taken in dressing appropriately for your job interview equates in an employer's mind with how much respect you have for the proffered job.

Even with a suit, mistakes can be made. For example, the monochromatic look—the same color suit and shirt—will not work in most job interviews, especially black clothing. Choose a color that flatters you. Avoid large patterns. A conservative pattern such as a muted pinstripe is acceptable but, if you choose a patterned suit, even a subtle one, do not wear a shirt with a pattern or design. Shy away from ties that have words printed on them or that resemble a vivid test pattern. Men have a lot more latitude than before in choosing ties with colors and patterns, but somewhat conservative ties still work best at interviews. Don't wear "bolos," string ties, or bow-ties.

Choose a shirt in a pale color that complements both the suit and your complexion and hair color. Be certain it is neatly pressed, collar and cuffs are not frayed, and all buttons are in place. Your shoes should be in good repair and polished. Athletic shoes are never appropriate, even if black or brown. Socks should be a solid dark color, without patterns and not sheer. Never wear white socks to an interview.

Most recent college grads aren't exactly "flush," what with student loans to repay and little savings from minimum wage jobs. It is not advisable to spend a fortune on clothes. Shop at discounted men's clothing stores. Or, do your initial shopping at thrift shops. You can purchase nice suits for little money. Mary often brings examples of interview clothes she has bought at secondhand stores to the classes she teaches, just to show it can be done. One suit she bought was a navy Brooks Brothers which she picked up for $7! A quick trip to the dry cleaners and you'll look great.

Hair

Face it. It's time to lose the ponytail and let the "fade" grow in. Employers are conservative about hair. Beyond extremes of style, however, your hair should be clean, neat, and out of your face. Facial hair doesn't pose as much of a problem. If you have a mustache or beard, it should be neatly groomed.

Hands and Nails

Years of talking to interviewers have revealed a common complaint from employers about male applicants: they do not like long nails on men. Include attention to your nails as part of your overall grooming habits. Also, be sure your nails are clean. Now, if you are an auto mechanic and an employer sees dirt under your nails, they think, "Yep. That's a mechanic." But if you are in, say, the health or food service industries, one speck of dirt under the nails can throw the interview.

Jewelry/Cologne

Limit the jewelry you wear—one ring, one chain, and so on. Instead of the earring, wear your Phi Beta Kappa pin. Use a tie tack or bar. Turn off the alarm on your watch! Cologne should be worn sparingly. This is an interview, not a date.

Hygiene

You should be freshly shaved. If your beard grows in very fast, shave just before leaving for your appointment. Use deodorant and mouthwash. Get a good night's sleep before the interview.

For Women

Clothing

The choices for business suits abound for women today. You are no longer limited to the navy suit with the white blouse and little scarf, once considered the "power suit" for interviews. By all means, use color. Choose shades that complement your coloring. However, you must wear a suit with a skirt. Slacks are not considered professional attire for interviews. Skirt length should be moderate, neither too short nor too long. Short skirts can be your undoing if you are constantly tugging at them during the interview. Your undergarments should fit properly, not slipping above or below your outfit.

The blouse you select can be any shade, as long as it goes with the suit. You can wear "shells" or button-front styles. Patterned blouses are not as professional as solids and you should never mix patterns of blouses and suits. Scarves are fine, as long as they don't overpower your appearance.

Polish your shoes. This is a grooming practice that is often overlooked by women. Be careful that your shoe heels are in good repair, with heel tips in place and no scuffing. Clean off the "black stuff" that gets on the backs of high heels when driving. Heel height should be moderate. Hose should be the color of your skin tone. Do not wear colored, patterned, or seamed hosiery. Carry an extra pair of hose in the car. A run in the stocking is sloppy and distracting.

Hair

Avoid extreme hairstyles. Hair should be clean and controlled. It is distracting when an applicant fiddles with hair during the interview. If you are interviewing for a job in healthcare or food service, pull your hair back if it is long.

Hands and Nails

Manicure your nails carefully. Employers really look at hands. Keep nails at a moderate to short length. If you wear nail polish, choose a conservative color that complements your outfit. If you are in the food service or health occupations, you should wear clear nail polish or none at all, and your nails should be shorter. (A French manicure, with clean, white nail tips, works very well for these careers.)

Makeup

If the employer can see you from a block away, you have on too much makeup. Use a light touch when applying makeup for an interview. Less is more. Avoid bright eye shadow and blush. Your lipstick should complement your clothing and nail color. If you're not sure how to properly apply makeup, consult a fashion magazine for tips on daytime makeup application.

Accessories/Jewelry

Your bag should match your shoes. If you carry a briefcase, you shouldn't also carry a purse. Pare down the contents of your purse so you don't need to fumble for a planner or a pen.

Keep jewelry simple. Earrings should be close to the head, never dangling or extreme. Wear just a couple of pieces. Jewelry that is noisy or gaudy or moves is distracting to the interviewer. The idea is to keep attention focused on you, not your jewelry.

Be Professional

You have mastered some complex theories and principles during college. The world of work is waiting for you to make a contribution with your knowledge and training. But, unless you can convince the employer that you know how to be professional on the job, you won't get your shot. This is accomplished by making a strong showing in the interview with proper grooming, preparation, and communication with the employer. Use the presentation skills you acquired in school to do a good job of interacting with the employer.

Keeping the Job by Keeping Up

Now that the dust has settled and you're safely ensconced in your new position, take a good look around you. Take the measure of the company once again, this time from the inside. What does it take to get ahead and succeed in this new job? The task of *finding* a job required hard work and dedication. You will now need to apply that same determination and diligence to *keeping* it. Job retention is the final step in the job search process. Following are some tips to make you indispensable to your new employer.

Hone Your Skills

Whatever skills you brought to the interview were sufficient to get you the job. The problem is that many employees stop there. Doing just enough to get in the door and no more will keep you at a fairly plodding pace in the company. Employers look for employees who go out of their way to improve their skills and job performance. These are the ones who get the promotions and keep their jobs during crisis periods. Volunteer for new in-house training if it becomes available. Take extension courses. Practice your craft, whatever it is, and become an expert at it. Try to "best your best."

Stay Informed

You got this job by means of the latest technology. Don't let your cutting edge become dulled. Read up on the latest techniques and trends. Do periodic research on the Internet. Stay up-to-date on the most recent events and changes in technology.

Contribute

Get involved in the discussion at staff meetings. Make suggestions for improvements—at least for your own job performance. Give your input when asked for it. Take an active part in your company's future. Bumps on a log don't grow.

Be a Team Player

Of course, you want to be the one who stands *out* from the crowd. What you want to avoid is standing *apart* from the crowd. Share your ideas and always credit others for theirs. Be generous in praise for your coworkers. The prevailing management concept in business today is Total Quality Management, or TQM. In TQM, everyone has a stake in the success of the company. You need to know how to play nice and share with the other kids to make this work.

Keep Your Private Life Private

Don't bring your personal "stuff" to work with you. Employers don't like to hire problems.

Don't Become Involved in Office Politics

Stay professional and courteous to your coworkers and superiors. Try to distance yourself from petty grievances and conflicts between other people. Be the one who builds consensus instead of creating divisiveness.

Keep a Positive Attitude

Don't be the one who always says it can't be done. Rise to new chal lenges. Be open to change. Stay flexible and willing to grow. Help lead the way into the future, instead of being dragged into it.

Stay in Touch with the Internet

The Internet was your best buddy when you were looking for work. You developed many contacts there and discovered a whole universe of data on a wide variety of subjects. This information is invaluable to you now. Make frequent contacts with the Internet. Through it you can stay current on world events, learn about advances within your company's field, watch the stock market (including your company's holdings!), and nurture future job contacts.

Using Your College Experience to Your Advantage

Your college experience will serve you well as you enter the labor market of the future. At school, you have been exposed to some of the very latest in technological advances, particularly the Internet. This exposure is a distinct advantage in a competitive labor market. You bring with you a fresh approach and a willing spirit, something that longtime employees sometimes lack. Stay engaged and interested. Don't leave your education at the university—make it a lifelong pursuit.

Advice for Employers

Perhaps you have been considering using the Internet for recruitment but are daunted by the sheer immensity of it. After all, you keep hearing these huge numbers: *"TWENTY-FIVE MILLION PEOPLE NOW USE THE INTERNET."* And you wonder, "If I put a job announcement on the Internet, how in the world am I going to interview and screen 25 million job applicants!?" You certainly don't have time to waste looking at all kinds of unsuitable applicants.

Electronic Recruiting

To many people the question is, what do you do now to prevent a crush of unqualified applicants? In the face-to-face world of recruitment and selection, employers are careful where and how they list position announcements. For example:

- They select agencies or "headhunters" who specialize in the kind of applicant pool they need.

- They pass the word through the "grapevine" to other employers that they are looking for good people.

- They write ads carefully, spelling out the minimum qualifications or setting the experience requirements very high.

- They place "blind" ads, where their name is not given.

- They begin with a "resume only" period, during which they do some preliminary screening to see how the applicant looks on paper.

- They contact college career centers where they think there might be a pool of graduates in their particular field.

These are the same steps you can take on the Internet. When you post your job opening in certain employment databases, you are asked to enter certain keywords. For instance, if your applicant must have a master's in marketing, ten years of experience, and live in the St. Louis area, your order would appear with the keywords: "MA Marketing, 10 years exp., St. Louis." You can narrow the field of applicants considerably just by adding specific keywords. This is akin to writing your ad with precisely defined requirements. Then, of course, within the body of the order, you may get even more detailed, thus further limiting your field of applicants.

Online Employment Services

Following are some examples of places where you can list your job openings online. One of the largest and most effective is the Online Career Center (OCC.) This is a very convenient place for job seekers to look because they can control their search area by controlling for different factors that employers have listed in each job opening, such as geographical location and the job itself. Within the OCC is also a huge resume bank accessible to employers and arranged geographically. Resumes are listed by subject line within each category.

What follows is a description of the OCC, its services, do's and don'ts, and frequently asked questions (FAQs) as they appear in USENET.

The purposes for which OCC formed are:

(1) To have a cooperative of employers through a nonprofit association, develop and manage an electronic employment advertising and communication system for human resource management;

(2) To share among a cooperative group of employers any and all available technology and use this technology to assist in employment advertising and communications;

(3) To develop and manage an electronic delivery system for processing and delivering employment advertising and recruiting information to other electronic delivery system vendors when appropriate;

(4) To negotiate agreements for electronic media services; control electronic media employment advertising, recruiting and communication services direction, development, and costs; and provide administrative services for its membership;

(5) To keep members informed about state of the art technology and to share this information with human resource professionals who are responsible for the employment process; and

(6) To develop, manage, and engage in all aspects of electronic distribution of employment advertising and communications for human resource management.

OCC membership is intended for the use of professionals engaged in organization development, employment, or recruitment for the organizations which employs them. Organizations engaged in "third party" recruiting are excluded from membership. This exclusion does not apply to contract recruiters whose efforts extend solely for the benefit of their contracted organization and who have not entered into contingency arrangement.

OCC member organizations may not engage in any "contingency" recruiting assignments while a member of OCC.

FAQs — Frequently Asked Questions about OCC

What is the purpose of OCC?

OCC's purpose is to work with the Internet, Prodigy, GEnie, CompuServe, America Online, and other national online networks to develop the most economical, effective network possible for employment advertising, outplacement services, and communications.

How can OCC help my company if we already use the Internet?

OCC provides a database, job and resume files, company information and profiles, and online search software to assist both employers and applicants in effectively using the Internet. This means employers greatly increase exposure to their jobs with the same distribution to the 250,000 USENET users they now have, plus access by millions of Internet users who do not subscribe to the USENET newsgroup feed.

OCC is available to Internet users by USENET Newsgroups, World Wide Web (WWW), Mosaic, Gopher, Telnet, and E-mail.

Online Career Center provides:

- desktop Internet access with online software specifically designed for recruiting and employment;

- a single source for placing state, regional, national, or international employment advertising for access by more than 20 million online subscribers (not just to the estimated 300,000 subscribers to USENET Newsgroups such as `misc.jobs.offered`);

- a "recruiting center" with a database for displaying and retaining recruitment information for an unlimited length of time. (With Internet access ONLY, employment ads reach a very limited number of Internet subscribers and have an online "life" of three to five days);

- a job listing database with KEYWORD SEARCH to assist both employers and applicants in effectively using the Internet;

- a resume database with KEYWORD SEARCH to assist recruiters in effectively using the Internet;

- a database of company information and profiles; electronic availability of ads and information to commercial network subscribers such as Prodigy, CompuServe, America Online, Delphi, National Videotex, BIX, Portal, GEnie, etc.;

- valuable outplacement assistance for employees through direct online access to hundreds of employment opportunities and full-text resume distribution to thousands of potential employers nationwide;

- online communications (including full-text resumes) with candidates from their homes or offices, if you choose; and

- member service (user) support for recruiters.

How will OCC reduce employment costs?

According to a cost study, 36 percent of a company's total recruiting budget is spent on advertising and search activities. While OCC will not replace current recruiting sources, it can provide phenomenal savings in high expense areas by strengthening current employment advertising and reducing agency and search fees. OCC can be especially effective in helping locate and identify hard-to-find professional, managerial, and technical candidates. It can also be a valuable resource for filling recurring vacancies, which are always challenging.

Who accesses online networks and how often?

OCC now reaches more than 20 million online users by consolidating the subscriber base of major online networks into a national audience of potential employment candidates. These networks are currently accessed more than 116 million times each month. Demographically, users are highly educated; work in all professional, technical, and managerial occupations; and demonstrate computer proficiency. Employment ads are available around-the-clock to users who are both actively and passively exploring employment opportunities.

How do I access OCC on the Internet?

Corporate recruiters may access the service using computer terminals, workstations, or PC's by telnet through company-provided or local Internet connections. Access options also include CompuServe's nationwide communications network and direct dial-in to the host computer.

Do I need to be a computer expert?

Absolutely not. OCC on the Internet is menu-driven with help files on every menu screen. As with traditional recruitment media, subscribers can advertise employment opportunities simply by forwarding job ads by fax, phone, or U.S. mail, or by entering them directly online. In turn, candidates may respond to ads by contacting employers directly —also by fax, phone, mail, or e-mail—as specified in your ad.

Which commercial network subscribers can view OCC?
OCC consolidates the more than 20 million subscribers of major online networks into a national audience of potential employment candidates. Subscribers to commercial online networks including the Internet, CompuServe, GEnie, America Online, The WELL, Portal, BIX, Delphi, and others can reach the Online Career Center by telnet, gopher, World Wide Web (WWW), Mosaic, e-mail, etc.

How do I receive responses?
Candidates may respond by phone, fax, or letter as specified in your ad. You may also receive full-text resume responses by e-mail from applicants who subscribe to commercial networks such as Prodigy, CompuServe, America Online, GEnie, Delphi, BIX, Portal, The Well, etc.

Can blind ads be placed on the networks?
Yes. Blind ads do not reveal a company's identity because the OCC's name and box number are listed as the contact source. Responses are received by OCC and forwarded unopened to the company.

Can multiple ads be placed on the networks?
Yes. Multiple ads may be placed on the networks at no additional cost. Multiple position ads can be one of the most productive and cost-effective forms of advertising. Multiple ads are used when a company has many positions open that cover various job titles. A general heading, opening, and closing may be used while inserting a list of separate job titles and descriptions.

Can I assist outplaced employees with OCC?
Yes. You may assist outplaced employees by providing access to the available job listings. You may also make their availability and qualifications, including full-text resumes, known to employers nationwide by placing the information online. As with employment ads, you may enter resumes online through your PC and modem.

Is the service international?
Yes. The service is available in the United States and in more than 100 foreign countries through the Internet with a strong presence in Canada, Europe, Asia, Australia, and the Pacific Rim.

How do I place ads online?
Online Career Center member companies may enter ads by either typing them in online or by uploading them from a word processor. OCC member companies also have the option of having ads designed, formatted, and placed online by their recruitment advertising agency. Employers who are not OCC members may have employment ads placed in the OCC database by contacting any one of the recruitment advertising agencies listed under "Recruitment Advertising Agencies" on the OCC main menu.

What is the cost for membership in OCC?

OCC is owned, managed, and controlled by employers through a nonprofit association. Employers pay a one-time association membership fee of $3,900 and a $60 per password annual access fee starting the second year. There are no charges to applicants.

How do I get started?

Call OCC at (317) 293-6499, or send an e-mail message to `occ@msen.com` and Member Services will set up your account.

Where can I look up job postings?

In a newsgroup called `misc.jobs.offered`. This group is for the posting of jobs only. Newsgroups tolerate no nonsense when it comes to inappropriate postings. We have printed it here just as it appears in USENET. The listings in `misc.jobs.offered` are not arranged in a particular manner, but the latest entries of jobs appear at the top. You are encouraged to put as much detail as you can about the job offered in the subject heading. This helps users browse more easily.

What is misc.jobs.offered?

It is a newsgroup for the posting of job offerings by individuals or companies with positions to fill. Job offers may be made by any company with a job opening or by a professional third party recruiting company which has been hired to fill an opening. Professional recruiters, however, should note that their being allowed to do business via USENET is an unusual exception to the general rule which forbids using the network for commercial profit. They should therefore be especially careful to adhere to the guidelines for posting. Violations and abuses upset readers, who may call for prohibiting these commercial postings.

Readers may note that postings are mostly computer related. This is due to USENET being a computer-based medium. (You have to use a computer to use USENET, and computer users are more likely to have computer-related jobs to offer.) Although, offers of noncomputer jobs are appropriate as well.

What isn't misc.jobs.offered?

It is not a discussion group or a group for posting resumes. General discussions concerning jobs should be held in `misc.jobs.misc`. Resumes should be posted in `misc.jobs.resumes`. Your cooperation is greatly appreciated. If you feel you must follow-up an article posted here, edit the "Newsgroups" line to Newsgroups: `misc.jobs.misc`.

`Misc.jobs.offered` is for offering jobs, not business opportunities. The posting must meet all legal requirements of the country where the work will be done. Readers should remember that USENET is an international network and that what is illegal in their country may be legal in the poster's country.

Why have posting guidelines?

Given the very high number of postings in these groups, it is now essential to be able to use the computer to quickly screen articles. As in buying a house, for many people the three most important things about a job are: location, location, and location. Someone in New York City may not be interested in relocating to Berlin and vice-versa. Brief job descriptions are also useful to screen. Thus, it is important that the location and brief job description appear in the subject line. There are a number of discussions which frequently occur in these groups. These discussions frequently result in long and unproductive arguments. These guidelines embody the consensus of opinion as to the proper form for postings of job offers.

What are the guidelines?

All postings must be for actual positions. Any job that is offered or alluded to must actually exist, and be "approved," if applicable. Do not submit postings for positions which do not exist. Do not submit vague postings in order to receive a supply of resumes. Resumes may be collected from `misc.jobs.resumes` if a source of resumes is desired. The name of the company making the offer must be present in the posting. Professional recruiters are requested to place the string "3RD PARTY RECRUITER" on the keywords line. Many universities are legally restricted from handling commercial traffic, and this will enable universities to comply with the law. This is especially true if there is a placement fee required of the person accepting the position. Other posters should use the organization line to indicate the name of the company making the offer and also include the name in the body of the posting.

No job offers should be cross-posted. All job offers should be restricted to `misc.jobs.offered` (except for contract jobs which go to `misc.jobs.contract` instead). Discussions of job offers and resumes requesting positions should likewise be limited to the appropriate groups. Again, judicious use of the "Follow-up To:" is heartily encouraged. Your posting may be the first time a potential employee has heard of you. Posting to the wrong group does not make a good first impression.

Offerings must be verifiable. The name and phone number or address of the person responsible for the position must be given. Provide information that is verifiable from anywhere in the world, such as a complete mailing address or a phone number usable from anywhere, (1-800 numbers are often only callable from specific geographic areas). Further information should be available on request. The more information you provide in your posting, the better the response will be. You should also consider providing an e-mail address and allowing resumes to be sent by e-mail.

The location of the job must be clearly stated in the subject line of the header and in the article. The format of the subject line is: country, state/province, city, job description, company. Here are some examples of subject lines:

```
U.S., IL, Chicago, Foobar Developer,
    Acme Widget Inc.
U.S., NY, New York City, Foobar Developer,
    Acme Widget Inc.
DE, Munich, Foobar Developer, Acme Widget Ag.
UK, London, Foobar Developer, Acme Widget Ltd.
    offsite, Foobar Developer, Acme Widget
```

In the subject line, use the country code, state, or province code and the largest nearby city. In the article, provide more detail if necessary to provide the reader with the job location for determining commuting distance. In many cities, this would mean a specific section of the city or a suburb. The street address of the company is usually sufficient. Be specific. A location in the Midwest, California, or Europe is needlessly vague. Give a specific city, such as Indianapolis, IN, Sunnyvale, CA, or London, UK. If the location is a small, little-known town or suburb near a major city give the major city as well, such as Lisle, IL, (near Chicago).

Remember that USENET is an international network. "Bay Area" may mean "San Francisco Bay Area" to you, but it may mean someplace entirely different to someone several thousand miles away. If the position is not of sufficient interest to the entire net, use the distribution line to limit the distribution of the article to your local area. Furthermore, you may wish to consider using local or intracompany newsgroups as a source for candidates. An example would be "trianobs" for jobs within the Research Triangle Park area.

If where the worker lives is not a significant factor, use "offsite" as the location in the subject line. For example, a job consisting mostly of work that can be done at home or one that is mostly travel would use "offsite" as the location. The details would then be provided in the body of the article. Note that not requiring a worker to show up on site will give you a larger pool of workers from which to choose. If some work can be done by telecommuting, but the worker is required to report onsite on a frequent basis, put the onsite location in the subject line and explain the telecommuting details in the body of the article.

A salary or salary range must be provided. Simply saying "competitive" or "commensurate with experience" is not helpful. Be specific. Again, remember that this is an international network and provide the monetary units (dollars, pounds, francs, etc.) involved. If the position is likely to require overtime, state how your organization handles it.

What about overtime pay? Flex time?
It is usually helpful to list both ideal or desired requirements and the minimum you will accept. There is a lack of uniformity in how people

map academic experience into commercial experience. If this is important to you, it may be helpful to explicitly state how they map at your organization. If you want entry-level candidates to apply (or not apply), say so explicitly. (Note that people sometimes return to school for a master's or Ph.D. after working for a few years. Therefore, the phrase "no entry-level positions at this time" is probably more accurate than "recent graduates need not apply." The definition of entry-level varies but usually means zero to two years of experience. If there are requirements such as being a citizen or permanent resident of a particular country, say so. If your organization has a dress code or standard working hours, say so. If your organization has unusual requirements, such as handwriting analysis, drug testing, polygraph tests, loyalty oaths, etc., say so.

How often can I repost my article?
If you do not get any interesting responses from your job posting or resume, you may want to post it again. But first, be patient. It can take several days or more for an article to reach all machines. Not everyone reads every group every day. If you need to repost an article, wait until 30 days have passed since the previous posting.

What if I made a mistake in my article?
USENET allows articles to be "canceled." This is usually done with a "c" or "C" command from your newsreader. For details consult the documentation for your newsreader software. If you have posted an article that contains a mistake, you can cancel the original article and then post a new, correct article.

What do I do once the job is filled (or I find a job)?
Once the position is filled (or you find a job), you should cancel your job posting (or resume). This will save people time from responding to your posting, and will save you time from responding to them.

What is misc.jobs.resumes?
`Misc.jobs.resumes` is a place for individuals seeking employment to post their resumes. If you feel you need to post a follow-up article to an article in `misc.jobs.resumes`, it should go to `misc.jobs.misc`. Many of the other suggestions made above apply here as well.

What is misc.jobs.misc?
This group exists for job-related discussion. Do not post job offers or resumes to misc.jobs.misc. Most topics relevant to seeking employment, seeking workers, or the workplace are appropriate here. For example: which items should/shouldn't be included on a resume, appropriate dress for an interview, salaries, references, degree versus experience, working from home, corporate culture, cubicles versus offices, dating coworkers, layoffs, etc. Also, follow-up articles from the `.offered` and `.resumes` groups go here.

Some topics can easily turn into flamefests, such as drug testing and affirmative action policies. Remember that other people have had different experiences than you and there is more than one valid opinion on many of these topics. Sometimes you may need to agree to disagree. Also consider the potential employers or employees who may be reading your article. Do they see a reasonable person? Or do they see someone they would never consider hiring or working for?

What is misc.jobs.contract?

This group is for discussion of contract work, as opposed to an "employee" full- or part-time position. Currently `mis.jobs.contract` serves for offers of contract work, offers of availability of contract workers, and general discussion.

How many people will see my posting?

According to December 1990 statistics, `misc.jobs.offered` is the third most widely-read newsgroup, read by an estimated 140,000 readers worldwide. `Misc.jobs.resumes` is read by 50,000 people worldwide, misc.jobs.misc is read by 71,000 people, and `misc.jobs.contract` is read by 37,000. Refer to the newsgroup `news.lists` for the latest estimates.

Where can I get more information about this network?

The `misc.jobs` groups are part of USENET. USENET is not the same as the Internet, although many sites use the Internet to transport news between sites. There are other methods of transport used, UUCP is a popular one. Read the articles in the newsgroups' `news.announce.newusers`. If you still have questions, ask the news administrator or another knowledgeable person at your site.

Examples of Job Orders

Now consider the following examples of how job orders look on the screen. The first were taken from the Online Career Center, the second from the newsgroup `misc.jobs.offered.`

• •

From: hwusa@mail.msen.com
Subject: Sr. Training Specialist (GA) / Unique Staffing and
Expo
Date: 02 Nov 1994 22:00:25 -0400
Location: in Texas in Southcentral

Sr. Training Specialist (GA)
(EMPLOYMENT AGENCY NAME)
Houston, Texas 77058
Fax: 000-000-0000

Description:
Instruct technical training classes relating to subscriber
Systems. Build instructional design programs for new
products. Train and administer program to train internal
employees. Develop training materials for all programs.

Qualifications:
BS Degree is preferred. 5+ years experience developing
training materials. Also experience as a System Manager 4/5
to 10, experience with Headend Controller, Scrambler,
860/8600X and interdiction Systems. Prefer developed skills
with computer systems specifically Hewlett-Packard and IBM
PCs.

All resumes must include job numbers

AAP Client

Status: FULL-TIME
Salary: $42,100 to $48,600
Job Number: BCD935
Location: Atlanta
Job Category: 19 Miscellaneous/Other
Starting date: ASAP
Source: TXHUSTN2

• •

Assistant Controller (PA)
(NAME OF HOSPITAL)
ADDRESS
Philadelphia, Pennsylvania 19124-2399

Contact: Human Resources Dept.
Business Line: Nonprofit psychiatric hospital

Description:
Responsibilities of this position include coordinating the
accounting, accounts payable and payroll activities.

Please mention you saw the position here!

Qualifications:
At least 3-5 years experience working in similar position,
which included handling third-party reimbursement and
general ledger.

Preference will be given to applicants with experience in supervising as well as working with computers. Preference will be given to applicants with either a CPA or MBA.

If you feel you are qualified for this position, mail your resume to the address listed above.

No phone calls please.

Community:
The Philadelphia area is conveniently located only a few hours from the Jersey Shore, the Pocono Mountains, Amish country, New York City and Washington, D.C.

For information on other job openings in the PA area, call the Online Opportunities voicemail hotline at 610-873-2168.

For maximum exposure of your qualifications, you are encouraged to place your resume into the Worldwide Resume Talent Bank, accessible on America Online and the Internet. The combined viewing audience with access to your resume is 20-30 million people and employers worldwide. For more information, send email to wwtb@jobnet.com.

Location: Employers Location - DELVAL
Starting date: Immediate
Closing date: November 7, 1994
Source: PAPHILLY2

(C) 1993, 1994 Gonyea and Associates, Inc. All Rights Reserved. Help Wanted-USA is a service of Gonyea and Associates, Inc., 3543 Enterprise Road East, SafetyHarbor FL34695.

● ●

/941102: Staff Registered Nurse - ICU (NY) /

From: hwusa@mail.msen.com
Subject: Staff Registered Nurse - ICU (NY) (NAME OF HOSPITAL) Glen Cove
Date: 02 Nov 1994 22:00:25 -0400
Location: in CANADA in Canada

Staff Registered Nurse - ICU (NY)
(NAME OF HOSPITAL) at Glen Cove
Glen Cove, New York 11542

Contact: Human Resources Department
Phone: 000-000-0000
Employees: 7000
Business Line: Part of Teaching Hospital

Description:
Candidate will work nights for 12 hours. Experience required, along with NYS Certification.

Qualifications:
SEE JOB DESCRIPTION. ((DON'T FORGET TO MENTION "HELP
WANTED-USA" WHEN APPLYING FOR THIS PARTICULAR POSITION))

Company:
Hospital, Glen Cove is part of a
network of Teaching Hospitals.

Community:
Some interesting Facts: Suffolk County is Eastern half of LI
with population of 1,328,622. Total LI population is
2,613,150, which surpasses that of 20 states. Median age:
36.6, Median disposable income: $53,425 (#1 in nation)
Unemployment: 7.1% (National avg.), Housing Median
Price: $159,240. Long Island is 120 miles long and is East
of NY City. It is between 12 and 20 miles wide and is
bounded by Long Island Sound to the North and Atlantic Ocean
to the South. Manhattan is 55 miles West from Suffolk
County line.

Status: Full Time
Salary: Open
Job Number: Help Wanted-USA/0411
Location: Glen Cove
Starting date: Soon As Possible
Closing date: When Filled
Source: NYSUFOLK

● ●

From: hwusa@mail.msen.com
Subject: Radiology, General Technician (CA) / ScrippsHealth
Date: 02 Nov 1994 22:00:25 -0400
Location: in California in West

Radiology, General Technician (CA)
ScrippsHealth
La Jolla, California 92037

Contact: Mail Resume to Human Resources
Phone: 000-000-0000
Business Line: Radiology, General Technician Hospitals and
Clinics

Description:
Radiology, General Technician

Qualifications:
This position requires a Registered Nurse. License and/or
Certification and experience in area of specialty is also
required.

Company:
ScrippsHealth is a bold new union of medical excellence
combining Scripps Memorial Hospitals, Scripps Clinics, and
Affiliated Business Services to provide quality, service
and value in health care. This position is at one of the
following locations in San Diego County; Del Mar, Chula
Vista, Encinitas, La Jolla or Rancho San Diego.

Community:
San Diego County is located in Southern California and
boasts to having the best climate on earth. It is the only
county in America where you can drive to the ocean, desert,
mountains, and visit a foreign country, all in one day.
While being a fast-paced Metropolitan Area, San Diego,
America's Finest City, has managed to maintain much of the
charm and mystique of small-town America.

Status: Full-Time
Salary: Salary Commensurate with Experience and Benefits
Job Number: HWUSA
Location: San Diego County, California
Starting date: Open
Closing date: When Filled
Source: CADIEGO1

● ●

FROM misc.jobs.offered

5/21Reading . . . Sat, 05 Nov 1994 08:53:28   ab.jobs
Thread 1 of 8
Waterloo, Ontario, Canada

Position of International Marketing Director available:

Plastic household products manufacturing company, with
facilities in Canada and U.S., is looking for an individual
able to fill the position of International Marketing Director,
who will be directing marketing of the company products
in the worldwide market.

Salary between 60K-100K depending on experience, plus other
remunerations. Language aptitude and European experience
welcomed.

Please do not respond to this post, but fax your resume
directly to 000-000-0000. You can also e-mail your resume
to us <   >, while we cannot answer any questions,

we can forward your resume to the company. Please put the words: "RESUME of <your name>" in the subject line.

Thank you.

• •

From misc.jobs.offered

Lines 24 Advertising Designer-Alkon Corporation-OH
No responses
occ@nero.aa.msen.com Online Career Ctr at Msen, Inc. —
Ann Arbor, MI (account)

       Advertising Designer

Excellent opportunity for an individual to start up an
internal advertising department for a Columbus, Ohio-based
manufacturer of PC-based control systems. Ongoing projects
include company newsletter, print ads, brochures, direct mail
pieces, and related materials. Creative skills are a must,
and copy strength is a real plus. Candidates must have solid
experience with desktop publishing systems, purchasing skills
with outside suppliers, and the ability for self-direction.

Send resume and current work samples to:

(NAME OF COMPANY) Corporation
Attn: LB
ADDRESS
Advertising Designer
Columbus, OH 43204

No Phone Calls, Please.

OH 43204

• •

From misc.jobs.offered

misc.jobs.offered   Thread 173 of 2924
Lines 37 Informtion Technology Consultants-CGA-MN
No responses
occ@nero.aa.msen.com Online Career Ctr at Msen, Inc. —
Ann Arbor, MI (account   )

(COMPANY NAME), headquartered in New York City, is part of
a major transnational information technology consulting firm.
With annual revenues of approximately $2 billion annually and
operations in 16 countries, (co. name) maintains a
worldwide, world-class professional staff of over 20,000
consultants.

The company's information technology service offerings include custom software development, applications management, systems integration, outsourcing, reeingineering, training and professional services across a broad spectrum of industries, including integrating manufacturing, financial services, retail, pharmaceutical, and the telecommunications industries.

We have needs for consultant to work in the MINNEAPOLIS, MN area. We select only the most ambitious technical professionals who are willing to do whatever it takes to help solve our clients' business problems. You could qualify for one of our Consultant positions if you've trained AND have experience in one or more of the following:
LOTUS NOTES, C++, Oracle, Ingress, CICS, DB2, COBOL, Visual Basic or Powerbuilder; IBM Mainframe, FoxPro, or Sybase. Successful candidates will have demonstrated business maturity, co-op or internship experience, leadership abilities, as well as excellent interpersonal and communications skills.

If you want to join a company committed to excellence and client satisfaction, if you enjoy a challenge and teamwork, and if you want to work with other exceptional people, we want to hear from you. Please send your resume to:
(COMPANY SNAIL MAIL ADDRESS) Minneapolis, MN 55401; or 000-000-0000 (FAX).

We are an equal opportunity employer. M/F/H/V

• •

misc.jobs.offered   Thread 174 of 2924
Lines 25 Programmer/Analysts
occ@mail.msen.com Online Career Ctr at Msen, Inc. —
Ann Arbor, MI (account in   )

(COMPANY NAME) currently needs:

- Sys38 RPG Analyst
(Will function as a Programmer/Analyst/Operator)

- Programmer Analyst
(Must have worked as a Programmer with ORACLE.)

Contact: Staffing Specialist
(COMPANY NAME)
Akron, OH 44308-1719
000-000-0000 - voice
000-000-0000 - fax

• •

• •

misc.jobs.offered   Thread 277 of 2924
Lines 37 Laboratory Safety Spclst-Univ of Medicine
occ@nero.aa.msen.com Online Career Ctr at Msen, Inc. —
Ann Arbor, MI (account   )

LABORATORY SAFETY SPECIALIST

Two (2) Positions:
One at Newark campus and one at Piscataway/New Brunswick
campus

UMDNJ, the University of Medicine & Dentistry of New Jersey,
the nation's largest comprehensive health sciences
university, is seeking a laboratory safety specialist.
Reporting to the local Campus Safety Officer, this
individual will identify, evaluate, eliminate and/or minimize
occupational and environmental hazards in laboratories and
related premises.

In addition to a Master's degree in industrial hygiene,
environmental or occupational health sciences, chemistry or a
related technical discipline, a minimum of three (3) years of
professional work experience in the field of industrial
hygiene, laboratory safety, or occupational/environmental
health prevention programs is required. A Bachelor's degree
and five years of experience in laboratory safety, industrial
hygiene, or occupational/environmental safety and health is
also acceptable. Thorough knowledge of laboratory safety
principles is imperative. Considerable knowledge of
industrial hygiene equipment uses and methodology as well as
the ability to calibrate and maintain monitoring equipment is
necessary. Knowledge of PEOSH/OSHA, NIOSH, ACGIH, and NJ
DEPE/EPA regulations is also necessary.

Ability to prepare clear, accurate and informative reports
including investigative findings, conclusions, and
recommendations along with superior interpersonal and oral
presentation skills needed.

UMDNJ offers a competitive salary and a comprehensive
benefits package. Please send your resume to:

• •

FROM misc.jobs.offered

   Insect Management Discovery Research - Biology   •

Associate Biologist. We are searching for a scientist
capable of working as a team member and collaborating on a
variety of projects in a multidisciplinary environment. The

successful candidate will be required to perform "in vitro" biochemical assays for insecticide discovery and mode of action studies. This person would maintain the equipment and supplies needed to run the assays, including maintaining insect and cell cultures and preparing media and buffers. Laboratory experience is required and experience in performing receptor binding assays is preferred. In addition to these operational duties, computer literacy is essential.

Requirements: Candidates should have B.S. or M.S. in biology, i.e., pharmacology, biochemistry, neuroscience, or related disciplines.

Applicants should send their resume, including names of at least three references.

Fee-Based Recruitment Services

Several private fee-based recruitment services are available to you online. Let's explore a couple of them.

Online Opportunities

Online Opportunities of Exton, Pennsylvania, is the regional representative for the commercial online services Help Wanted-USA and E-Span, both national distributors of employment information. Affiliation with this service allows employers to advertise positions nationally and/or search national databases of resumes.

To enter a job order into the database, you dial the BBS directly. Then, you place your "ad" with the service, much like you would with a newspaper. The similarity, however, ends there, says Ward Christman, executive director of Online Opportunities. "With a job ad placed in a newspaper, employers are limited to what they can put in the ad because of expense and space limitations. With so little detail, a candidate responding to the ad may not even come close to meeting an employer's needs. With our service, the flat rate means employers are not limited to how much information they place in their ad. In fact, many companies place the entire in-house job description. Then, the ad is indexed, so every word of the ad is searchable. This means that job seekers can type specific keywords at the prompt and get a much better match with the employer's requirements. More detail means that employers can expect fewer responses from a higher rate of qualified applicants—more like 50 to 60 percent."

Christman says the advantage of using a fee-based service like his is that employers can place job orders in a private database that is not swamped with other ads.

"Previously, newsgroups were the primary space where job seekers looked for work. Over time, they have grown too much. Now, job seekers simply don't have time to wade through all the postings. With

Online Opportunities, the employer's ad is placed into a more functional service. The keywording device allows them to reach a narrower, more qualified field of applicants."

Another advantage, he says, is maintenance. "Private databases are maintained and updated frequently, whereas newsgroups may not be. Our jobs are updated every two weeks." Online Opportunities also offers employers access to resume databases. Says Christman, "They can advertise their job or search the resume database, whichever suits their needs. When employers subscribe to a resume database, they get a corporate account which gives them keyword access to the database. Then, they enter specific keywords at the prompt line to search. This gives them a one-line summary that matches the search. From that, they can determine if they want to see the full text of the resume. It really saves time."

Christman has recently taken his service into another dimension in the electronic job search arena. Each month, he makes Help Wanted-USA available to listeners in the Philadelphia area on a local radio station. On a call-in program, Christman links job seekers with jobs throughout the country. He has also made his service available to companies that are downsizing. He recently assisted a major local manufacturing employer with outplacement services by uploading the resumes of 500 displaced employees to his computer network for distribution on commercial online services.

Access to Online Opportunities is available through dial-in to the BBS. If an employer doesn't yet have a modem, they may fax their job opening. Employers pay a flat fee of $2,000 per year which gives them access to Online Opportunities' resume database. They may run their job ad through Help Wanted-USA for a fee of $50 for two weeks or $90 a month. No membership fee is required to run a job ad and ads may be placed on an as-needed basis. Online Opportunities is available by phone at (610) 873-6811, fax at (610) 873-4022, and BBS at (610) 873-7170. You may also contact Ward Christman by e-mail at **sysop@jobnet.com**.

Job Finders

Another fee-based online employment service is Job Finders in Leominster, Massachusetts. Job Finders belongs to a network of employment consultants. Their database is posted in the Career Center section of America Online, the Online Career Center on the Internet, and many local bulletin board systems. Job Finders also places ads in the Help Wanted-USA database. Mary spoke with the proprietor of Job Finders, David Davidowicz, about his service:

> **MN:** How does Job Finders work?
>
> **DD:** Employers just forward their help wanted notices by fax, e-mail, or postal service. We format the ad and upload it into the database.

MN: Is there a flat fee per year for unlimited service?

DD: Yes, $500 per quarter for ten or more listings in that period. Individual listings are $50 each.

MN: What do employers get for the fee?

DD: They can advertise an unlimited amount of information about the position, the company, and the local area nationally, via our network, 24 hours a day. Listings run in forums on networks, newsgroups, etc. This gives the employer a combined audience of more than 30 million potential applicants.

MN: How does the fee payment work?

DD: Though my service is affiliated with Help Wanted-USA, the rates and terms quoted here are Job Finders'. Job Finders invoices advertisers either after the listings have run or quarterly, depending on which option they choose. If an employer elects to pay for each listing individually, they are billed after the listing has completed its cycle (two weeks). If employers elect unlimited listings (ten or more per quarter), they are invoiced quarterly and must pay by the third upload for that quarter.

MN: How does keywording work?

DD: Keywording is used to streamline the matching process. Let's say you are looking for a job in marketing and have experience in the healthcare field. The job seeker would simply type "marketing and healthcare" at the search prompt and all the listings that contain those two words would appear. The same is true with our resume database, but employers or recruiters search for individuals with specific experience to obtain resumes instead of job openings.

MN: Do you have special software that helps you screen for appropriate applicants?

DD: Yes, I make the software to access the databases available to employers free of charge. There are some network fees associated with it, though. The software allows the employer to upload job openings directly to me. It also permits an employer to be very specific in the job description to discourage unqualified individuals from applying. Not all employers are concerned with unqualified applicants, but it does add additional cost to the process. The resume database is designed to only pull resumes that include the words the searcher has entered. Help Wanted-USA is testing an updated, much improved version that will be marketed sometime in 1995. This will be available to job seekers and employers allowing them to interact directly with our service.

MN: What is the advantage to an employer of using a fee-based service versus a newsgroup or other free service?

DD: An important advantage is maintenance. The listings are deleted two weeks after they are posted, automatically. The employer doesn't have to go back and do it after the position has been filled. I upload them every two weeks until the position is filled and make sure they get deleted on time.

Another plus is convenience, a sort of "one stop shopping." Employers do not have to post their openings in five or six different places. We save them time—lots of time and for a minimal fee. I like to explain it to people as if they were buying or selling a house. Could you do it on your own? Sure. Is there still a need for realtors? Yes.

Expertise is another factor. Online recruiting is a new concept and not many experts are out there yet. You do need to know where and how to find and post the information. I'm available at short notice to any employer using my service. They can talk to me directly and I will, 99 times out of a 100, be able to fix any problems or explain glitches in the system right away.

The classified employment advertising market is a 5+ billion dollar a year affair. Why? It costs a lot to reach people conventionally, but not electronically. I've seen articles that list executive recruitment as one of the top paying careers in the '90s and beyond. My reaction is and always will be, "not if I have anything to say about it."

David Davidowicz can be reached at Job Finders by e-mail at `MAWORCTR@aol.com` or voice at (508) 840-4479.

The Job Company

Yet another fee-based service available to employers is a resume service called The Job Company. This company will take your job order, input all the resumes received for it and sort them to arrive at the top candidates for your consideration. John Malone, President of the Job Company, explains his Search One Assistance service:

> "You simply run your classified advertisement, listing your job opening as usual, but you have the incoming resumes sent to The Job Company instead. If you have been receiving resumes already, just call us and we'll pick them up within 24 hours.

> "As the resumes arrive at our company, we open, sort, take out the staples and scan them into our computer system. We use the most advanced scanning and OCR (optical character recognition) program in the world to input each resume. This program enables our software to actually "read" each resume. The software contains nearly a 100,000 word employment-oriented vocabulary, for automatic candidate categorization.

> "Our system analyzes each resume for a match to your specified employment criteria. Immediately after we have loaded all your resumes, we can instantly sort to find the few candidates

who meet all your criteria. Once we have completed our search of candidate matching, we forward the top ten resumes in their exact form through fax or mail."

The fee for Search One Assistance is $295.

Another service offered by the Job Company is called Global Search. This feature allows employers to offer job openings to the widest range of candidates in the system. Here is how Malone explains Global Search:

> "We search our entire database for the basic job parameters of the position," says Malone. "With literature supplied by the employer, our system will automatically mail this job information personally to each candidate, explaining the position, salary, job location, benefits, etc. We can even conduct exact area searches by area code to eliminate candidates who may reside too far from the job location. The candidate can review this information and, if interested, can contact the employer directly."

The minimum charge for this service is $250 for 500 candidate contacts or 50 cents per candidate.

The Job Company can also create and mail any number of letters to the applicants on the employer's behalf. They then scan your signature and print it at the close of each letter. This allows you to "handle" the task of responding to cover letters and notifying applicants. John Malone may be reached at The Job Company, 3189 Danville Blvd., Alamo, CA 94507, 510-831-6707, e-mail `jgmalone@ix.netcom.com`

The process of electronic recruiting is different from the conventional kind, but perhaps more effective. As we have seen, it is easier to find a narrow field of qualified candidates through online applicant databases, even though the pool of applicants is much larger than what is available to you through other means, such as the newspaper. This is due to the ability of employers to write detailed job descriptions and to search for applicants by using keywords. There are also other distinct advantages that electronic recruiting has over conventional methods. Let's take a look at some of them.

Advantages of Online Recruiting

E-mail. The ability to use e-mail to conduct prescreening interviews is a tremendous benefit to electronic recruiting. As you respond to the resume postings, you do so through e-mail, a much more expedient process than callbacks and so-called "snail mail" (the regular postal service). Through the ensuing messages between you and the candidate, you get much more detail than you normally would in a single phone call or by reading a work application.

The other advantage to e-mail is that the results are immediate. Generally, you can expect replies within eight hours, and usually even sooner because the job seeker is eagerly awaiting your "new mail" message. (Overseas responses usually take longer.) With e-mail there are no busy signals or answering machines or waiting on hold. You simply post your reply or request and go on with your business.

> **Note:** Remember that a human being is waiting on the other end for your answer. It is disheartening and frustrating to be left dangling while waiting for an employer's decision. It doesn't take a minute to send an e-mail if you have decided not to consider the applicant. A good way to handle this unpleasant task is to compose a courteous rejection note in your word processor which can be easily uploaded to all your applicants. Be friendly and wish them success. It gives the job seeker closure.

The Right People. With conventional recruiting, you spend a lot of time interviewing the "wrong" people. Usually, when filling a position, you have first received a resume and maybe made a brief phone call to schedule the applicant. Often when you finally meet the applicant, you find he or she doesn't have the qualifications or qualities you really need. However, you are committed to that 15 or 20 minutes of an interview, after having brought the applicant in. It is a waste of your time and the applicant's. (Understand, applicants are no more willing to waste their time than you are. Indeed, with the expense of job hunting and no income to offset it, they are even less willing to sit through a futile interview.)

Thanks to e-mail prescreening interviews, you already have a "handle" on applicants before you ever meet them. You are able to delve into certain areas a bit more deeply, asking for examples or samples. These prescreening e-mails are a service to the applicant as well. They may be able to expand on some point in the resume which may have been overlooked at first glance. They get that "second chance" to impress you by giving you a little more than a mere piece of paper can provide.

Every employer we spoke with extolled the virtues of the e-mail prescreen. They found it a major convenience in terms of getting to the right people.

The Lobby. Electronic recruiting has it all over the face-to-face variety when it comes to the lobby of your company. During conventional recruitment, applicants—qualified and otherwise—crowd your office, making it difficult to conduct normal business. Entire weeks get blocked out on calendars, meetings get postponed, and alternative space arrangements have to be made when a company is in "hire mode."

Not so with electronic recruiting. Your "lobby" is the screen on your computer. You access it at your convenience. The business of your organization does not grind to a halt while your receptionist deals with a lobby full of applicants.

Phone Time. Thanks to e-mail, you won't be inundated with phone calls, as you are during conventional recruiting. Unless you have listed your phone number or have given it to certain candidates, job seekers will contact you by e-mail. It's a good idea to specify "no phone calls" in the job order and not include your phone number if you don't wish to get calls. (However, we received some complaints from applicants who wondered why employers recruiting in an e-mail medium would specify "no e-mails" in their postings, as sometimes happens. If you have a rational reason for not accepting e-mail submissions, by all means state it in your order. It will make more sense to applicants and spare some hard feelings.)

Cutting Edge People. All the employers and recruiters we spoke to were agreed on this point. If you find your applicant on the net, you are probably getting someone comfortable with technology, familiar with current developments, and who is not afraid to try new things. These are people who will know how to work with that new computer you just installed to help with invoicing and may even be able to help you troubleshoot problems with your system.

You Control It. With electronic recruiting, you call the shots. You decide when to pull your ad. You revise your announcement as needed. You can start recruiting immediately when you need to fill a position. You are not at the mercy of a newspaper ad or a busy calendar. Your computer can receive applicants 24 hours a day, 7 days a week and hold them until you can deal with them. This puts considerably more control of the recruitment process in your hands and simplifies the task of finding your candidate.

Legal and Ethical Aspects of Electronic Recruiting

As you begin your applicant search on the net, you need to remember that your legal obligations don't change simply because you are recruiting in another environment. The same laws that apply in "real-world" recruitment apply in cyberspace as well.

As we have discussed, several employers observed that the anonymity factor in applicant search over the net actually helped to impose fairness on the process of hiring and made them better recruiters. The absence of visual clues forced them to treat candidates impartially and to judge them on their merits rather than on external factors such as appearance.

We should note, however, that in a couple of cases, applicants expressed concern that craftily written questions could elicit information which could possibly be used to screen out "undesirable" candidates. One older job seeker told us about an employer who asked when he'd gotten his degree in a clear attempt to ascertain his age, a violation of the Age Discrimination in Employment Act. (Don't forget, though, that with the recent economic conditions many older adults have returned to college in hopes of bettering their employability.)

Illegal questions don't become magically legal just because you ask them over a computer screen instead of in person. For example, questions about marital and family status are still very much off limits in electronic interviewing. This gets a bit tricky because through e-mail contact, you and the applicant may have established a fairly friendly and informal rapport. Just remember: If you wouldn't ask it during an interview, don't ask it online.

Limitless Recruiting Opportunities

Employment recruiting over the Internet can be the most expedient and rewarding way you have ever utilized for finding and hiring applicants. It is a cost-effective way of uncovering the best pool of qualified applicants available. This wonderful new technology has changed the face of the recruiting and employment process. Used properly, it can prove to be your company's most important tool.

Summary

The Internet is no longer an elite instrument of a few computer specialists or university personnel. In the last few years, it has become an indispensable tool for business and private citizens alike. It is an electronic marketplace for countless services and resources. As a job search and recruitment tool, it is unparalleled.

As members of the Internet community, you now have access to the most expansive assortment of jobs and applicants available anywhere. If you apply what you have learned about the process of job hunting on the Internet, coupled with a positive attitude, you cannot help but succeed in this or any other labor market.

In the parlance of the Internet:

```
        logon> every day
         get> motivated
help> your Internet neighbors
          DON'T> quit
```

See you on the net!

```
      > bye
```

GLOSSARY

access A means of connecting or "getting on," as in having access to the Internet

address One's computer address for receiving e-mail—for example, `mnemnich@acme.csusb.edu,` which is read as "M Nemnich at acme dot c-s-u-s-b dot e-d-u"

alt (1) part of newsgroups (sometimes called bulletin boards or discussion groups) that tend to be on controversial or lighter subjects—for example, `alt.fishing;` (2) the Alt key on your keyboard used with another key to execute a command

America Online One of the more popular commercial (for a fee) networks providing access to the Internet

anonymous A way to login to public storage sites on the computer

AOL The abbreviation for America Online, read as "a-o-l"

archie A database of all the names of files stored at known public archive sites

archive A place where files are stored

ASCII (American Standard Code for Information Interchange) One of the two main types of files (binary is the other); also known as a text-only file containing no special formatting codes, such as bolding or underlining

baud rate The switching speed of a line

BBSs (Bulletin board systems) services available through modem dial-up that can include "read-only" information, conferences, e-mail, live chat, and Internet access

binary One of the two main types of files (ASCII is the other); as a program file rather than a text file, it is undecipherable without a computer program

bit Short for "binary digit," the smallest unit of information stored on a computer

bounced message Undelivered e-mail returned to its sender

bps Bits per second, a way of designating the speed of a modem

browser A program that searches and presents information in an easy and time-saving manner

bulletin board systems Services available through modem dial-up that can include "read-only" information, conferences, e-mail, live chat, and Internet access

bullet (1) A dot for marking lines or otherwise calling attention to a part of a text; (2) a condensed statement of information on a resume

byte (1) A character of data (consisting of eight bits) representing a single letter, number, or symbol; (2) a unit for measuring computer and disk storage capacity

caps Uppercase letters

capture "To grab" information off a file and store it in your computer

case-sensitive A warning that upper- and lowercase letters cannot be interchanged; for example, some computers can read only lower-case letters

CD-ROM A disk with "read only memory"; that is, a disk for information retrieval only

chat Real-time interactive communication; that is, as you "type" your words, another person is able to read them

command Directions or orders entered into a computer

compressed Files that are "squeezed" to conserve disk space and to make transfer time faster

CompuServe One of the more popular commercial (for a fee) networks providing access to the Internet

cursor A blinking indication of where the next character you type will appear

cyberspace A term created by science fiction writer William Gibson for the electronic zone where information is exchanged and contacts take place through computers

database A large amount of data stored in a well-organized format

Delphi One of the commercial (for a fee) networks providing access to the Internet

directory An index to a location of files

disk drive A part of the computer that stores information on disks

document A text (word) file

dot The word spoken for a period in an address

download Transfer of information from one computer to another

electronic interview An employment interview that takes place over e-mail rather than in person

electronic job application A computerized employment application form, in which information is entered by the applicant on-screen

electronic resume A special type of resume for use in a computer-assisted job search

e-mail (electronic mail) A written message sent to one person or a group of people by computer networks

e-mail address One's computer address (see "address")

emoticons Facial expressions made up of punctuation marks used to convey emotion, such as : -) for happiness or : - (for sadness, viewed by moving your head sideways and downward to the left (see also "smileys")

error correction A way of filtering out telephone line noise in modems

error message A computer message that the user has done something incorrectly

escape How one "gets out of" an application

execute To accomplish the command

exit To logout or leave a session

face-to-face (or ftf) Communication that is face-to-face rather than by computer

FAQs Frequently Asked Questions; answers to the most common questions compiled into one document

FidoNet A large BBS network

file A document or other collection of data

file server A computer that stores data and programs that are shared by many users in a network

finger A program for finding and displaying information about the users of a computer

flame An angry or hostile message or reprimand directed to an individual in newsgroups and IRC

floppy disk A small disk used in a disk drive to record and store information

font A particular style and size of letters or characters

freenet Community-based bulletin board systems funded and operated by individuals and volunteers; many offer Internet access free or at low cost

ftp File transfer protocol; program allowing you to connect to another computer and view and copy files back and forth between the two computers

global village Refers to the way in which our "real world" has been made smaller by computer and other communication technology

gopher A fast and easy menu-driven application that organizes and presents Internet resources

hard drive The memory storage device built into a computer

hardware The computer itself and computer equipment, such as modem, monitor, and printer

header/headings The identifying data at the top of an e-mail message, such as date and sender

headhunter A recruiter who charges a fee to an employer to find applicants or to an applicant to find employers

home pages A site for information on the World Wide Web

host (1) A computer with a permanent connection to the Internet; (2) a service provider

hypertext A technology for linking documents for the rapid retrieval of data

icon A symbol for a computer program

interactive A means of "give and take" between the user and the computer program

interface The connection between one compatible system and another

Internet The interconnection among computer networks

InternetMCI A new commercial network from MCI Communications

IP address Internet protocol address; usually four groups of numbers separated by periods, such as 140.147.254.3 – the IP address for the Library of Information System

IRC Internet Relay Chat; a many-to-many live interactive discussion

job bank A centralized listing of job openings

job search process Includes online search, resume, application, interview, and hire

keyword A word denoting an important job or applicant characteristic (such as "marketing") used to narrow search criteria

line length The number of characters (letters and numbers) available on a line

list Electronic mailing list or discussion group

list administrator The person who runs a list

LISTSERV List server; an automatic discussion list service capable of responding to requests for subscription

load To put information and data into the computer or memory

login (1) The process of signing on to a computer network; (2) the prompt for your userid (shortened and combined form of "user identification")

lurker One who observes or reads a newsgroup or IRC without joining the conversation

Lynx A text-only hypertext browser

megabytes One million bytes of information

megahertz An indicator of the speed at which a computer processes information

memory The capacity of a computer to store information

menu A list of available sites, documents, or commands

message An e-mail letter

Microsoft Network A new commercial network from Microsoft

MIPS The number of millions of instructions a mainframe computer can process per second

modem (from *mo*dulate-*dem*odulate device) The device for sending and receiving data over telephone lines

monitor The screen on which information is displayed in a readable form; monitors can be monochrome or color

Mosaic A hypertext browser with picture and sound capability

mouse A device used to point, select, and move information or to draw figures on-screen

multimedia A combination of picture, sound, and text

net A shortened form of Internet and USENET

netiquette Internet etiquette; proper behavior on the Internet or USENET

network news Discussion groups on USENET devoted to a single topic

networking groups Traditionally individuals who work together to provide mutual support and job search assistance to other members

newsgroups Discussion groups on USENET devoted to a single topic

online Being connected to the Internet or other computer networks

Online Career Center One of the largest job banks available online

online employment services Fee-based employment agencies available online

password A secret word used to verify userid

path Menu choices selected to arrive at a particular information site

pc Personal computer

point-and-click Using the mouse to select a choice

port A dedicated line for linking up to a mainframe computer or peripheral

posting A message or article on a newsgroup

Prodigy One of the more popular commercial (for a fee) networks providing access to the Internet

prompt The point at which a command is entered

real-time At the moment as it is happening

scroll key The key to "freeze" and "unfreeze" the display scrolling or rolling on the screen

server A program to find requested documents

service provider An organization that provides access to the Internet

site Location on the Internet where information is available

smileys Facial expressions made by using punctuation marks used to convey emotion in e-mail (see also "emoticons")

snail mail Mail delivered by the U.S. Postal Service

subject line A headline highlighting the most important part of a message

subscribe Adding your name to a list

sysop Short for *sys*tem *op*erator, the person in charge of a BBS or other computer system

talk Real-time interactive conversation, such as keying in words another person is able to read as you key them

telnet What allows you to access another computer through remote login

terminal emulation Enables a computer to recognize your terminal as a compatible terminal

UNIX An operating system originally developed for networking individual workstations

upload The transfer of information from one computer to another

URL (Universal Resource Locator) The address of a World Wide Web site

USENET User's Network; a very large distributed BBS that carries network news

userid Short for *user id*entification, the name you use for login

user name The name you use for login

Veronica A way of searching gopher menus

VT-100 A standard terminal emulation

WAIS Wide Area Information Service; an application to search databases using keywords

WELL Whole Earth 'Lectronic Link; a BBS started by *Whole Earth Review*

World Wide Web An organizing system with the Internet that makes it easy to establish links between computers

Zip To compress a file

INDEX

More Good Books from JIST Works, Inc.

Using WordPerfect in Your Job Search

By David F. Noble

This is a new, focused kind of computer book that shows readers how to use the power of WordPerfect to create best-quality resumes, cover letters, and other important job search documents. Detailed, step-by-step instructions make it easy to create many different types of resumes, such as:

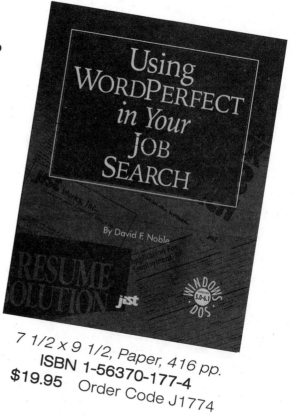

- ✓ Chronological resumes
- ✓ Scannable resumes
- ✓ Combination resumes
- ✓ Hypertext resumes
- ✓ Resumes from templates

Using WordPerfect in Your Job Search also provides valuable information on how to organize and conduct an active job search, as well as modify different WordPerfect templates to create resumes. Appropriate for beginning and advanced WordPerfect users.

7 1/2 x 9 1/2, Paper, 416 pp.
ISBN 1-56370-177-4
$19.95   Order Code J1774

Other Information

- Step-by-step instructions on how to use WordPerfect to create and desktop publish quality resumes and other job search documents.

- Contains many examples of resumes, cover letters, and other job search documents.

Look for these and other fine books from JIST Works, Inc. at your full service bookstore or call us for additional information

More Good Books from JIST Works, Inc.

The Customer Is Usually Wrong!
Contrary to What You've Been Told. . .What You Know to Be True about Customer Service!
By Fred E. Jandt

The JIST QUICK SERIES

Quick Resume & Cover Letter Book

by J. Michael Farr

Write and Use a Superior Resume Within 24 Hours

jist the job search people

6 x 9, Paper, 224 pp.
ISBN 1-57112-067-X
$12.95   Order Code CUW

Emphasizing the use of win-win negotiation skills, this revolutionary book explains why the popular adage, "The customer is always right," has failed. Includes a frank discussion of customer expectations and the types of services that workers are actually able to provide. Also includes:

- Real-life examples of effective supervision and positive employee morale

- A Model Service Organization

Sales Information

- Important training tool for every customer service representative and supervisor
- Demonstrates effective supervision and positive employee morale
- Provides actual examples of the win-win strategies at work in a customer service setting

Look for these and other fine books from JIST Works, Inc. at your full service bookstore or call us for additional information

More Good Books from JIST Works, Inc.

The Quick Interview & Salary Negotiation Book
Dramatically Improve Your Interviewing Skills and Pay in a Matter of Hours
By J. Michael Farr

8.1/2 x 11, Paper, 220 pp.
ISBN 1-56370-162-6
$9.95   Order Code J1626

More than 80 percent of job applicants do a poor job of presenting their skills in job interviews. Even more people are baffled by problem questions, such as:

- What salary are you expecting?
- Why should I hire you?
- What is your major weakness?

The simple yet powerful three-step process explained in this book unravels the secret of answering these and other difficult interview questions. *The Quick Interview & Salary Negotiation Book* contains features that will enable readers to quickly improve their interviewing skills and avoid being screened out of a job before the interview.

Other Information
- Includes basic and advanced interview techniques
- Contains many specific examples
- Helps develop a powerful skills language.

Look for these and other fine books from JIST Works, Inc. at your full service bookstore or call us for additional information

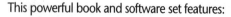